AF577020

# WALKING IN THE WILD

# WALKING IN THE WILD

---

## The Complete Guide to Hiking and Backpacking

---

ROBERT J. KELSEY

Funk & Wagnalls NEW YORK

 Published simultaneously in Canada by Fitzhenry & Whiteside Limited, Toronto.

Manufactured in the United States of America

ISBN 0-308-10083-2

1 2 3 4 5 6 7 8 9 10

**Library of Congress Cataloging in Publication Data**

Kelsey, Robert.
Walking in the wild.

Bibliography: p.
1. Backpacking. 2. Hiking. I. Title.
SK602.2.K44 1973 796.5 73-8907
ISBN 0-308-10083-2

TO TEDDY

*who has always given me the encouragement, the time, and the means to climb higher and farther*

# Contents

# INTRODUCTION—
# *A New Way to Walk the Trails*

People go hiking for many reasons, perhaps the most important of which is an instinctive need to take a temporary break from civilization and to draw a renewed strength of spirit from nature. There is no mystery about why the outdoors is increasingly popular today with both young and old; the beat of modern city and suburban living drives people to seek occasional haven from the noise and strife of crowded pavements.

Yet a short afternoon stroll in a park or at a public beach is not enough for many of us who want to get away from all the crowds and man-made complications of public spots for a weekend, a week, or even longer. When we do, walking becomes backpacking—lightweight living in which the hiker carries on his back everything he needs to survive and, indeed, to live very well.

Today there is a revolution in backpacking. Not only has the variety of equipment increased at a bewildering rate, it has changed so vastly in principle and in construction materials that outdoorsmen of a generation or two ago would hardly recognize some of the new gear. It's an on-going change, too, that will continue with the rapid growth of the sport. The trend has been both good and bad.

On the one hand, a great deal of the modern equipment incorporates significant technical advances, enormously useful in reducing weight, relieving effort, and promoting comfort and safety. On the other side, there is also a lot of useless and frightfully expensive gadgetry that is a sheer waste of money.

This book will serve as a guide, first to the principles of backpacking and, second, to the old and new types of equipment actually necessary for extended stays in the wilderness.

There is another change in backpacking that has been spawned by its increasing popularity and by the resultant pressure of many people on some wilderness areas. The outdoors is no longer immune to "urban blight," and so traditional old-time practices such as the construction of browse beds, the burying of trash and garbage, and even, in some areas, the building of campfires are either banned by law or are morally indefensible.

While some people may question the wisdom of writing a book that may further increase the popularity of backpacking, I believe that the impulse to get away from urban pressures is so intense that people will continue to undertake the experience even if nothing further is ever written about this great sport. The problem is not so much the numbers of backpackers as it is their actions in the outdoors.

Therefore, this book will also stress modern methods of camping that are not destructive, methods that foster solid conservation practices, which, it is hoped, all readers—both newcomers and old pros—will adopt. Failure to take care of our outdoor heritage will inevitably result in the urbanization of rare wild areas or in the closing of these areas for long periods of time, until nature can patiently restore the beauty that people are now squandering through ignorance and carelessness.

Backpacking *is* for everyone who shares these goals. On the side of Mount Marcy in the New York Adirondacks, I once passed a white-haired gentleman of nearly seventy, his hair bound up in a sweatband, who was leaping cheerfully down the trail from the summit. And in the Cathedral Mountains of California's Tuolumne area, I recently talked with a teen-age couple carrying a tiny baby in an aluminum back carrier.

I know young and vigorous hikers who pride themselves on their ability to climb seven mountains in a single day. And there are older (and perhaps wiser) friends who hike no more than seven hours a day and who dally at every beautiful view or glimpse of wildlife. Some people use backpacking as a means of getting to a favorable base-camp position, from which they fish or hunt or hike or climb, unencumbered by a pack. There are backpackers who live on spartan survival rations and scorn the art of camp cooking. And there are others who pride themselves on turning out a campfire meal that is every bit as elaborate and fine as that possible in a home kitchen.

For some, backpacking is a complete sport; some use it to pursue other hobbies—photography, painting, and nature and rock study. While most people enjoy these pleasures in small groups, others favor large club outings and a few challenge safety by going it alone. There are enthusiasts who go out at all times of the year, traveling winter snows on either skis or snowshoes.

In short, the wilderness is wide enough to satisfy every desire, and there are trails and techniques suitable for all ages and numbers.

I started backpacking when I was five, forty-one years ago in the Sierra Madre mountains of California where we lived. My older three children—Rob, Pat, and Chuck—all started at four. My wife, Teddy, started with our third child, Chuck, and, although she had never been off concrete before in her life, has become an enthusiastic and very competent summer/fall backpacker. Her ideas on feminine needs for hiking are interspersed throughout the book. Our much-later youngest, Chris, started at two, because we couldn't bear to put off backpacking until he was four and because he was so brainwashed by a houseful of gear and outdoor enthusiasts that he couldn't wait any longer to hit the trail. Therefore, we have practiced all of the techniques described in this book on one trip or another.

I will cater to all these levels of outdoor interest—and all pocketbooks. Many would-be beginners are turned off by the amount and cost of equipment that they see in outdoor stores. No beginner who starts with an occasional outing in summer need buy expensive gear. And lightweight food is available in any supermarket.

On the other hand, professionals and advanced amateurs, who do extensive backpacking over all kinds of terrain and at all times of the year, need sophisticated equipment and specialized foods that are ultra-light in weight and can deliver maximum utility.

Therefore, the discussion of equipment and techniques in this book will start with fundamentals and work up to more elaborate procedures. Chapters 2 through 7 are on equipment and how to use it: clothing for both warm and cold weather, sleeping bags, packs, tents, and camp gear. The last five chapters are on techniques for planning trips and hiking, both on trails and off them, for setting up a camp and taking it down, for selecting food and menus, for creating your own camping gear at home, and on how to deal with emergencies. There is an extensive appendix of other useful publications and of equipment and camping food suppliers in every part of the country.

Obviously, it would be impossible for me to have used every piece of equipment mentioned in this book. However, I have either personally examined all the gear that is discussed or know experts who have used every piece. Because the amount of equipment on the market is increasing at an astronomical rate, with new suppliers and outlets opening up almost weekly, I have emphasized the principles of construction and use which are less likely to be outdated.

In this regard, I would like to express my personal thanks to two fine outdoor stores in my area—Kreeger & Son Ltd., 30 West 46th Street, New York City, and Recreation Unlimited, Inc., 926 Route 17, Ramsey, N.J.—who loaned me much of the equipment shown in the photos in this book. Kreeger, which carries many of the leading brands, supplied all of the gear from Alpine Designs, Kelty, K2-Jan Sport, Ocaté, Optimus, Primus, and Sunbird. Recreation Unlimited supplied the Gerry items. The rest is our own gear.

In the chapters on equipment, prices are frequently cited for comparative purposes. Every attempt has been made to insure their accuracy. But this is a period of rapidly changing retail values, and suppliers bring out catalogs at different times of the year. Therefore, a few prices may have been superceded, so the reader should use figures as close approximations in determining relative values.

Like any outdoorsman, I have personal preferences and a few prejudices. I have tried to be objective and to point out where judgments are personal in nature.

In any work of this scope, there are bound to be some omissions and some overemphasis on the techniques, gear, and hiking areas that most appeal to the author. As a result,

I ask the indulgence of the experts who read my book and would welcome as a real favor any comments or criticisms by readers with other points of view.

It should be pointed out that no one can learn backpacking or the love of wild places from a book. The only way for you to build experience is to tramp many trails with a load on your back, make camp in every type of place and in every kind of weather. Range farther and farther from established trails and campsites until you achieve the ability to bushwhack across untracked wilderness to hidden ponds, alpine valleys, and remote shores where there is no sign that another human being has ever stood. Experience the thrill of surmounting a high and cold mountain, of lying under a clear night sky filled with a billion billion stars, of hearing the call of a lonely loon far down a wilderness lake, and of sharing a snug camp with one or two trusted friends.

Even if you never attempt an ambitious expedition, wild areas on a small scale are everywhere. There is virtually no city or town in this country that is far removed from some seashore nook, lake, stream, or mountain that a hiker can call his own for at least a weekend. These are the memories that make routine living possible, that lure backpackers back again and again to borrow and savor and protect the far-flung places that still exist in all corners of this great land.

Read on. Then put this book aside and step out to walk with the rocks and the water and the trees that will renew your life.

# WALKING IN THE WILD

# 1

# WALKING IN THE WILD

There is a hidden beaver pond in the Catskill Mountains that can only be reached by bushwhacking over a mountain along deeply worn game trails. Once, on a sunny afternoon in early fall, my oldest son, Rob, hooked his first trout in this pristine pond, which shows no sign that any other man has shared this experience. Yet the pond lies only two hours as the crow flies from Manhattan. Even if someone else has been there, he has concealed the evidence as carefully as we do our traces, for each time we return we know the same thrill of discovery that excited us the first time we succeeded in finding this insignificant dot on a topographical map.

Just as nearby is an isolated and magnificent cliff of rock in the western reaches of New York State's Bear

Mountain Park where my middle son, Chuck, learned to climb on rock, which was part of his training toward his eventual goal of expedition climbing. We have spent many spring afternoons there in complete isolation, linked both by the rope between us and by the magnetism of the earth under our hands and feet.

We share the same feeling for a little-used trail on the shoulder of Mount Marcy that allowed us to retreat before bitter cold and an approaching storm while winter mountaineering in the Adirondacks. Despite some need for

haste, we lingered along the way to gaze in awe at the towering icefalls, delicately yellowed by the juice of spruce roots, that cascaded down rock cliffs beside the trail. No other human was within eight miles of us and not a single sound broke the stillness except the sigh of our snowshoes breaking trail in the deep and virgin drifts.

The reward for a long day's hike over rough trails is an ice-cold brook where we can wade or swim—most of all, the opportunity to be a family together in the woods. This is the way it was when our older children were little on a week-long backpack in the Smokies.

A place that will always live in the memory of my wife, Teddy, and daughter, Pat, is a secluded "fork" in the Smokies into which my family and I stumbled one summer afternoon. We were footsore from a wet and rocky tramp of five days on the Appalachian Trail and this little sunny glade with its ice-cold brook for bathing tired bodies looked like heaven. We pitched camp on the bank of the stream, swam in its deep pools, and admired a flock of bright blue butterflies, which had gathered to sip sap that had dripped from a tree onto a rock beside the stream. Although we were less than five miles from one of the largest campgrounds in North Carolina, not a soul intruded on our wilderness home for the day and a half we spent there.

I have personal memories of some lone camps. Perhaps the most vivid is of a solo bushwhack in the Kings Canyon of California, which followed a hectic week of business in Los Angeles. It took eight hours on Friday night and Saturday morning to reach the trailhead. After a day-long climb, I reached a solitary saddle between two unnamed peaks at 9,500 feet—just below the snow line on this date in early July. Several thousand feet below me in Kings Canyon swarms of people scurried up and down the main trail. But up where I snuggled down between the boles of two downed spruce, I was not only alone but owned the whole world and all of the countless stars that shone above.

I had a similar experience a few years later in the Northern Sierra in a high valley between Mount Dana and Mount Gibbs, the eastern bastions of the Tuolumne Valley. Again, I had completed an exhausting week of business, this time in San Francisco, and late on Friday afternoon I raced across the valley and up the foothills intent on getting as high into the mountains as possible before dark. My goal was to see the sunrise over the Mono Desert from Dana, described by the great Sierra naturalist and explorer John Muir as one of the world's most magnificent sights.

At seven in the evening I started bushwhacking up the series of terminal moraines that guard the col between Dana and Gibbs, stopped at dark near 11,000 feet, and went to sleep with the music of a melting snow stream in my ears. I was up at five and, after munching a handful of raisins and nuts, started climbing in the predawn gloom by flashlight, skirting patches of the unique dwarfed evergreens that carpet this high-altitude valley. I gained the col as the sun broke the horizon and bathed Mono Lake and its nearby cinder cones with a shimmering red light that resembled neither the sun nor the moon alone, but a strange combination of both. The luminescent orb transformed the lake and desert into things of unearthly beauty. For an hour I stood alone, the only man on earth to witness this miracle that morning. Then the sun rose higher, broke free of the air-borne minerals that must account for this optical rarity, and also broke the spell.

These are the kinds of memories that can be treasured by those who venture beyond the end of the road. The rewards, though, are much deeper. The physical release of backpacking is accompanied by a complete psychic rebirth as the sophisticated human being becomes once again, even if for just a while, one with the rock and the earth and the water that are his fundament.

Teddy started backpacking with us after she had observed many times that I came back from such trips looking ten years younger; she wanted to share an experience that could transform someone so deeply, for since I was often physically battered and aching, the change could only have come from within. She has found the same peace of mind in the woods. And she has also been able to share the experiences and the thinking of a growing family, which is hard to attain in busy, busy suburbia.

Perhaps these are some of the answers to the perennial question asked by those who don't go into the woods, "What makes you do it?"

Wilderness wanderers have responded to the question in various ways—from George Leigh-Mallory's cryptic classic about Mount Everest, "Because it is there," to the puckish rejoinder of Art Davidson after the first winter ascent of Mount McKinley and an agonizing six-day bivouac at a chill factor of $-148$ degrees Fahrenheit, "Because the mountains give me a tremendous opportunity to eat raisins and peanut butter sandwiches . . ." It is hard for outdoorsmen to put into words why they travel trails, sometimes for long periods of time and occasionally with hardship, because the reasons are not only complex and intensely personal but, I believe, spring from ancient urges that rise from below the level of consciousness.

But after I had a family, I discovered another reason for walking in the wild. I go there with my children because I have found it the easiest place to teach them the fundamental virtues needed in civilization. In the city, lessons on cooperation, honesty, courage, thrift, forethought, and mutual concern all seem somewhat fuzzy in outline. But no preaching is needed in the wild, where neglect of any of these evidences of maturity by a single person in a party can cause all to be cold, hungry, or in danger.

It was as much for this reason as to share with them the beauty of the outdoors that I started my children on the trail at an early age. And while I will never tempt fate by claiming any success in rearing the young, I am reasonably satisfied with the results. All should be able to hold their own now with either man or the elements.

His first shot at a big trout by floating dry flies with a makeshift rod. It doesn't matter whether one is caught for dinner or not, Rob will always remember the experience.

Principally, though, it has been darned good fun. We have enjoyed experiences together that we would never have had if everyone had gone their separate ways in the town where we live. We have struggled up steep mountains, been soaked and cold, suffered illness and minor injury. We also have sat around snug campfires, toasted marshmallows, sung together, and shared mutually the triumph of a high and wind-swept summit, experiencing a range of human emotions that some take a lifetime to find, but which we have enjoyed in little more than a decade. I am confident that my grown children will continue to follow their own trails for the rest of their lives.

Fine, you say. But how does someone enjoy such an experience today? Things have changed even in ten years and the public areas are thronged with millions of people. Popular areas are being increasingly regulated, even closed to people. Where can an ordinary person or family go for a walk in the wild?

It is true that the budding misanthrope is often forced to travel a little farther to get away from people than he did a decade ago. Many near-in parks, lakes, woods, and beaches have become little more than semi-rural extensions of the urban evils they seek to cure. This is true of some areas near roads in even the largest wilderness areas. So a seeker of solitude must take to his feet. When the distance becomes too great to manage in a single day, he spends the night out. At this point, he or she graduates from simple hiking to backpacking and enters a new and freer world in which the few real necessities for supporting life in reasonable comfort can all be carried on the back.

Millions have already discovered this freedom to roam where they will. Many more millions are expected to follow suit in the next few years. And while these escapees from the pressure cooker of modern life could severely overtax the most popular wilderness spots, I believe that with broad utilization of *all* the wilderness areas that now exist or are proposed, we can support many times the number of backpackers now forecast.

But people must be encouraged to extend their experiences beyond the traditional two-month "summer season" and also to seek mountains, forests, deserts, and shores beyond those that are the goals of traditionalists and of record seekers. As illustrated by the personal examples just described, this doesn't require elaborate expeditions to far-flung corners of the earth.

In fact, many millions of backpackers overlook some of the most obvious places because they are right under their noses. There is no urban center in this country that is more than a few hours from wilderness. And while it may be measured in a few square miles instead of thousands, it can serve anyone just as well for weekend tripping. For longer vacations, there are still trackless wildernesses measured in hundreds or thousands of square miles in existence in this country, preserved by the foresightedness and stubborn work of a few amateur and professional conservationists over the last hundred years and defended with vigor by their descendants today.

Within these areas, both vast and small, are opportunities for everyone to enjoy the outdoors—by foot, boat, ski, bicycle, or even motor vehicle. We will consider only the footpath, for it is by foot that you can best escape from the press of people and enjoy both the peace and the beauty of the outdoors.

The first step on this long trail should be a modest weekend tramp near your home. This is the place to shake down gear—or the lack of it—and to decide what equipment will satisfy your needs out of the wealth that is now available, and which will be discussed in the chapters that follow. Be modest in these first explorations. I find many people are far too ambitious at the start. They buy equipment (instead of borrowing or renting it) without knowing what they need or how they will use it. They set off on stiff week-long climbs without planning, training, or physical conditioning. They drag along friends with even less experience and conditioning, or perhaps young children, who not only suffer these drawbacks but also lack the stamina and resilience that are only acquired with age. I might add that male ego and a residual myth that we are all descended from pioneers are usually responsible for these mistakes.

Start simply, both in equipment and ambition. It takes very little gear to enjoy warm-weather camping, as we shall see shortly. And some of the most beautiful spots on earth are those that you see for the first time with a close friend, the most enjoyable times those quiet moments shoulder to shoulder in front of a snug campfire—no matter where it is built.

As you gain in experience, your awakening sense of adventure should lead you to sample the joys of crisp spring and fall days and even the exhilaration of a backpack over deep snow in the crackling cold of winter. Inevitably, you will probably be drawn to high ground. There seems to be a magnetic attraction between man and mountain, a basic desire to stand on top of the highest rock and to glory in this view of the world and in the triumph of will over body that made it possible.

And it doesn't take a remote peak in a far country to achieve this state of mind either. For the very young and the beginner of any age, the attainment of a local tor may hold the same thrill as experienced by a mountaineer in his struggle up one of the world's giants. And some local peaks that are climbed regularly by tyros from the easy side are not despised even by professionals when climbed by a more difficult route or "out of season."

As an example, the White Mountains of New Hamp-

A brother and sister have a good talk to make a long trail shorter as they plod down a woods road at the end of a happy trip in the mountains.

shire and the Adirondacks in New York, which are tramped by thousands during the summer, have many exciting rock climbs for experienced cragsmen and can be among the most challenging experiences in the world in winter, even though their highest peaks rise no more than 5,000 or 6,000 feet. The same challenges can be found in other mountain ranges from coast to coast.

Beginners should savor every experience and gain maturity at the same deliberate pace used in hiking the trails. Haste is something that belongs in the city, if it belongs anywhere.

Take time to learn and enjoy some of the other rewards of the outdoors—the identity of flowers, bushes, and trees that make up the woods and fields, the geological history of your hills and mountains, the significance of animal signs and glimpses of wildlife that will gradually appear to your opening eyes. One does not have to be a trained geologist or biologist to become knowledgeable in these arts, which increase the pleasure of the wild.

Like anything else that's worthwhile, a knowledge of nature and of equipment and techniques is not achieved without some work. That's what the rest of this book is all about. In it, you will find a detailed account of the materials and methods needed for every kind of backpacking trip in all parts of the country, a distillation of forty years of trial-and-error experience on how to walk with comfort and safety in the wild.

# 2

# HOW TO DRESS FOR MODERATE WEATHER

Stay-at-homes accustomed to evenly heated and cooled homes, who decide to take to the woods, cannot at first appreciate the importance of proper outdoor clothing. One chilly or wet outing usually convinces them. But then what is the proper wear for backpacking? The outdoor stores and catalogs now show a wealth of gear at all prices, some of it good, some worthless.

Let's start at the bottom and work up because absolutely the most important article of wearing apparel is what goes on your feet. Since your feet are the only means of locomotion for carrying you into—and safely out of—the wilderness, it pays to pamper them. Unfortunately, there is no one perfect type of footgear for all conditions. However, get set now for the first of my

A late-summer backpacking bonus is picking blackberries on the trail. Teddy and Chris harvest dessert on the way up Balsam Lake Mountain in the Catskills of New York. Another bonus of August is a minimum of insects, which permits short sleeves and generally lightweight clothing.

prejudices. The one that comes closest to ideal is a sneaker.

Yes—you heard me right—a sneaker; either the low tennis kind or the high basketball type. I know most of the experts knock them, but I wore sneakers for thirty years on all kinds of trails and never bruised my feet, never twisted an ankle. And the sneakers available now with steel arch supports and molded from plastic instead of sewn canvas are even better than the ones I wore.

Consider the advantages. Sneakers are lighter than any boot. True, they also get wet fast on sopping trails. But the water runs out as fast as it runs in and sneakers will quickly walk dry after an inadvertent wetting. When it comes to drying your footwear over a campfire at night, you can hang sneakers close to the fire, rubber soles turned away from the heat, and really get them dry. Leather boots cannot be put close enough to a fire to dry them in an evening—or even in a whole night.

Sneakers are also inexpensive—a fifth or even less the cost of good boots. This makes them attractive for rapidly growing children who move through shoe sizes too fast to warrant expensive boots. So, if you have strong arches and ankles, and the trails you tramp at the start are reasonably smooth, don't be afraid to use these practical rubber-soled shoes. Now, having got that off my chest, I also have a good word to say for the more professional hiking boots.

When the going gets really rough, as on some trails in western mountains and in northern New England, or just about anywhere that you wish to bushwhack off trail (or if you're getting into your late thirties and want to pamper yourself), there is nothing like a sturdy, well-broken-in pair of leather boots with lug soles. So important are they, in fact, for the health of your propulsion units that we will spend some time talking about boots.

First problem is that footwear is now getting as fancy as

skiing equipment—with prices to match. So, how do you get a good buy for the money?

First, some general principles. For all practical purposes, a summer backpacker only needs low, standard boots that are six or, at the most, eight inches high. He should stay away from insulated boots, which are hot in summer and take forever to dry out after a wetting. Although suede or "rough out" finishes are now popular, a smooth outer surface on the leather is easier to treat with waterproofing and leather conditioners. It shows scuffs more, of course, but you aren't wearing your boots to a formal dinner. Some of the newer boots have a plastic-coated exterior for water and scuff resistance and are said also to be superior on ice and snow.

Boots should have a steel inner shank for permanent arch support, and the fewer pieces of leather they are made from the longer they will last (and the higher will be the price tag). The heel should be covered with a rock guard of leather and padded scree tops are useful to keep out pebbles, twigs, and snow. Coated nylon gaiters from seven to eighteen inches long, with elastic tops and bottoms that zip and fasten in place with Velcro tabs over the boot tops, are also useful to keep out debris or snow (price at Recreational Equipment is $3.49 to $9.95). Remember, you can get into snowdrifts and snowfields at high altitudes even during the summer. Foam-padded ankle and heel sections and a padded tongue are comfortable and an inner soft-leather lining adds even more comfort. Some people also swear by the addition of foam or sponge-rubber inner soles, but I have found them to wear out rapidly and to be unnecessary with good boots.

The soles should be of tough Vibram or similar composition material with a deep lug pattern that grips slippery surfaces. These soles are commonly vulcanized to the uppers and may also be screwed in place for added security. The welt should be sewn with nylon thread to resist rot. But it is not necessary for the ordinary hiker to have closely trimmed soles and welts. Such shoes are needed only by rock climbers who stand on narrow ledges. Also rock-climbing klettershoes are very light in weight. While this might be okay for light hiking, backpackers usually prefer sturdier gear.

Hooks, eyes, or speed laces? There's no easy answer. It's true that eyes are more secure, in general, and do not catch weeds and brush. But they also ice up in cold weather and take a devil of a time to thread. If I were starting from scratch, I believe I would pick sturdy speed laces, which are little pivoted loops of steel that lie flat and pull up very fast. However, I have been very happy for the past seven years with a pair of Dunham boots ($35) that have all hooks; so happy, in fact, that I just had them resoled for $10 after the original Vibram wore out.

Rawhide is my preference for lacing because it grips tighter when pulling up and tying. But I admit that braided nylon laces are sturdier and I wouldn't fight anyone who opted for them. Just remember to tie a double knot in the tops of such laces to prevent them from slipping. And after you are on the trail for a little while, you may have to stop and re-tie, because both nylon and rawhide tend to stretch.

An important point about lacing is that it should be done in two levels. The bottom part is pulled quite snug—how snug is a matter of experience and personal preference. My view is that the bottom of the boot should be only tight enough to prevent a shifting of the foot in the boot and not so close as to shut off circulation.

However, the tops should be looser to allow the ankle to bend. A trick for obtaining this two-level tension is to lace the boots to the instep and pull tight, tying a half-knot to secure the tension. Then lace the rest of the boot with moderate tension and finish off with a double bowknot. I do not wrap the laces around the boot, since I believe this impairs movement and circulation.

How much should a good boot with all of the features described cost? Anywhere from $20 to $70; the average is about $30 to $40. Frankly, I would advise buying, for the first time, a sturdy but not elaborate pair of boots of either Italian or American make for between $20 and $30. They are obtainable from practically every outfitter. You will probably be completely satisfied with them. By the time they wear out you may be so experienced, or wealthy, that you will want the more elaborate gear crafted by Fabiano, Raichle, Val D'Or, or one of the other famous bootmakers. However, no matter what you pay, the success of a hiking boot is as much in the ordering and in the care of the boot as in its construction.

There is no substitute for being fitted in person. But if you live too far from an outfitter to get to the store, at least order your boots properly. First, put on the socks you are going to wear when hiking (see next section for this information). Then stand on a sheet of paper and draw a heavy line around the outside of your larger foot, holding the pencil vertical for accuracy. (One outfitter advocates sitting down for this operation to avoid spreading the foot, but I believe in full weight, which is the way you are going to wear them.) Send the pattern along with your regular shoe size. With this information, a good outfitter should be able to fit you.

When you get your boots, don't rush right off for the mountains. They must be checked and broken in, if you expect to avoid painful and dangerous blisters. To start, put the boots on over your hiking socks and lace them up snugly. Is your heel firmly against the back of the shoe? Does it move from side to side? Does it shift forward when you kick the toe?

Since boots are made for average sizes, you may have to adjust for variations by putting various degrees of tension on different parts of the laces to compensate. But if this doesn't work, send the boots back before you wear them outside. Any reputable outdoor store will exchange them and make sure you are satisfied as long as you haven't damaged the boots.

Once you have a pair that fits, wear them around the house for a couple of weekends, gradually increasing the hours of wear. Then take some short hikes. At all times, keep a careful watch on your feet for rough or reddened spots.

Some boots can be really stubborn. Mine, for example. I wore them for six months, and they were still painful. So I finally resorted to a trick I probably should have performed in the beginning. I put them on over my socks and stood for about fifteen minutes in a tub of lukewarm water. Then I wore them for the weekend while they dried as I worked around the house. This molded them perfectly to my feet. Now they're scarred till hell won't have 'em, but ever since that first treatment they've been as comfortable as a pair of bedroom slippers.

Following such treatment, of course, the boots should be coated with a leather conditioner and the welts sealed with waterproofing. In fact, this is always a necessary part of continuing boot care. Every time you return from a trip you should wipe boot uppers with a damp cloth to remove mud and grime (and dig mud out of the cleats, too, if you want to preserve a happy home). Stubborn dirt should be scrubbed away with saddle soap.

Then treat the leather after it is dry with one of the boot preservatives. I like neat's-foot oil, but some people prefer boot greases. My winter boots are treated with a silicone preservative, and I believe that this is considered better for preserving the insulation value of leather. Whatever you use, apply it completely but sparingly. Too much preservative will soften the leather unduly and reduce its support. The welt should be coated with a sealing compound such as Leath-R-Seal or Sno-Seal. And all preservatives should be kept away from the soles.

Naturally, boots should be dried away from artificial heat, which deteriorates leather. Stuffing the boots lightly with newspaper or paper towels helps to absorb inner moisture. Boots should be dried and stored while held securely in boot trees or clamps to prevent the soles from

Boots for all occasions include (top row) eight-inch insulated shoewear for cold weather and six-inch boots for all kinds of climbing and hiking. But many people can wear sneakers (lower left) and for extra-wet conditions and for snowshoeing in cold weather felt-lined shoepacs (center) are favored. A low-cost answer for growing youngsters is the vinyl "Mickey Mouse" boot (right).

curling. Sometimes these clamps, which are usually designed for ski boots, will not cling to the heels of close-trimmed hiking boots. What I did in this case was to insert a brass screw in the middle of each heel, leaving about a quarter inch of the shank protruding. This is enough to grip the boot clamp, but has never interfered with hiking or climbing.

If you follow these simple maintenance procedures, your expensive boots will last for many, many years and then can be resoled at least once.

But low-topped leather hiking boots are still not the answer to every need. In the Southeast, where trail conditions can be very wet, and in northern snow areas, a good case can be made for shoepacs or "Mickey Mouse" boots.

The former were originally developed by L. L. Bean and are called the Main Hunting Shoe by this famous outfitter. It is a rubber-bottomed and leather-topped boot that comes in six heights from six to sixteen inches. It is also made with Ensolite foam insulation for winter wear in ten- and twelve-inch heights. Felt liners can also be obtained for even greater warmth. The advantage of these boots is that the leather tops allow the feet to breathe while the rubber bottoms keep them dry. These boots are really very good for hunting and snowshoeing and cost from $18 to $30. A minor drawback is the chain-tread sole, which tends to slip in mud or on ice, particularly after they are a bit worn. And for long-distance backpacking, in my opinion, these boots just do not give as much support to the foot as leather boots.

The Mickey Mouse or pile-lined Korean-style boots were developed by the Army, but are now molded abroad from vinyl, presumably by gnomes who never eat, because they are very cheap—under $10. They do have a lug sole with a good grip. They are also quite heavy and, because they are impervious to water, retain sweat and quickly soak stockings and feet. This is not necessarily a drawback, so long as you are hiking and camping at temperatures above freezing or are spending the nights in a cabin or other heated shelter where your stockings can be thoroughly dried.

But these plastic boots are slow to dry because of the pile lining and can't be put anywhere near a fire or stove without ruining them. The eyelets are another weak point; they tend to tear away from the vinyl, particularly if the laces are frozen. On balance, I'd say these boots are mainly for wet- or cold-weather wear by rapidly growing children.

Two other famous types of footwear should be mentioned. One is Bean's Maine Guide Shoe in both men's and women's models (it's actually a lightweight boot) and Bean's Men's Country Walker, a sturdy and lightweight shoe good for both men and women. These economical items of footwear ($27, $25 and $18, respectively) are both good for tramping. Personally, I prefer a sturdier boot for rough trails. But my mother-in-law, in her youth, hiked all of the rugged mountains of New Hampshire and Maine in Country Walkers and swore by them. If they were good enough for this intrepid New England woman, they ought to be good enough for anyone.

Two types of footwear that any hiker should stay away from are knee-high boots and moccasins. There is really no useful function served by the former in backpacking. The high tops cut off circulation, heat up the feet, and surround the legs with a great deal of unnecessary weight.

Some hikers in heavy snake country claim knee-high boots are necessary. However, a good pair of gaiters with special wire-mesh linings are just as good and are lighter in the palmetto and swamp country where snakes can lurk on high brush-covered banks. Elsewhere, it would take a powerful snake with a lot of persistence and luck to strike over the tops of regular six-inch boots and through stockings and twill pants. Snakes have more important things to do.

Moccasins are good for camp, period. A modern hiker would take forever to toughen his feet enough to wear such thin footwear over even the smoothest trails. And in between trips, his feet would simply soften again.

### *The Great Sock Controversy*

Once you have your outer foot covering, the next most important question is what to wear inside. With sneakers, this requires little decision. You draw on a pair of standard white athletic socks, tuck a couple of extra pairs in your pack for daily changes, and away you go. But with boots, there are a number of theories on what kind and how many pairs of socks to wear.

The minimum number is two. Even here, though, there are three schools of thought: wool and cotton, all wool, and a combination of wool and the new Wick Dry socks. Look out! I have another prejudice.

I don't like cotton socks. In theory, they are supposed to wick moisture away from your feet and transmit it to the wool socks, which exhale the vapor under the heat of walking friction. In practice, I have found that cotton socks get soggy and stay that way. Further, they stretch out of shape no matter how snug at the start and then wrinkle, setting you up for a king-sized blister.

If you are allergic to wool, well, at least try to get a cotton-synthetic blend that keeps its shape better. Or try the new Wick Dry socks. They are all synthetic. The inner sock is 70 percent olefin and 30 percent nylon. The outer variety is 65 percent orlon, 25 percent wool, and 10 percent nylon. I haven't tried them yet, not because I'm skeptical, but simply because I'm satisfied with my own combination.

There's no question about the need for two pairs of socks, both for the cushioning and for the slip between the two pairs that keeps feet from abrading. I wear a light pair of wool stretch socks in hot weather and, over these, a sturdy pair of Norwegian Ragg knit socks. In slightly cooler weather, I favor a heavier pair of wool athletic socks under the Ragg socks. For the inner socks, I buy a wool-synthetic blend that costs a little more but lasts infinitely longer. However, Teddy prefers lighter socks and wears cotton/synthetic blends against her feet with a light wool athletic sock outside.

A secret for keeping any socks soft and increasing their life is in the laundering. First, frequency: wash them daily, if water is available. Use a soap such as Woolite that is designed for wool. Wash in cool water, never hot. Air dry and with all-wool socks use stretchers (at home) to maintain shape and size. Store socks flat, not rolled. In the field, dry them preferably on a warm rock out of the sun. If you follow these procedures, your socks will last a long time. But when they finally go, throw them out. Even the finest darns can cause blisters. The saving in socks is not worth the personal cost.

While we are on the subject of shoes and socks, equal attention should be paid to your feet. Naturally, you should keep your toenails trimmed close and square to prevent in-growing and pain when going downhill, at which time your toes jam against the front of the boots. If, in spite of this, you still have to excavate an in-grown nail, put a tiny twist of alcohol-soaked cotton in the cavity and keep it there for a week or so with a Band-Aid, replacing when necessary. This will force the nail to grow outward.

If you should start to get a blister, treat it at once. For procedures, see Chapter 12 on first aid.

Keep your feet dry, particularly between the toes. Some experts advocate frequent alcohol baths and application of foot powder. It's a good idea, I guess, but my feet have never given me any problems with simple washing and drying. I change socks every night and immediately wash out the dirty set. These are hung up for the night, then are tied to the outside of my pack the next day to dry completely. People with tender feet might change socks more often.

In any case, don't walk around with wet feet. If you slip into a stream or pond over the tops of your boots, stop at once and wring out your socks. Use them to sponge out your boots. Then, put on dry socks, changing them again and again as fast as you can dry the wet ones until your boots walk dry. Wet feet soften, and no long-range backpacker can afford this.

### *Clothes That Make the Backpacker*

What to wear when backpacking is a matter of where you walk and at what time of year. There is also a healthy share of personal preference. Colin Fletcher, who wrote *The Man Who Walked Through Time*, wore nothing but a hat and boots during much of his epic hike through the Grand Canyon. I haven't made that trip, but I shudder to think what sharp eastern branches and brambles or thorny western desert growth would do to various tender parts of my torso—as well as the outrage it might cause among any other backpackers I met on the trail.

So, I advocate clothes. And since we're already there, let's start at the skin. A great problem for many hikers is chafing in the crotch. The longer you hike and the more powerful your thighs become, the more they tend to rub together. Add a great deal of heat and sweat and a little grime and you have abrasion, and then trouble.

My solution to this problem is a pair of knitted undershorts with a slight leg. The leg is softer and looser, soaks up the sweat, and doesn't cut my crotch as briefs would. I suppose a pair of cotton drawers would work okay, but I prefer the snugger-fitting knits.

Teddy prefers cotton bra and panties to nylon, which she declares itches in the heat. And she says that a woman should not wear a panty girdle—too tight and rides up.

The second step is to change shorts every day, washing and rinsing the dirty pair thoroughly, again if water is available. They can dry on the outside of your pack, too (yes, you do look a bit like a walking clothesline on the trail).

The most important step is to wash yourself every day—summer and winter. (You can at least sponge off in the coldest weather.) Then, dry carefully. I use no talcum powder because I have found it abrasive and irritating. Some backpackers use a hike as an excuse to get dirty. If you can stand yourself this way—and if your companions don't object—go ahead. But I think most people will be more comfortable with a daily plunge in a lake or stream and a change of clean underclothes.

Teddy agrees and maintains that women can be just as dainty in the woods as at home. For period times, she advocates tampons, which are more compact than pads. But either can be carried along in a plastic bag to keep them clean; used ones are completely burned in the campfire. Other feminine needs are discussed in Chapter 7.

Almost as important is what you wear over the shorts. Tight Levi's are out for long-distance walkers; they chafe.

Other than that, you can wear any sturdy and comfortable clothes you have around the house, at least in mid-summer. Teddy says that a woman should wear straight-legged pants, slightly larger than would be fashionable, for comfort. And the belt should not be too wide.

In the late summer when it is hot and the bugs are few, I wear shorts. For years, I had a delightful pair of sawed-off chinos, cut very short and wide of leg. They were the last word in comfort and coolness, I believed. An outraged wife and daughter, who claimed I was indecent every time I sat or bent over, converted me recently to a pair of L. L. Bean Hiking Britches.

Now I'm glad they did. These cotton-twill short-shorts ($9) are really sturdy and have four full-depth front pockets, two with flaps, and two rear button-down pockets that all hold gear securely. On a day hike, you can carry everything you need including a light lunch in them. The attached belt has ring tighteners on each side for adjustment. Very practical. Every major outfitter has shorts that are just as good, I'm sure. Similar shorts are available for women.

In the hottest weather in eastern woodlands, above the waist I wear a terrycloth sweatband with a Velcro fastener ($1 by Bauer & Black) and nothing else. However, on high, bare mountains either east or west and in deserts, I wear a shirt with long sleeves, metal-framed sunglasses, and either a red felt "hillbilly" hat or an ancient Australian digger hat with a broad brim to protect my face and thinning thatch.

People who haven't been outside very much, or who have tender skin, should be very careful about hiking anywhere in only shorts. You get far more sun in clean wilderness air, particularly at higher altitudes and in highly reflective desert and beach areas. Therefore, it is only simple good sense to expose your body for short periods, even if you have a tan.

The best kind of shirt is one with long sleeves and with two button-down breast pockets for secure storage of gear. It should also button all the way down the front so that it can be opened to any degree for ventilation. A T-shirt is also handy for intermediate conditions.

But if you go out from early spring to late fall, you will need a lot more than just a shirt and shorts. In the eastern half of the country and, particularly, in just about the entire northern half of the United States, the bugs can be unbelievably fierce in the spring and early summer. Even the mountains on the West Coast have snow mosquitoes and gnats that breed in melting snow water. Seashores that back up in bays and marshes can also turn out hordes of biters.

On the desert, I am a believer in covering up. The naked body can absorb up to 230 calories per hour from the sun on a clear day. Clothing reduces this surface-heating effect, thus minimizing the evaporation of body moisture. Furthermore, evenings and mornings can be cold in mountains everywhere, and an offshore breeze can turn a hot beach chilly in minutes. Even deserts can get perishingly cold at nights.

I believe that minimal clothing for comfort most of the year is a sturdy chino or twill shirt and pants. For ruggedness and long life, I like the dark-green Scout Explorer uniform ($30)—with insignia removed, of course. But any similar and relatively inexpensive work uniform will do. I carry a T-shirt to wear under this, when needed, and an old boating sweatshirt with hood. A light windproof of nylon for windy or chilly times is also included.

In the fall I often wear a beret, not one of those fancy military models that are sold in outlet stores but a genuine, soft, Basque beret that can be pulled down over the ears in

Universal clothing that can go anywhere is a long-sleeved twill shirt and pants. I top them with sunglasses and a broad-brimmed hat that wards off both sun and rain. The belt pouch holds reading glasses, pipe, tobacco, and matches.

the evening and in the sleeping bag. It can be rolled up and stuffed in a pocket when you don't want it and is just about the most practical and versatile hat ever invented.

These clothes have been sufficient for me, east and west, at altitudes above 14,000 feet in all kinds of summer conditions. But I run a very high thermostat. People who tend to get chilly (which appears to include all women and growing boys) should probably take along some lightweight long johns and an extra sweater or a light, insulated vest or jacket.

Teddy wears soft corduroy pants and a cotton shirt, topped with a floppy-brimmed suede hat. She always carries a sweatshirt and a fleece-lined cotton jacket for cool evenings. She braids her hair or ties it in a ponytail with yarn to keep it off her neck in the heat.

Then, there is rain. Don't tell me it doesn't "at this time of year" where you live. I have been misinformed so many times that I would take rain gear to the middle of the Sahara.

The standard answer is a poncho. One can be made quite simply and for little cost from a section of polyethylene drop sheet used by painters. Just cut a slit near the center for the head to go through. A hat diverts any rain that would run down the slit. Be sure to cut the sheet plenty long in back so it covers your pack and sleeping bag completely. Or you can buy a tougher vinyl or an even tougher waterproofed nylon poncho. The vinyl ponchos with snaps on the sides and a hood over the slit can be bought for as little as $2. Polyurethane-coated ripstop nylon ponchos with snaps and grommets for using the poncho as a tarp or as a shelter can cost from $9 to $18; the price is governed by weight, size, and finishing details. To be fair, Teddy prefers a nylon windbreaker or a poncho; the latter, a long nylon model, is waterproofed

My collection of hats reflects many needs. The western straw, conventional felt, and "Digger" (bottom to top, left) are good sun and rain shields, as is my wife's floppy suede hat (center, right). I wear the beret and knit balaclava in colder weather and the floppy felt at lower right is for climbing. The baseball-type cap I picked up from a manufacturer in Japan—it came in handy in the Japanese Alps.

with a polyurethane coating. All of our kids have used vinyl ponchos.

However, except to cover the woodpile, I have little use for ponchos—another personal prejudice based on long experience. They are as hot as hell, for one thing. And they usually let enough rain in at the sides, despite the snaps, to soak you. In any event, they end at the knees, thus draining all the water onto your pants and into your boots. Inevitably, they also hike up in back, exposing your sleeping bag. You can tie a nylon cord around your waist to improve this situation a bit, if you want to, but why try?

The only thing that will really keep you dry is a rain suit, even though it is also hot. They are supplied by Morsan, for example, for a little over $5. Better ones of coated nylon are obtainable from Morsan, Moor and Mountain, and Recreational Equipment for from $9 to $20. Other outfitters have similarly priced suits. How do you keep your pack dry? I do it with a homemade hood or cover that I will describe in detail in Chapter 5.

My own camouflage-pattern coated-nylon rain suit from Eddie Bauer, with tapered and zippered legs (for pulling on over boots), is so appallingly costly that I won't even discuss it. The only excuse for such frippery is an indulgent wife with a career and income of her own who believes that I deserve the best in backpacking gear. God give every backpacker such a wife!

The final essential, as far as I'm concerned, is a pair of doeskin or horsehide gloves. Their main purpose is to guard my citified hands when cutting and dragging wood, building rock fireplaces, and doing other manly chores. But they also come in darn handy when you top a sunny rise and come out on a high mountain shoulder straight into the teeth of an icy wind or when you are climbing on ice and rock in the winter and must feel for handholds.

There are other garments that you may wish to consider

Rain gear is a matter of personal preference. Chris likes his sawed-off poncho. Teddy gets along with a nylon windbreaker. A slightly longer model is called an anorak and an ankle-length type is called a cagoule. I prefer a rain suit of waterproofed nylon.

and will regard as either just nice to have or completely essential, depending on your personal preference. One is a cagoule, a cape-like parka with a hood that stretches to below the knees and is usually made of waterproofed nylon for about $21. Its purpose is in case you have to make a bivouac some night without a sleeping bag or other gear. You just draw your feet up and sort of curl into the thing. Having done this once on the side of a mountain, my heartfelt advice is, don't. It's a damned cold way to live.

Then, there is the anorak, a shorter windproof that is often supplied with a crotch strap to keep it from blowing in the wind. Because they are generally made from fine cotton, they're expensive, up to $35. Personally, I prefer my less costly nylon windproof, which has a draw string at the waist to prevent flapping.

You can wear knickers instead of pants. Most rock climbers do. The best are tough corduroy or tweed and cost from $23 to $37 at Recreational Equipment, for example. With the knickers go knee socks ($3 to $7) in traditional Swiss-guide white or bright patterns. You'll probably top this with a hand-knit sweater.

The real point is to know the conditions you are going to face. Then wear what is necessary and comfortable and warm. And then forget it.

# 3

# WHAT TO WEAR IN WINTER

Those who camp only in summer have seen only a tenth of the beauty in the outdoors. If they extend their outings to spring and fall, they get 50 percent. Winter backpacking is another whole world of beauty equal to all the rest of the year lumped together, and it is a specialized game that deserves attention all by itself.

However, even summer backpackers should know how to keep warm because cold snaps can occur at any time of year, particularly at higher elevations. In fact, at really high altitudes, it is winter the year around.

Summer hikers should remember that the temperatures they will encounter depend on a number of factors: latitude, altitude, cloud cover, and relative humidity. Anyone knows that, in general, the farther north you go, the lower the average temperature and the cooler the nights. But it is easy to forget this fact when you are planning a trip while sweltering in your suburban home.

No matter where you climb, temperatures also drop with altitude—about 4 degrees Fahrenheit for every 1,000 feet of elevation. Therefore, if you are going to climb a 10,000-foot mountain when it is 80 degrees Fahrenheit at the foot, you should expect a temperature of no more than 40 degrees Fahrenheit at the top. If the humidity is high, the difference could be somewhat more. And wind creates a chill factor that makes the apparent temperature seem even lower.

Therefore, you should always be prepared in the woods for chilly conditions, and in winter you must be even further armed with both special knowledge and clothing to stay safe and warm.

Okay, if you buy that, what *does* a nut wear who can't stay sensibly at home in front of the fire like everyone else? An intelligent answer requires a little knowledge of how the human body works. No one has described this better than Gerry Cunningham in his booklet "How to Keep Warm," which is available at any dealer that stocks Gerry backpacking and camping equipment. I will paraphrase him.

### *The Theory of Metabolism*

The body is a heat machine that turns out from 70 calories per hour when sleeping to 524 calories per hour with strenuous work. It also loses 1½ pints or more of water every 12 hours, depending on activity. Since clothing only conserves heat, it is this body heat that keeps you warm—or overheated, as the case may be.

The body loses heat mainly by convection, but since the

The magic world of winter in the woods is missed by fair-weather backpackers. It takes some special—and rather expensive—gear, but one view of snowcapped Mount Algonquin from Indian Falls in New York's Adirondacks is worth the training and effort.

air layer within $\frac{1}{8}$ inch of a surface—skin or clothing—tends to stick to that surface, any material that interrupts the flow of air at such intervals can be used for insulation. Interestingly enough, goosepimples, which erect body hairs, are an automatic device by the body to increase the amount of surface-still air.

When a body loses heat faster than it is being created, a protective mechanism called vascular constriction comes into play. To guard the vital organs in the torso, the body decreases the diameter of blood vessels in the extremities, thus reducing blood flow to these major heat-loss areas. That's why your hands and feet get cold. However, it is important to know that the head, with its rich supply of blood vessels to the brain, does not undergo vaso-constriction (for obvious reasons). Therefore, the head continues to be a prime heat radiator even when you are cold.

Now you know where the old saw about keeping your feet warm by covering your head came from. It is true—but only if you stop heat loss before vaso-constriction occurs. It is a much harder and longer process to reverse this automatic reaction. Incidentally, both tobacco and alcohol also constrict blood vessels. So, when you are backpacking in severe winter weather, it is wise not to smoke or drink.

To stay warm, the trick is to start covering up the minute you stop violent activity (such as climbing a mountain in snow on a bright day). First, you roll down your loose pants cuffs and roll up your long stockings. Then, on with the gloves or mittens. Next, button up and tuck in your shirt. Finally, after fluffing up your hair, you pull your cap well down over the sides of your head and neck—exactly the reverse order in importance of body radiation areas. Undressing must be resumed when you start up again, so you can see that life on the trail in winter can be hectic.

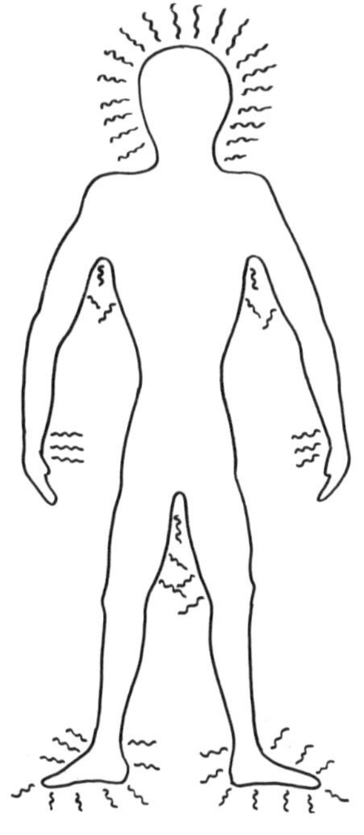

Major radiation areas of heat and moisture are in the body extremities. These must be ventilated during exercise and covered to retain heat when resting. This is particularly true of the head and neck, which always continue radiation. If too much heat is lost, the veins in the arms and legs constrict, causing them to feel cold.

Remember, vaso-constriction can be induced either by inadequate insulation or by insufficient production of body heat. Even the warmest clothes won't keep you warm if your metabolism is low for such reasons as poor health, lack of food, or inactivity.

The dressing and undressing game is essential in winter because moisture is deadly to insulation. Sweat can condense on outer layers of garments in the cold and then wick back to the skin, where it draws more heat from the body to re-evaporate. You may get away with this cyclic process while you are moving—even feel more comfortable. But when you stop on cold days, or even on mild days, in a wind, the chill strikes fast.

## WIND CHILL CHART

| | Actual Temperature (°F.) | | | | | | | | | |
|---|---|---|---|---|---|---|---|---|---|---|
| | 50 | 40 | 30 | 20 | 10 | 0 | −10 | −20 | −30 | −40 |
| *Estimated Wind Speed (mph)* | *Equivalent Temperature (°F.)* | | | | | | | | | |
| *calm* | 50 | 40 | 30 | 20 | 10 | 0 | −10 | −20 | −30 | −40 |
| 5 | 48 | 37 | 27 | 16 | 6 | −5 | −15 | −26 | −36 | −47 |
| 10 | 40 | 28 | 16 | 4 | −9 | −21 | −33 | −46 | −58 | −70 |
| 15 | 36 | 22 | 9 | −5 | −18 | −32 | −45 | −58 | −72 | −85 |
| 20 | 32 | 18 | 4 | −10 | −25 | −39 | −53 | −67 | −82 | −96 |
| 25 | 30 | 16 | 0 | −15 | −29 | −44 | −59 | −74 | −88 | −104 |
| 30 | 28 | 13 | −2 | −18 | −33 | −48 | −63 | −79 | −94 | −109 |
| 35 | 27 | 11 | −4 | −20 | −35 | −51 | −67 | −82 | −98 | −113 |
| 40 | 26 | 10 | −6 | −21 | −37 | −53 | −69 | −85 | −100 | −116 |
| | Little Danger | | | | Moderate Danger | | Great Danger | | | |

NOTE: Wind velocity can be estimated, as follows:

5 mph—Slight breeze that can be felt, rustles grass and leaves
10 mph—Leaves and small twigs in motion, ripples on lake water
15 mph—Dust swirls, branches move, heavy ripples on water
20 mph—Small trees sway, water ripples crest, snow drifts
25 mph—Large tree branches sway, water whitecaps
30 mph—Large trees sway, loose snow creates clouds in air
35 mph—Leaves and twigs break off trees, walking difficult
40 mph—Large branches break, trees lash wildly, water breaks in waves, walking is very difficult against wind

The latter is because of a factor called wind chill. In a wind, your body loses heat faster than in still air. The wind not only disrupts the surface-still air, but actually penetrates your insulated clothing. From experiments, a wind-chill table has been developed that plots wind velocity against actual temperatures in degrees Fahrenheit. The factor is roughly equivalent to the chilling effect of still air at that number of degrees Fahrenheit. The significance is that with proper clothing there is little danger of freezing at chill factors above −20 degrees Fahrenheit, moderate danger from there down to about −50, and great danger regardless of clothing at values below −60.

Okay, enough background. How do you actually stay warm? Experts say that the most important factor is to avoid sweating, but they don't tell you how. If you have a metabolism like mine, it takes some doing.

### *How to Prevent Sweating*

The conventional answer is to wear a number of layers of light garments that entrap still-air layers: fishnet long johns of at least a 3/8-inch mesh under a conventional wool shirt and pants, with whatever outer torso covering is appropriate to wind and temperature, a light parka or windproof, an insulated vest or sweater, or a heavy hooded parka. These garments not only create the desired layers of entrapped still air, they also transmit body moisture outward most efficiently.

In addition to wearing the proper clothing, to avoid sweating the hiker must proceed slowly. If your metabolism is normal or a little slow, this should do the trick. Since I sweat with not much more activity than blinking my eyelids, I have to take further steps.

I generally leave off the long johns, reserving them for the end of the day. (I carry a light, insulated undersuit that can be slipped over my regular clothes at long, cold stops.) Sometimes, I even have to take off my wool shirt and put on a loose, thin nylon windproof over a T-shirt when moving in the sun. It is important to remember that some covering should be maintained over tender skin to prevent frostbite, and all the exposed areas of the skin should be watched constantly for numbness or the white patches that are the evidence of freezing.

Since it is impractical to roll up your pants in deep powder snow, you might consider a new kind of pants that have side zippers, which can be opened from the top for ventilating the legs. I don't have them, but I do treasure an old-fashioned pair of gabardine ski pants that are cut full in the leg and allow moisture to "exhale." They have another advantage, too. They're so roomy I can wear my insulated pants under them in really bitter weather. I once had to do this during a February expedition into the Adirondack Mountains when the temperature dropped to −25 degrees Fahrenheit with a 10 miles per hour wind (about −50 degrees chill factor).

At night or when there is no sun or in a wind, the problem for everyone is staying warm. Forget the cheerful campfire, unless you simply want one for psychological reasons. In the open at low temperatures, a campfire is not only difficult to start but provides very little warmth. We usually don't even waste the energy to start one. Clothing is the answer to conserving heat. In this regard, any ads you read about miracle-thin space-age garments that are as warm as down are pure nonsense. Insulation is achieved by thickness and by the amount of entrapped air in that thickness.

In a World War II experiment, says Gerry Cunningham, cotton, kapok, and No. 000 steel wool were all tested for insulating value at densities below 4 pounds per cubic foot. All provided the same insulation. The lesson is that at these densities it is bulk that conserves heat, regardless of material.

*The Value of Down*

The most efficient type of bulk is that achieved by goose down, which is not a feather but a multi-filament pod that grows next to the bird's skin and protects it in the fiercest weather. The reason goose down is tops (with duck down second) is that it is extremely light (1.85 pounds per cubic foot density). It is also flexible and fluffs up to a high "loft," or bulk, yet compresses to about $\frac{1}{30}$th of its fluffed-out bulk for storage. It is also resilient and washable, and it breathes. In other words, it is a most practical material for use in outer garments and in sleeping bags for winter camping.

Next is duck down. In fact, it may be just as good as goose down today, according to Eastern Mountain Sports. This outfitter reports that goose down is being harvested from younger and smaller birds (grown for food), which reduces the bulk (loft) of the down. By separating duck down from the feathers, a process known as fractionalizing, a product with a bulk of 650 cubic inches per ounce can be obtained. This compares favorably with the virtually unobtainable Siberian goose down, which bulks at 800 cubic inches per ounce.

Some synthetics are now pretty good, too, particularly crimped and curled polyester fiber and, lately, some foam plastics. These materials are also a lot less costly than down, and this is important because, in my opinion, for ordinary winter camping the difference between materials in clothing is less critical than it is in sleeping bags (which will be discussed in Chapter 4). This is because heavily insulated garments provide less of your total protection, most of which is provided by other clothing. So, if you can only afford polyester- or foam-insulated jacket and pants, don't worry. You can easily get by with them on ordinary winter hikes.

In fact, if you shop shrewdly and know what you need, you can get by at modest cost even for quite severe winter backpacking. An example is the outfitting of Chuck two years ago when he was fourteen and started winter mountaineering with me.

Since he was growing like a weed, we didn't feel we could afford the more than $300 it can cost for gear suitable for conditions up to 15,000 feet of altitude (and you get these conditions regularly in the much-lower Adirondack and White mountains). But we wanted him to be safely clothed. In the end, we did it for a little over $100.

Our major source of clothing was a marvelous discount and surplus outlet called P&S Sales. A pair of heavy wool-serge surplus flight pants with double knees and seat and knitted anklets came to $6, with $10 more for local tailoring to make them fit my lean son. Long johns were $7. An orange balaclava with a dickey, front and back, was another $3.50. Long wool-and-nylon stockings came to $3.50 for two pairs, and there was another $4 for wool-and-nylon inner socks.

A pair of Mickey Mouse vinyl boots with lug soles added $8 more. Surplus Army ski goggles with interchangeable lenses were only $1. A heavy CPO shirt cost $11. And I loaned him a heavy knitted cotton sweatshirt that was worth $5. Two pairs of wool mitten liners and leather over-mittens or shells came to about $10. A foam-lined nylon ski parka was finally found locally on sale for $25. Plastic snowshoes ($15) and an ice axe ($19) topped off the rig. Total cost: about $128.

We loaned him one of our low-temperature down sleeping bags (about $150), and he has been snug with this outfit for two years now. The only thing we have added is some down "sox" ($7 from Eddie Bauer) for nighttime wear. Basically, this outfit would be suitable for anyone of any age.

### *Clothing for Severe Weather*

My gear, which has been acquired over many years, is a little more elaborate. On top of my old ski pants, I wear a wool Army shirt with an inner overlapping front flap that can be buttoned in place to give double protection. It was given to me by a friend, so I don't know what it cost. I also carry the Dacron-insulated undersuit, which I have worn occasionally as an undersuit, but more often as an outer suit when my regular clothes become wet and frozen. This 5.5-ounce Dacron-filled suit costs $15. And I carry a $20 nylon windproof for ordinary protection.

For outer wear in severe weather, I advocate a heavy-duty parka similar to my Kara Koram by Eddie Bauer ($70). Other makes of parkas from this and other outlets range in price from $40 to $95, depending on fill and construction. They pay off. The last time I climbed Mount Marcy in winter it was 40 degrees Fahrenheit and raining at the Adirondack Loj. On top, it was 20 degrees with winds estimated at 50 to 60 miles per hour. That's a chill factor of −21 degrees, which is the generally accepted dividing line between "cold" and "really cold" weather that necessitates high-altitude garments.

Other useful cold-weather clothes are down vests and lightweight down jackets that are priced from about $17 to $40. Combined with an under-sweater and an outer nylon windproof, they can carry you at rather severe conditions. Insulated and waterproofed ski mittens are also okay to protect hands.

The hardest areas to keep warm are the hands and feet,

as we have already learned from the facts about body metabolism. And it doesn't get any easier as you get older and your circulation slows down, either. The main answer is dryness. Keep snow out of mittens and boots and, when it inevitably gets in, have spare mitten liners and stockings in abundance. Make sure, too, that mittens and stockings and boots are not so tight as to restrict circulation.

Wet mittens and stockings can be dried by wringing them out and letting them freeze at night; in the morning bang the frost out and then complete the drying by putting

Largely surplus clothes costing just over $120 carry Chuck (left) through a 10-below bivouac at Lake Colden in the Adirondacks. The nearly buried lean-to (right) is also walled up with snow blocks to keep out wind.

them inside your clothes next to your skin during the day or by sleeping with them at night.

In deep powder snow, even with snowshoes, the short hiking boots worn during the summer are impractical. A higher boot, preferably insulated, is much more comfortable. Also, a sturdy boot is almost essential for wearing crampons. My own boots for winter wear are 8-inch K-99 insulated boots by Eddie Bauer ($47). Bauer and other suppliers have a wide range of similar boots in a wide range of prices. Such boots should be protected with silicone dressings, which are much more durable in cold, wet conditions. For short hikes, insulated Maine hunting shoes or felt mukluks inside galoshes are favored by some.

A good way to keep snow out of boots is with gaiters. I have a 16-inch pair, red nylon with rear zippers and Velcro top tabs, that really does the trick, for $6 from Recreational Equipment, Inc.

Since you can't work in mittens—to operate a stove, camera, or even open your pack—you also need gloves. I take along the same doeskin gloves I use in summer and keep them dry by carrying them inside my T-shirt. I have tried silk, a marvelous insulator in incredibly thin layers, which is available in gloves, stockings, and underwear. But silk is too fragile. The gloves I had, which protected my fingers very nicely during the cooking and eating of whole dinners at 25 below, developed holes in the tips of the fingers in a matter of days. If some genius would only laminate nylon fabric to the silk to form a tough outer layer, we might really have something. Alert, all of you geniuses in the supply business!

The topper is your hat or cap. For ordinary winter woods cruising, I like the beret mentioned in Chapter 2. For high-mountain work, though, a balaclava like my son's with a tuck-in extension fore and aft that works like a scarf is the ticket. When the wind rises, it can be rolled down over your face. Goggles cover most of the open space around the face.

Last, but far from least, is the critical matter of what you put over your eyes. I suppose, if you are just taking a stroll through shaded woods, ordinary sunglasses are okay. But don't be foolish enough to think these will suffice at high altitudes or on any bare snow slope. In the mountains, sunlight and particularly the powerful actinic rays that cause sunburn and eye damage are particularly strong—and the snow reflects the rays at all angles. The only safe protection is goggles that enclose the eyes on all sides. Lenses should be of dark safety glass or plastic, preferably a neutral gray that does not distort natural colors. Always wear such protection, even on cloudy days. Clouds do not screen out these radiations. Ski goggles are another possibility, although they are seldom dark enough and tend to steam up.

Remember, too, that sunburn in such conditions is extremely rapid—even faster than on a summer beach in Florida. Be very careful about exposing any skin and protect your face and neck with sun cream—not oil—or glacier cream or zinc-oxide ointment. I cringe every time I see tyros climbing or skiing in warm weather stripped to the waist or, even worse, in shorts. A dangerous burn can occur in as short a time as a half hour on snow, and a burn is even inevitable for a person with a heavy suntan.

### *How to Get About on Snow*

Now that you're dressed, let's have a word about transportation. Snowshoes are the only practical method of getting around on tightly wooded and narrow-trailed Eastern mountains. Nordic skiing in more open areas is a great sport as well as a method of travel, but it's a complete subject in itself, on which a number of good books have been written. We'll just have to define it, arbitrarily, as beyond the scope of backpacking.

Many winter hikers turn up their noses at anything other than traditional wood-framed snowshoes with either rawhide or neoprene-coated-nylon webbing. These snowshoes are admittedly very good. They come in either long-tailed models—Maine, trail, cross-country, or pickerel styles, in increasing order of slenderness and length—or in short, round bear-paw or modified bear-paw (with a slight tail) styles at prices from about $29 to $45. The neoprene rigging is about $2 more than rawhide, but is not as susceptible to moisture damage or to the hungry nibbles of mice and squirrels. The bindings are extra, $6 to $15.

For heavy woods and trails, the Maine and bear-paw models are best, since they are shorter and more maneuverable. You should look for smooth, well-varnished hardwood frames, preferably of white ash. If you elect rawhide webbing, it should be thoroughly shellacked or varnished and should be kept that way with regular maintenance. Snowshoes are stored out-of-season in a cool and dry place, safe from rodents.

You will find that the shorter and broader snowshoes can be difficult to walk in for long distances so, if the terrain permits, you may be happier with a trail shoe. These 5-foot snowshoes give excellent support in loose and deep snow for even the biggest man with a heavy pack. The tail helps keep the snowshoe on track and the high turned-up toe clears the drifts with efficiency. However, conventional snowshoes should be kept outside a warm cabin and away from campfires, to prevent them from softening and absorbing melting snow and from icing up. They weigh about 6 pounds.

Because of these objections, we use plastic snowshoes, called Snowtreads, that are made from a modified polypropylene and have a woven-web nylon binding attached to a toe plate that is plastic-hinged to the body of the waffle-patterned molded shoe. They only weigh a pound apiece, and although they are much smaller than conventional snowshoes (and hence, easier to manuever), they do not sink very far in deep powder even when carrying a heavy load. They require no care, either.

I have used mine for six years, and they show no signs of wear or cracking, although I have bridged them over logs and rocks at low temperatures on many occasions. One problem they did have. It was impossible at first to keep the foot snugly in the binding because the toe plate space was too short to push the foot far enough forward and because the webbing was threaded through slots over the top of the plate. The foot slid out when the webbing iced up.

We corrected this by threading the webbing under the toe plate and by cutting away the plastic directly in front of the plate in a sort of gothic arch. This permits the foot to be slid farther forward into the binding, which can then be secured over the instep. The snowshoes now work perfectly and we have been quite satisfied—particularly with the price, which is $15 complete.

People who snowshoe over rough terrain sometimes carry a ski pole for balance. We go one better and use two cross-country ski poles, which are longer and have bigger baskets than the downhill variety. These help a great deal on steep slopes and keep you upright and steady when you are carrying a heavy pack in deep powder.

Another aid that many people construct is snowshoe crampons for traveling over hard crusts or on icy slopes. I have never used them, but I am thinking of making a pair because they are really handy.

The best that I have seen were some owned by an old gentleman who was staying at the Adirondack Loj one winter weekend and who also used plastic snowshoes. He had taken two strips of ¼-inch-thick aluminum bar, each about 12 inches long, and had riveted them together to form an X. About 1 and 2 inches from each of the four ends, he drilled and countersank two holes, then inserted flathead aluminum bolts in the outer holes, securing them under the bars with nuts and lock washers. The ends of

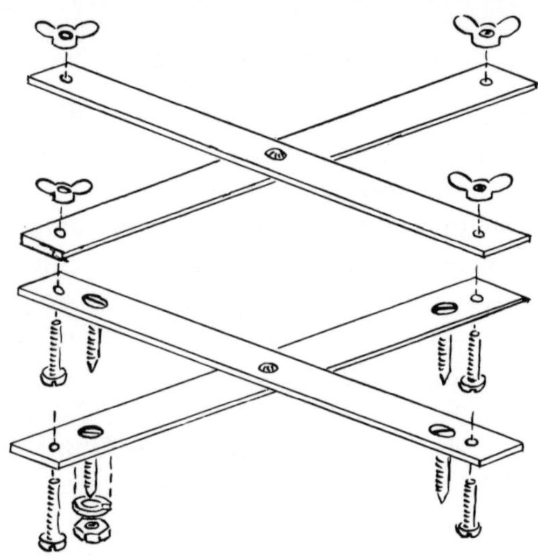

Snowshoe crampons can be made from flat aluminum bar stock, riveted into X-shaped members and held together above and below the shoe with bolts and wing nuts. Spikes are sharpened flathead bolts, held in place with lock washers and nuts.

these bolts were sharpened to points on a grinding wheel.

A similar X was made from two other pieces of bar stock and drilled with four holes that matched the four inner holes in the first X, 2 inches in from the ends. The only additional materials were four more flathead aluminum bolts with wing nuts. To assemble, he placed the spiked X under the snowshoe just behind his foot. The other X was placed on top of the shoe and both were fastened together with the four bolts and wing nuts, which passed through the wafflled openings in the shoes. Attachment took less than a minute per shoe.

When not in use, he folded the X-shaped pieces flat and carried them in a little bag—a very light and practical rig.

If you climb mountains, though, you inevitably come to the place where snowshoes are useless and where ice and wind-hardened snow require the use of crampons. These devices can be useful, in fact, even at low altitudes on icy surfaces. They represent a considerable investment but are worth it for the safety they provide.

The simplest type is ice creepers, which can be obtained from a surplus outlet for $2. They have blunt points, but these can be sharpened to needles on a grinding wheel and they will take care of you on the level. Slightly better are four-point instep crampons ($2) that can also be used as snowshoe crampons. But for upland work, you need the real thing.

Unless you are going to climb near-vertical walls, you can get by very well with 10-point crampons. And if you know the boot that you will always wear, get a non-adjustable crampon. They cost less. A representative range of prices is found at Recreational Equipment, Inc.: 10-point, $18; 12-point, $20; adjustable 10- and 12-point, $22 to $25. Add $3 to all of these prices for nylon straps, or make your own, which will do just as well, from nylon cord. The heavy-duty Chouinard 12-point adjustable crampons that I own go for $35 plus $4 for nylon straps.

Non-adjustable crampons must be fitted precisely to your boots because any flexing of the hardened steel points will cause them to break. So, take your boots along when you buy, or send an accurate cutout tracing of your boot to the outfitter. Both adjustable and fixed crampons should fit the boot so snugly that they will not fall off when the boot is waved in the air with the crampon in place but unstrapped. This is one reason why my winter boots are of sturdy leather with Vibram soles.

One other thing about crampons: they are murderously sharp (and should be kept that way). When you walk in them, keep your feet slightly apart, as when snowshoeing, to avoid spiking yourself in the trousers or, worse, in the leg. And when they are not in use, get some rubber protectors ($1 to $2) that fit over the spikes for storage in your pack. What a loose pair of crampons can do to a pack and its contents is too horrible to mention.

The last piece of gear, which you may or may not consider essential, is an ice axe. Think you don't need one? Well, just get to a lean-to where you plan to spend the night and find the outhouse door frozen in by 4 to 6 feet of successively crusted snow and ice layers. The temperature is coasting down past 20 below, there's a brisk little breeze blowing, and you don't want to frostbite your tender parts by hanging them in a snowbank. You can cut and shovel that door open in ten minutes with an ice axe and your snowshoes.

But an ice axe is useful to the average winter hiker in many more ways. Some people use them instead of ski poles when snowshoeing (you can get a basket attachment for about $2). They can serve as an emergency or extra tent pole or stake, particularly in high winds. There are always icy banks where a few steps cut in the ice add safety. And if you camp by a stream and can't find a natural hole in the ice, an ice axe can enable you quickly to obtain a water supply that would take an hour to melt from snow. Of course, if you climb, an ice axe is as essential as your arms. On steep scrambles, this tool is a must for safety, enabling a climber to arrest himself in case of a slip or fall.

The proper length is a matter of changing fashion, but I like one that is long enough to reach from the ground to the flat of my hand when the arm is extended. This enables it to be used as a walking stick and also eases the cutting of steps below me on a descent, if I can't avoid such an unhappy circumstance.

There are a great number of types. Recreational Equipment, Inc., has a larger assortment than anyone else I know. They range in price from $15 to $35. I paid $17 for

A weasel on the prowl leaves record in woodland snowdrifts. Following the tracks of these rarely seen animals is one of the many reasons for roaming the woods in winter.

my Stubai Aschenbrenner model, which has a curved adze, carbiner hole, and long, slender pick. The handle is straight-grained ash and carries a strap and guide ring. Any other features, among the many that are touted, I would think are a matter of personal preference.

But be sure to get a leather guard ($1) for the head and a rubber guard for the spike. An ice axe is almost as dangerous as crampons in its unguarded state.

One more thought about cold-weather camping. Don't let the details of winter equipment put you off. Winter mountaineering may be a bit formidable, but winter backpacking need not be. It would be a shame if you never tried it, once you know the ropes of warm-weather camping. A winter woodland is a wonderland. Every ordinary shape is excitingly different. And where most wild animals pass unseen in summer, in winter their every movement leaves a trail for you to unravel.

I recall a trip many years ago to Balsam Lake Mountain in the western Catskills in midwinter with my two young boys. As we neared the summit, plowing through nearly three feet of snow, we spotted the tracks of a bobcat on the prowl for food. Suddenly, the tracks changed in pace. We saw where the cat had spotted a rabbit under the low branches of a hemlock. The rabbit made a prodigious leap of over seven feet in his flight to safety. Back and forth the chase ran across the trail. We patiently followed. Finally, the desperate rabbit made a mistake and zigged when he should have zagged. The final story of a predator's meal was told in a few blood spots and a tuft of white fur. My boys have never forgotten this woodland lesson, available only to those who venture forth "out-of-season."

# 4

# HOW TO SLEEP WELL

My experience with sleeping bags is of fairly recent vintage. I don't know how it was in the East, but in the mountains of California where I grew up only effete—and very wealthy—sportsmen owned real sleeping bags. We rolled up a blanket or two, occasionally pinned it into a double-fold bag, and headed for the hills. At night we just rolled up in them, put our feet to the embers, and corked off—as the mountain men had done a hundred years before us. It wasn't exactly comfortable, but we didn't know any better.

Much later, I swiped a brand-new L. L. Bean kapok-filled sleeping bag from a careless relative and discovered a different way of living. What a monster! It had a canvas outer liner and weighed about twenty-five pounds, rolled into a sausage about three feet long and a foot in diameter, and caught on every tree I passed in the woods. But I used it for twenty years until one night, on top of a mountain, the temperature dropped to 15 degrees and I felt the cold air rushing through every part of it. I knew then that the kapok had finally disintegrated.

I have much fancier gear now, but I don't regret the earlier experiences. They gave me a much stronger appreciation of the great technical advances that have been made in sleeping bags. Even so, it is not necessary to turn up one's nose at blanket rolls. They are low in cost and very efficient for summer camping. We started our first three kids off in blanket rolls and they say they were very comfortable. So, if you have a slim wallet, some old blankets, and some young children, it's probably the cheapest way to get into business. See Chapter 11 for how to arrange them.

But when all is said and done, man has only one real haven in the wild—his ever-lovin' sleeping bag. So, it pays to have a good one. No matter how cold and wet and tired you get during the day, at night you can strip down and slip into that soft, warm, fluffy bag and be in heaven. You can, that is, if you have chosen well and if you have adequately protected your investment. With the zillion claims being made for sleeping bags of all kinds today, selection is not always the easiest thing in the world to do.

### *Sleeping Bag Construction*

First of all, let's look at some fundamentals. We have already discussed the nature of insulation and its purpose in clothing. For sleeping gear, these facts go double. Remember, you're only turning out about 70 calories per hour when you're cutting zees.

But insulation isn't insulating unless it's where it's supposed to be and stays there. This requires some pretty fancy construction in sleeping bags—and that's what the claims are mostly about and also why the cost of sleeping bags varies so much.

Basically, there are five types of construction to hold loose insulating material in place: sewn-through tubing, slant tube, box tube, overlapping tube, and various tube-on-tube buildups. These structures run the vertical

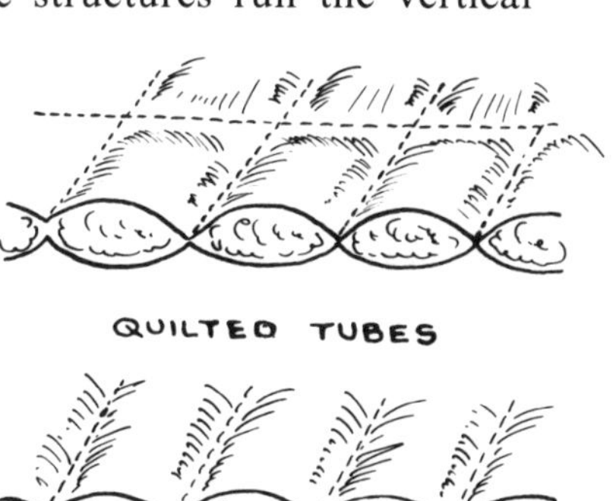

Five basic constructions on which all filled sleeping bags are based, starting with the simplest at the top and progressing to the more complex and warmer—and more expensive—at the bottom.

length of the bag or can be wrapped around horizontally or can be veed in a transverse manner.

The simplest and most economical structure is the sewn-through tubing, which is also sometimes quilted with cross-stitching. Obviously, this whole operation can be conducted on machines, which cuts costs. Without cross-stitching in this type of structure, however, the filling tends to settle under pressure from the body into the head and foot of the tubes, reducing the insulation around the torso. But where the stitches bring the two layers of fabric together, there is virtually no insulation and the cold can come through. Nevertheless, this construction is used in most low-cost bags where only moderate protection in summer weather is needed.

The other types are all attempts to overcome the deficiencies of the simple tube. They are more costly because they demand a lot of handwork, sometimes including special internal baffles that keep insulation from shifting without stitching the two liners directly together and thus creating a cold spot. Generally, these structures also use more of the expensive insulating material, too. But for cold-weather use, this extra work and cost pays off big.

There are other costs. A sleeping bag with a full or even a partial zipper is easier to get into and to air out between uses. Nylon zippers are rapidly replacing metal zippers for this purpose, since the former don't jam as easily. Full zippers are necessary to join mating bags to create a double bed.

But a zipper lets in about as much cold air as a screen door. To prevent this, better sleeping bags have an insulated baffle that hangs over the zipper inside the bag. Then, there are auxiliary insulated hoods that zip on and can be drawn over the head and shoulders to keep out drafts and nylon cord ties to tighten various sections of the bag. Bags are made in various shapes, too—rectangular, tapered, and mummy—which use different amounts of insulating material and are constructed with varying degrees of difficulty.

The inner and outer liners of a bag are important to its construction, too. They must be proof against the passage of insulation, but must transmit body moisture. They must be tough enough to resist tearing, light enough to reduce weight, and easy to keep clean.

Today, most liners are of ripstop nylon. North Face believes, and I agree, that the minimum weight for such an outside liner is 1.9 ounces per square yard.

## *What Is Loft?*

There is another factor in the insulating value of a sleeping bag—a rather intangible quality called loft. Loft is the total thickness of a sleeping bag, measured by fluffing up the bag and smoothing it out evenly, as nearly as possible, with no weight in or on the bag.

It should be noted that prime duck down has only about 80 percent of the loft of prime goose down. And it takes from one and a half to two times as much polyester fiber

Thickness of insulation needed at various temperatures for different types of activity. Temperatures are in still air.

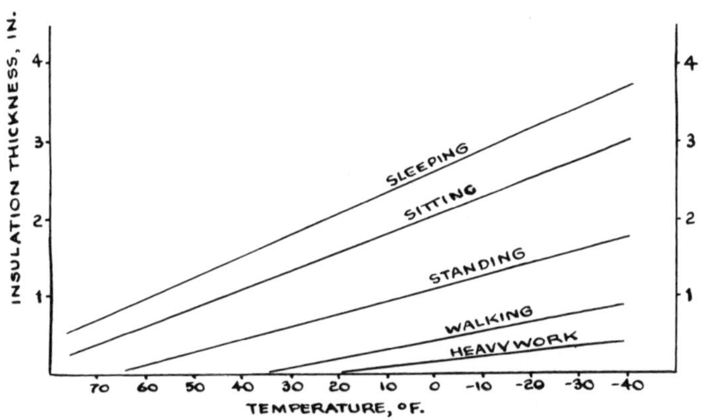

to give as much insulation as a given quantity of goose down.

Based on studies originated by the Army, it has been determined that a sleeping man needs from 1½ to 3½ inches of insulation at still-air temperatures from 50 to –40 degrees Fahrenheit (as shown in the graph reprinted with permission from Gerry Cunningham's booklet). Since loft is a total of both sides of a sleeping bag, a loft of from 3 to 7 inches is necessary to meet Army specs.

The intangible part of the thing is that loft is not constant. It varies with the way an individual prepares and takes care of his sleeping bag. And the minute he climbs into it, there is little or no loft left under him. Insulating value also varies with the amount of moisture in the insulation.

However, one thing the chart does demonstrate is the importance of still air. Check again the Wind Chill Chart in Chapter 3 and see how you can get a still-air temperature of –60 degrees at only –10 degrees Fahrenheit when exposed to a 30 mile per hour wind. Chuck and I, in company with three other young men, just achieved this dubious distinction at a night's bivouac on top of Slide Mountain in the Catskills. Such conditions emphasize the need for wind-screen protection around your sleeping bag, if it is to do its job. We'll see how such protection is achieved in Chapter 6. As for loft, use it as a guide in selecting a sleeping bag, not as the final scientific determinant.

### *Mummy Versus Tapered Bags*

But, enough of theory. What kind of bag should you choose, insulated with what kind of material? Hold on, we're headed again for a big, fat prejudice.

I don't like mummy bags. However, before a lynching party is formed from all of their adherents, I will try to cite their advantages objectively.

Pound for pound, mummy bags are the warmest kind of bag. They weigh less than any other bag of comparable material and comfort range and, of course, they stuff into a smaller space. Generally, they cost less—at least a little less—than comparable larger bags.

They are warmer because they conform more closely to the body, particularly if they are made with a "differential cut," where the inner liner is smaller than the outer liner. The close-fitting drawstring hood, which is inherent, prevents body heat from being lost at the neck or top opening. Today many mummy bags are also being cut in a sort of hourglass shape that provides more room for the feet.

How much do they cost? Well, in goose down, you can pay from about $46 to $83 for bags with a low comfort point of 25 degrees Fahrenheit. The average, though, seems to be about $50. These bags are horizontal-tube structures with from 1 to $2\frac{1}{4}$ pounds of down fill and have gross weights of from $3\frac{1}{4}$ to $3\frac{5}{8}$ pounds. The lowest-cost bag, from Olin's Comfy Division, and the highest-priced bag, from Alpine Designs, have full zippers and can be mated to other bags. Middle-priced bags from Morsan and Eddie Bauer have a short zipper and no zipper, respectively.

But mummy bags are made in greater quantity for the lower temperature range of 10 degrees to −40 degrees Fahrenheit minimum-comfort points. These bags cost from $65 to $135, with the average somewhere around $90. They are insulated with from $2\frac{1}{2}$ to $5\frac{1}{8}$ pounds of down and total weights range from $3\frac{7}{8}$ to $7\frac{1}{8}$ pounds. These bags are all made with single- or double-overlapping or slant-tube constructions, and all but two have full zippers. In addition to the companies mentioned before, this sampling includes Blacks, North Face, Recreational Equipment, Inc., and Sierra Designs, all of which make mummy bags only for the colder conditions.

While many of the standard right-hand bags can be mated to left-hand-opening bags (which generally cost a little more), it should be recorded that Sierra Designs has a true double-mummy bag for those with other than backpacking on their minds. It has full zippers on both sides, individual hoods, is loaded with 3 pounds 9 ounces of down and weighs 6 pounds 23 ounces. For obvious reasons, the firm doesn't give an estimate on minimum temperature, but I agree with them that, if you can't be comfortable at zero, you should stay in the lodge—or sleep alone.

At least two firms have junior-sized down bags for kids under five feet tall that cost $48 for a North Face mummy and $37 for a rectangular Eddie Bauer. They have comfort ranges of 10 and 25 degrees Fahrenheit, respectively. We have the Eddie Bauer bag for our six-year-old Chris and it is a real bargain, weighs only 25 ounces and has a built-in hood. (As the last in line, he is being pampered, I'm afraid!)

How do the figures given above relate to materials other than down? Well, Morsan has three mummies rated from 20 to 30 degrees minimum comfort that are filled with either 2 or 3 pounds of different polyesters. The bags weigh from 4 to 4½ pounds and cost from $23 to $40. Swiss Ski Sports also has a $45 bag in this comfort range with 3 pounds of polyester that totals 4⅝ pounds. And White Stag has one, too, stuffed with 2 pounds of polyester and weighing in at 3 pounds 5 ounces for only $25.

Comfy and Morsan, for two, also have fiber-filled junior mummy bags that are a little less in price than comparable adult bags: $25 to $40 for 25- and 10-degree ratings.

However, a trip to any outdoor store will reveal a host of cut-rate bags of questionable virtue and dubious construction for as little as $15.

A new concept in sleeping gear is a mummy bag made with a solid inner layer of foam plastic and covered with nylon fabric both inside and outside. It's made by Ocaté and is rated for zero. Diagonal cords, laced through loops in the outer liner, enable the shell to be drawn close to the body. The jury is still out on this innovation. One of my young friends has one; reports that while it is warm, he has trouble rolling and stuffing it into its bag.

If a mummy bag is your ticket, and you are going to start with occasional backpacking, or have a youngster entering the Scouts, I would opt for a good polyester-filled bag. Obviously, they are lower in cost, but they are also easily machine-washable and are not as fragile as good down bags. In other words, the kid can drag it through the mud and you can still restore it at home.

Since the better mummy bags are good values for the benefits delivered, why do I object to mummies? There are a number of reasons, the first of which is conventional, but also very personal. I like to move around when I sleep and a mummy bag gives about as much freedom as a coffin. But, I also have another objection: lack of versatility.

There is very little you can do to improve the warmth of a mummy bag. There's no room for liners. Nor is there room for all the stuff you have to take to bed with you on a winter backpack at low temperatures: your cameras, flashlight, wet clothes, water bottle, and boots. You have to share sleeping room with all of this plunder to keep it from freezing, and it does take up some space.

Now, no one is suggesting that a backpacker can afford the weight and bulk of a conventional rectangular sleeping bag either. Those are good only for car campers. But a tapered bag. Ah, there's a real bed. This bag is a

Representative types of sleeping bags in clockwise order are Eddie Bauer's tapered down bag (right foreground) that I use, a barrel-shaped down bag by Alpine Designs, a new foam-filled bag with drawstring tighteners by Ocaté, and Chris's down-filled junior bag with hood by Eddie Bauer.

modification of the rectangular bag with a full-width top, but tapering in either a straight or curved line to a smaller base. It has all of the roomy advantages of a rectangular bag with less weight and bulk. Unfortunately, there are not too many on the market.

Two that Teddy and I have had for years are so-called Four Season bags by Eddie Bauer (which were called Forest King, when we bought them). One has a 3-pound down fill, weighs 6 pounds 2 ounces and is rated to 5 degrees. The other has a 2 pound fill, weighs 5 pounds 3 ounces and is rated to 30 degrees. (The current list prices are $109 and $104, respectively). They mate together with full side-and-bottom zippers.

We have nylon fleece liners and down hoods that were especially crafted for these bags and can be added whenever we want to get another 20 to 30 degrees of warmth. The cost of these attachments totaled another $50 for each set. This firm has also recently come out with a tapered down liner with a 1-pound fill that could add another 25 degrees of warmth for $35 and an extra 2 pounds of weight, if we ever needed it. I don't think we ever will.

The weight of our bags with hoods and liners is between 8 and 9 pounds each. And as I said earlier, both of them have been used at chill factors as low as −60 degrees Fahrenheit in perfect comfort. Okay, so we paid about $15 more than the highest priced mummy, and our fully equipped rig weighs from 1 to 2 pounds more than the heaviest and most expensive mummy. To be fairer about it, we are about $50 to $70 more and 3 to 4 pounds heavier than the average low-temperature mummy. Without the extras, we're 2 to 3 pounds heavier than comparable lightweight mummies.

But our bags are not only more roomy and easier to air out and clean, they can also be adapted more easily for the wide degree of temperatures backpackers find in the field. And the price and weight comparisons for our older bags are not the whole story. There are lighter and less costly tapered bags that have come along since we bought ours.

Blacks has a tapered Ice Cap at $96 with 2¼ pounds of down that is rated to 10 below. It also has a barrel-shaped Norland for $78 with 1½ pounds of fill, zero rating, that can be slipped into a $105 Norland Special containing 2 pounds of down and rated alone to −10 degrees. The combination gives year-around versatility for an out-of-this-world price of $183.

North Face has a Unimog tapered bag for $98 with 2¼ pounds of down and a weight of 3¾ pounds that's good to zero. Recreational Equipment, Inc., has a Skier model with a barrel shape and fills of 2, 2½, and 3 pounds of down and gross weights from 3¾ to 5⅜ pounds. The prices are from $59 to $83 and minimum comforts are from zero to −40.

Sierra Designs has an Omni model at $98 with just over 2 pounds of duck down and a gross weight of 4⅝ pounds that is good for 15 degrees. Finally, White Stag has another barrel shape with 50-50 down and polyester that weighs 5¼ pounds and costs $43. All of these bags can also be fitted with extra liners to extend their ranges. Some have attachable hoods. However, you can also buy a separate hood with shoulders from Blacks for $11.

Just to complete the picture, there is also a thing called an elephant's foot, which is a half bag for emergency mountain bivouacs and is used in conjunction with a down parka. They usually weigh less than 2 pounds and cost about $35 or so. Having once made such an emergency bivouac on a mountain in a sudden and savage storm, I can say with feeling that only such an emergency would make me repeat the experience.

There's one last thing that should be said about tapered bags. They are definitely more comfortable for summer use. All bag makers claim fantastic ranges for their products. Eddie Bauer, for example, says that its heaviest Kara Koram is comfortable all the way from −20 to 50 degrees. Other outfitters make equally absurd claims.

But the fact is that at normal summer-night low-altitude temperatures, you have to open these bags up and even then you may almost die of heat prostration. The tapered bags are capable of being fully opened and are much more adjustable in ventilation, in my opinion. However, for another and even lower-cost solution to this problem, see Chapter 11.

But enough. I have gone into all of this detail to show you the wide variety of prices and constructions now available. In the end, you will have to assess their value for your personal needs and peculiarities. If you have never camped before, don't just rush into a store and buy a bag from these or any other specs, though. The first time you go backpacking, try to borrow a bag or rent one from an outdoor store. Even one night of experience will tell you more about your particular metabolism and likes and dislikes than all the textbook theory in the world.

An inadequate sleeping bag can be improved by what you wear in it. In summer, I don't advocate wearing anything except, perhaps, clean underwear and socks. Dirty clothes can soil the bag, and clothing is unnecessary. But in cold weather, you may want to wear your clothes to bed, even donning an extra sweatshirt or sweater and extra dry socks. Dry clothing can improve the temperature rating of a bag by at least 20 degrees.

If you have a short-haired dog with you, he may be more comfortable if you carry a small piece of flannel blanket to wrap around him at night. Our long-haired pooch is happy just curled up between us at the outside foot of our bags.

## *Under the Sleeping Bag*

And now, on to an equally important subject. A sleeping bag alone is not the whole bed. Without something under it, the finest sleeping bag in the world will not keep you warm, particularly in winter. The something that does is a ground cloth and some kind of support to raise and insulate the bag from the ground.

In the old days, this support was browse, the tender little branch ends from balsam, spruce, or fir trees that were painstakingly plucked and shingled into a foot-thick layer. Today, anyone who cuts green limbs of any kind should be locked up—and could be, too, because it is against the law in most state and all federal parks.

But just in case you think you missed something of the old days, let me reassure you. You didn't. The smell was lovely, but it took nearly an hour to construct such a bed properly and they had to be rebuilt every day because they crushed down. Furthermore, evergreen boughs weep resin, which used to get all over clothes and blankets—and would be disastrous on today's nylon bag liners. All in all, we're much better off with modern air mattresses and insulated pads. But which to use? We have both for different reasons.

For many years, I scorned any padding; just hollowed out a little space under hip and shoulder and dropped off. When Teddy first started backpacking with me, she dutifully tried the same routine—once. Being a sensible woman under no illusions of masculinity, pioneering forebearers and so forth, she said, "There must be a better way."

Still not really convinced that it wasn't indecent for a mountaineer to idle the night away in sybaritic luxury, I nevertheless bought some Japanese-made "balloons" for, I believe, about $2 each. Incredibly, these lightweight air mattresses lasted for a couple of years with only occasional patching. And before their last seams expired in the middle of a night, I was ruined forever for the spartan life.

We now own $10 Stebco mattresses in the three-quarter backpacker size. Five-tube units made from nylon laminated to a low-temperature-resistant vinyl, they measure

28 by 50 inches deflated, somewhat less when full of air. They weigh 1 pound 12 ounces and fold very compactly in the pack. They have a simple rubber-plugged inflating tube, a pop-out button that warns against overinflation, and a handy-dandy 1-inch drain valve that lets the air out almost instantaneously. I heartily recommend these features and warn against buying a mattress with a single air valve or a metal one. The single valve takes forever to drain the bag in the morning. And a metal valve can rub a hole in the mattress when it is folded in the pack and also tends to freeze open or shut.

Many people become disillusioned with air mattresses because they don't know how to inflate them properly. If a mattress is blown up too hard, you will find it almost impossible to stay aboard. The trick is to blow it up, then

Practical pads for support and insulation under sleeping bags are (left to right) a backpacker air mattress with quick-release valves, Chris's Japanese vinyl full-length mattress with pillow, and a nylon-covered foam pad that is similar but thicker than an Ensolite pad. These are shown on a 9- by 12-foot polyethylene ground cloth.

lie on it on your side. Let air out until your hip just barely clears the ground and you will be comfortable.

There are air mattresses with over-sized outer tubes, lengths to 72 inches and attached pillow sections. Buy 'em if you wish. But they generally weigh a great deal more, and I find all of the extra features unnecessary.

Naturally, no backpacker will waste from 8 to 18 ounces of weight on an air pump. You blow mattresses up by mouth. If you do it immediately upon arrival in camp after a hard climb, you'll see stars and constellations never before visible to man. If you wait until after dinner, you'll throw up. Oh, yes, and there seems to be an immutable law of nature that an air mattress—no matter how carefully tested at home—will only develop a leak in the very middle of a dark, cold night (usually when you have forgotten or can't find the repair kit).

For these trivial reasons and the fact that air mattresses are rather heavy, many people shun them in favor of foam pads. We have both ensolite and foam pads.

The best thing about a closed-cell Ensolite pad is its incredible ability to insulate and its imperviousness to the transmission of moisture. A pad only ¼ inch thick can protect you at sub-zero temperatures, although the ⅜-inch pad is even better. But Ensolite is virtually non-compressible and is bulky when rolled. It is light, all right. A 21- by 56-inch pad of ¼-inch Ensolite weighs 14 ounces; the same size in ⅜-inch material weighs 20 ounces. They cost from $4 to $5, respectively, and are just about imperative for winter mountaineering.

However, for all practical purposes, I get the same results from a more comfortable polyurethane foam pad that measures 20 by 42 inches and is enclosed in a removable, washable nylon cover that prevents moisture from wicking through the open-celled foam. It costs $6 and can be compressed in rolling to a diameter of about 4 inches.

One or the other type of foam pad is an essential in winter camping, because an air mattress permits cold to strike through from the ground and provides very little insulation. I feel that with either rig, a pillow is unnecessary either in summer or winter. I put my clothes in my sleeping-bag stuff bag and that serves as a very comfortable pillow.

Since the pad or mattress is only three-quarter length, something must be done about the legs. In summer, I do nothing. The sleeping bag is soft enough for me. In winter, I put my down parka under my legs to insulate them from the ground. You could also put your pack, or dried leaves or grass, under your legs if you feel the need for extra padding. Teddy carries a pair of terry cloth bed socks, which she keeps in her sleeping bag at all times. She puts them on at night to keep her feet warmer. We used these for all our kids when they were young, too.

Next in importance is a waterproof ground cloth, which prevents moisture from traveling from the ground to your sleeping bag and also keeps this expensive item clean and protected from small sticks and stones. And don't kid yourself. There is *always* moisture in the ground and there are *always* sticks and rocks, no matter how carefully you choose and police your campsite.

The least costly and lightest material for a ground cloth is polyethylene film. You can use a painter's drop sheet obtained from the nearest hardware store, although these are usually only 3 or 4 mils in thickness (0.003 to 0.004 inches)—a little thin for long wear. Many camping stores now carry 5- and 6-mil sheets in various sizes. An 8x10-foot sheet can be obtained from Morsan, for example, for $3. This gives enough room for your bag and gear and some cooking space on the side. After the first night's use, you'll see how much water has been drawn from the ground by the heat of your body and has condensed on the underside of the sheet.

As a matter of course, we generally carry an extra ground cloth. They are handy things to have around. The spare one can cover a woodpile or shield one end of a tent or tarp from driving rain or it can even be used as an emergency tent, as we shall see later in Chapter 6.

The three elements, then, that are required for a good night's sleep are a sleeping bag suitable for the temperature conditions you expect, adequate shielding from the wind, and a ground cloth and pad or air mattress to shield you from ground cold and moisture.

### *How to Care for Sleeping Bags*

To protect the very substantial investment you have made in your sleeping bag, you must care for it. Sleeping bags should be carried in stuff bags, generally nylon and sometimes equipped with tightening cords to compress the bundle to its smallest possible size. The stuff bag also wards off dirt and moisture. A down bag should always be stuffed randomly into this bag to avoid creating set fold lines that can break down the down. At home, the bag should be either hung up at full length in a closet or folded loosely on a shelf.

In the woods, take your bag out as soon as you make camp and shake it out for several minutes to fluff up the loft. Every morning, as soon as you get up, unzip the bag and hang it over a line in the sun or under cover if it is raining to let it air out and to evaporate the body moisture it has collected during the night.

When you inevitably get some dirt spots on the liners, wash them out at once at home with fairly dry suds of a mild soap. Use only enough to remove the dirt and then sponge all of the soap from the fabric with clean, lukewarm water.

When your bag begins to get lumpy and loses its loft after many years, don't give up. The bag can be restored to like-new condition with proper cleaning. Down can be either dry-cleaned or washed. If dry-cleaned, take the bag (or your down garments) to a cleaner experienced in down who will use the proper solvent and will dry the bag completely afterward to eliminate vapors that can be deadly if left in the down to be inhaled on the next camping trip.

However, many backpackers wash their bags themselves because they believe that it preserves loft better than dry cleaning. It can be done in any large tumble-type machine. Set the washer on delicate cycling and use only lukewarm water and mild soap, not a detergent. Rinse the bag at least twice to get rid of every trace of soap.

The real trick is in the drying, for which I am indebted to Eastern Mountain Sports. Set the dryer on low temperature and throw a pair of rubber sneakers in with the bag. The static created between rubber and nylon develops a higher loft in the down and also breaks up large wet clumps of down for more effective drying. Follow up the drying cycles with a fresh-air hanging. Since bulky bags can jam or tangle in washers and dryers, never leave the scene while the equipment is in motion.

One way to help keep bags clean in the first place is with inner and outer liners. Sleeping bag covers of ripstop nylon that can be easily removed for washing are available at about $4.

Inner liners are made from flannel or nylon fleece. They are held in place inside with either snaps or Velcro fasteners that pass through loops sewn into the bags. I have found that the nylon fleece liners are very comfortable and stay in place, since the body or clothing slides smoothly over the synthetic. But the flannel liners never seem to stay in place; they stick to my clothing or my skin and end up wound around my legs in a tangle. Perhaps more fasteners would solve this problem, or maybe the liners should be made from a synthetic (there are a few nylon inner liners now on the market). Teddy feels very strongly about women having a clean liner. She says her face breaks out if she doesn't have a clean liner to lie on—but also agrees that a small square of cloth for the top of the bag would be sufficient.

All of this care may seem a little fussy to the uninitiated, but a little experience will convince you of the wisdom of taking good care of your best friend in the woods.

I recall one winter mountaineering trip with Chuck when everything seemed to be going wrong. First it thawed and then rained. Next the temperature dropped, freezing the rain-covered ground. Then it snowed. It was nearly impossible to see deep pools of water under the thin ice-and-snow covering. Although we took every care, in the late afternoon we both broke through to our waists, soaking ourselves to the skin. Only with great difficulty were we able to extricate ourselves and our snowshoes from the slushy pools.

The temperature plunged even further and, at 5 below, we started to freeze as we stumbled into our lean-to. It was only a matter of minutes, though, before we were stripped and tucked into our warm sleeping bags with dry stockings and down booties helping to warm our chilled limbs. Parkas kept our upper bodies warm as we heated up some soup over the Primus and followed this steaming brew with a good hot supper—all without wriggling from our down cocoons. As we finally snuggled down to sleep, Chuck said, "Boy, even a warm cabin couldn't beat this!" That says it all about a good sleeping bag.

# 5

# CARRYING THE LOAD

It sure would have been nice when I was a kid to have had the equipment that is available today. And just about the first item I would have bought is a modern pack.

We used to gather our gear—mostly some lard tins with wire-bail handles for cooking and a few cloth bags of staple foods—and arrange them in a line on our blankets. The whole thing was rolled into a sausage, secured at either end with a rope, which also formed a loop to hang the business across the shoulders. A .22 was hung over the free shoulder and away we went.

The rope cut into our shoulders, the roll banged against our hips, and it was obvious that there just had to be a better way. When I read about the Trapper Nelson packboard in a boy's magazine, I built one just about as fast as I could scrounge wood from an old packing crate and a piece of canvas from the ranch supply.

With a packboard, you arrange your gear on a sheet of plastic film or nylon (we used oilcloth), fold the parcel into a neat package, and lash it onto the board with rope, preferably with a diamond hitch, but at least with a crisscross pattern. Although this frame is said to have been developed by an Alaskan sourdough, the basic idea is probably the most ancient type of backpack known to man.

After World War II, I picked up a surplus Army A-frame rucksack. It was a further improvement. I still have this pack and, although I haven't used it for years, I keep it around just in case I may have to tote a big load. It has a mammoth sack and can easily carry up to a hundred pounds of gear in reasonable comfort. It's probably impossible now to buy one of these antiques, but packboards are still available. And there just isn't a better or more economical way to move giant loads, if you should ever be faced with that backbreaking task.

Made from aluminum instead of wood, packboards are still the preferred way to haul supplies on Himalayan or other large-group expeditions. If you ever build a camp deep in the woods, you might want to make a wooden one to help haul weighty supplies and materials. I'll show you how in Chapter 11.

However, the average backpacker doesn't—or at least shouldn't—face this kind of peonage. Modern aircraft technology in the working of aluminum, together with some real cool research in the carrying of loads, has now made equipment available that eliminates struggling on the trails. The biggest problem, with backpacks today, as with other gear, is selecting the right one to fit your needs from the dozens of styles now on the market.

Again, the first thing to do is to look at the fundamen-

The pack should be positioned and loaded so that center of gravity is fairly high and in a direct line with the hips and legs. This puts up to 70 percent of the weight where it belongs—on the body's strongest members.

tals. How should a load be carried and what kinds of trips require what kinds of loads and equipment?

To start with, a vertical line drawn through the center of gravity of a load (usually the heaviest and densest part) should pass through the hips and legs of the hiker, which are the portions of the body best equipped to carry a load. Therefore, weights should be carried as close to the back as practical and fairly high on the shoulders. But, if the load is too high, it tends to overbalance the hiker when he leans forward a bit to scramble up or down difficult slopes.

Also, since it is very tiring to have a load suspended only from the shoulders for long periods of time, most of the weight should be carried by the hips and legs. However, if the load is too low on the back, it puts a great deal of strain on the spine, which wasn't even designed for man to stand erect, much less to carry a load.

In short, the correct positioning and distribution of a load for maximum efficiency and comfort is a complex engineering problem. It's no wonder it took so many centuries to work it out. Man, how did those Indians ever survive without us!

Anyhow, there are a few other things to consider. Different kinds of hikes make for different kinds of loads. On a simple day hike, you may be carrying only a light lunch, rain gear, first-aid kit, maps, compass, and, perhaps, a camera and binoculars. With this comparatively easy load, you could be happy with a belt pack or a light rucksack. I have a 16-ounce nylon rucksack by Eddie Bauer ($10) with two outside pockets for this purpose.

A high mountaineer or rock climber must use a narrowly tapered pack with smooth contours and no outside pockets that can be eased around rocks and pulled up chimneys on the end of a rope. A ski mountaineer needs a rucksack with a low center of gravity that sits down near his hips so that he can keep his balance on rough trails and sharp turns.

Likewise, bicycle campers have other special requirements, pannier packs that hang over the rear wheel on either side and a handlebar pack that is compact—both designed to keep weight low and evenly distributed.

But the average backpacker on weekend or week-long trips has other needs. He will carry between twenty-five and about forty pounds of weight—in comfort, if all goes well. The pack must serve as a storehouse for all his gear, which must be instantly available when it is needed without unpacking the entire load. This calls for a cross between the packboard and the rucksack and also some careful packing.

The first requirement is inherent in the design of modern packs and frames. The second takes a little practice to acquire.

In Europe and Japan, the rucksack is still the overwhelmingly popular way to carry hiking loads. In Japan, in fact, they have huge double-width rucksacks that hold immense loads. But, having recently tried one of these on a mountain-climbing weekend in Japan, I'll take my own pack and frame anytime. A rucksack suspends just about all of the weight from the shoulders and positions it too far

Asians and Europeans still prefer rucksacks, sometimes big double-sized ones like my partner carries on a climb in the Japanese Alps. While these carriers do have built-in frames, they do not ride as well as American pack-and-frame combinations.

out from the back. Generally, the weight also sags down into the small of the back, even with sacks that have stiffening frames built in.

The pack-and-frame structure, now used universally in America, combines the best features of the packboard with a special rucksack that is constructed to hold its contents in a narrow plane close to and high on the back. As a matter of fact, if you only just toss your gear into such a carrier, you can't go far wrong. If you do a little arranging, you can almost forget you have a load on your back. Well, I said *almost.* Let's look at each element separately and see how each works.

Thanks to pioneering research by two or three of the major pack and frame manufacturers, most modern frames are not straight-line structures, as in the early Trapper Nelson and even in the first tubular-aluminum frames. Viewed from the side, they form a slight S-curve that conforms to the natural contours of the back and also forces the pack to follow these efficient weight-distribution lines.

Obviously, this contour is only effective if it matches the back it is placed on. Therefore, such leading designers as Camp Trails, Gerry, Himalayan, and Kelty make frames in three or four different lengths from 22 to 32 inches that are scaled to fit people from five to over six feet in height.

Frame materials are either high-tensile aluminum or magnesium alloys, generally tubular, and most often welded by a heliarc process. However, at least one frame by White Stag is of square-tube construction. Some are held together with mechanical couplings. There is a new one from North Face that is injection-molded in one piece from polycarbonate, an engineering plastic of great strength and light weight.

There are also a few frames that are adjustable in height, notably a 33-inch frame by Alpine Designs that has a top

Representative of the best in modern packs and frames are (top to bottom) Kelty, Camp Trails, K2 Jan Sport, Sunbird, and Gerry. Kelty and Gerry packs are compartmented with zipper access. The rest have pockets only. My pack is the one at center left.

extension bar that can increase it to 38 inches. Incidentally, this frame is put together with polycarbonate couplings that also hold the pack on. So the frame can be adjusted to fit any of three Alpine packs. Eddie Bauer has an adjustable crossbar on its packs, too, that enables the load to be shifted up or down as desired.

While more experience is needed to judge the effectiveness of plastic frames and fittings, I believe there is little to choose from between welded and mechanically joined frames, despite competitive claims. If the frame is well built, it has been my experience that either structure will give almost infinite service.

Magnesium alloys are a little lighter than aluminum for frames of the same strength, but they are also more expensive. For example, a medium-sized Camp Trails Cruiser frame of welded aluminum weighs 31 ounces and is priced at $14. The Summit Cruiser of the same size in welded magnesium weighs 29 ounces, but costs $28. For all practical purposes, a backpacker should be perfectly satisfied with a high-quality aluminum frame.

To keep the crossbars on the frame away from the back to allow air to circulate for cooling, any good frame is equipped with two back bands of nylon cloth or mesh, 5 or 6 inches wide, that are fastened tightly between the side bars either with nylon laces or turnbuckles. These bands should be positioned to press against the wearer at the waist and shoulder blades. Alpine Designs does away with guesswork on positioning by supplying a full-length panel of nylon mesh.

On all modern packs, the shoulder straps are attached at the bottom of the frame and at some distance below the top, thus forcing the load to ride high—level with the top of your head or even higher, depending on the size of the frame. These straps, at the point where they pass over the shoulders, should be from 2 to 2½ inches wide and be made from urethane foam covered with nylon. The lower portion is of nylon webbing with buckles for adjusting the length.

The final essential is a waist belt, preferably padded with nylon-covered foam. This item is generally sold as an accessory, but it is a necessity, not a luxury. Fastened at the bottom of the pack at the point of shoulder-strap attachment and equipped with a quick-release buckle, this belt is what enables you to carry from 60 percent to 75 percent of the weight of the load on your hips, where it belongs.

A good point to look for when you buy a frame is how the straps are attached. On cheaper frames, they are riveted. But straps wear out and have to be replaced, so better frames are drilled for special, aluminum clevis pins, which are secured with snap rings. At the point of attachment, the straps should be grommeted, too, for additional strength and life.

If the frame terminates at top and bottom in cut-tube sections, these should be plugged with plastic caps to prevent wear on the pack at the top—the pack on this type of frame is hung over the projections by little pockets. The caps at the bottom keep out dirt and water. An increasing number of frames are made from continuous tubing. On these, the pack is attached along the sides by clevis pins.

Some frames are still made with bottom shelves of tubing in an L configuration, either fixed or folding. Accessory shelf attachments are generally available for any frame, if you buy the idea that these enable a pack to stand erect for loading and unloading when it is placed on the ground. The fact is that the pack won't, so my advice is to save your money. A shelf is unnecessary except for big-load frames, such as The Freighter by Camp Trails that is designed to carry game animals, chain saws, and other back-bustin' goodies. Here, the folding shelf helps support the load.

That should be all there is to say about frames, but progress keeps going on and new ideas are continuous. Three deserve mention. The first is by a new company called Sunbird Industries, Inc., and is an improvement in waist suspension for frames. The Sunbird frames are raked sharply forward at the bottom and are equipped with C-shaped tubing extensions, mounted on swivels, to which the wraparound waist belt is attached. The pitch is that these extensions automatically conform to the waist and helped suspend the load on the tops of the hips. Rob and Chuck and I tried one, recently, and we all agreed it was so comfortable as to be sinful.

Another frame built on this principle is an Alpenlite carried by Swiss Ski Sports. Here, the frame is bent sharply forward to put the weight on the center of the hips. This also enables the frame to stand on three points for loading. Eddie Bauer has a similar model.

The third recent innovation is an articulated pack frame by K2 Jan Sport that is pinned together rather than welded. It flexes diagonally and in and out as the wearer moves over the terrain, and has a dynamic rather than static loading. Padded back pads and a differentially cut wraparound waistband, which is smaller at top and bottom to contour to the hips, are supposed to create more comfort. I haven't tried one, but Chuck did for the accompanying photo and says it is a beauty.

### *Picking a Pack*

Most important, of course, is what you hang on the frame. And to me, the most important thing about a pack

Most modern packs are tested by my two sons. Chuck (left) shoulders one by K2 Jan Sport that has an articulated frame, which flexes with body movements. Rob strides along with Sunbird's cantilevered model, which has extensions at the waist belt that position weight on the center of the hips.

next to its size is how many pockets it has. I like a lot of pockets.

Therefore, I'm not shot down with the compartmented carriers that have no pockets: Alpine Designs Packmaster and Gerry's Vagabond and Traveler CWD (Controlled Weight Distribution). These packs are divided horizontally into four zippered compartments. The bottom, and slightly larger, compartment carries sleeping bag and pad. The top one is big enough for a mountain tent. The rest of your gear goes in between. It's neat and streamlined, and if that's what you like, fine.

Personally, I like exterior pockets—at least two on either side, a large one in the back, and a map pocket in the top flap. These enable you to organize your gear better and to get at items you need on the trail—cameras, cup, first-aid kit, compass, maps—without blindly rummaging inside the pack.

Gerry and Alpine Designs have these packs, too. And so do Eddie Bauer, Camp Trails, Eastern Mountain Sports, Himalayan, Jonas Bros. of Seattle, Kelty, K2 Jan Sport, Moor and Mountain, Morsan, Recreational Equipment, and White Stag—to name just about all of the leading fabricators of packs and frames. In addition to plenty of outside pockets, some of these packs also have internal dividers with zippered access—so you can have everything in one pack, if you want.

These packs come in a variety of colors, in duck or nylon, and with a gaggle of different features. Are there any universal things to look for? You bet.

First, material of construction. Cotton duck is rugged, no question. I had a bag from Morsan that lasted through years of heavy service. But nylon is stronger, pound for pound, and is more easily and permanently waterproofed. So, I would opt for nylon. But make sure it is heavy enough in weight and preferably urethane-coated to protect against rain.

The 6- to 8-ounce nylon weaves used by most of the better pack makers are the ticket. Packs should also be reinforced at stress points where the bag is attached to the frame or where ties are attached.

Color is a personal preference. I happen to like quiet dark green or brown, but I'll admit that the bright reds, oranges, yellows, and even red-white-and-blue stripes that have appeared recently are easier to spot on a mountain and look prettier in color slides.

Second is size. This depends on the kind of backpacking you will be doing. If you never intend to take more than a weekender in your whole life, it would be foolish to get a large expedition pack. You will be tempted to fill it, just because the space is there. And you'll never learn the valuable self-discipline of making every inch and ounce count.

On the other hand, if you are equipped with a small pack for weekends and suddenly decide to take a two-week expedition away from sources of supply, you're going to look like an itinerant peddler with stuff tied all over the outside of your pack. You'll be uncomfortable, too.

One solution has just come on the market. It's an extendable bag by Camp Trails that is available in three models. The slim-built Ponderosa has an extendable 8½-inch top sleeve with a drawstring and cord lock device that provides a total volume of 4,430 cubic inches. Alpine Designs also has a convertible Omni ski-touring rucksack that can be fitted to a frame and has a 14-inch sleeve extension that increases its capacity from 1,500 to 2,200 cubic inches. Price is $33.

Camp Trails Moose Medium has a 9-inch extendable

top and is also extendable in depth (that is, front to back) by means of tightener cords of nylon that are threaded crosswise through rings on the back of the pack, which can be loosened or pulled up tight to fit the load and can be secured with a cord lock. The combo enables this pack to hold 4,860 cubic inches.

Then, there is the mammoth Yukon, a normally 31-inch pack that has a towering 16-inch extension. These four packs cost from $30 to $50. White Stag has a similar pack that extends its depth by 7½ inches, and another pack by this maker has side zippers that increase the depth 7 to 10 inches. How much more flexibility do you want?

But for the ordinary backpacker and for trips from a weekend to two weeks, almost any of the medium to large packs, measuring between 22 and 31 inches high, are perfectly adequate. Width is usually standard at 14 to 15 inches and depth is generally between 5 and 7 inches. This gives you between 1,500 and 3,100 cubic inches. Plenty. You shouldn't carry more.

Now as I said, some bags are attached to the frame by pockets and some by clevis pins. Both methods are okay if the bag is well made, and I don't have any personal preference. I do have a preference—or prejudice, if you will—about pocket closures. I distrust zippers—any kind of zipper. I like nylon tie-downs. They never freeze or pop on you, and they also permit the pocket to expand a bit in capacity so you can cram an extra large something in, such as a big camera.

Pack prices are generally between $20 and $30 for the size we have been discussing. Frames vary all the way from $11 to $29. This would seem to say you can get in business for from $30 to $60. But there are good combination deals at almost every outfitter that cost only $17 to $20 and are completely adequate for the occasional camper. And at the end of the season almost every outdoor store has sales on even the better packs. If you really want the nitty-gritty of specs and prices, the best presentation I have ever seen is in Eastern Mountain Sports' catalog, which carries most of the leading brands.

What about the extras? There are a jillion. You can get packs with hold-open frames, ice-axe and crampon and ski carriers, outside add-on pockets, extra clevis-pin attachments, and you name it. Backpacking approaches golf, fishing, and skiing in the amount of gadgetry available. If you *need* the stuff for some special reason, buy it. But remember, everything you hang on a pack weighs just as much as if it were put inside, something that people often forget. So, don't get anything you don't absolutely need.

Before leaving this subject, though, I just have to say something about the Cadillacs of the backpacking world. Everyone likes to dream about ultimate luxury and, for my money, K2 Jan Sport and Sunbird Industries take the prize at this time.

To fit on its articulated frame, K2 Jan Sport has what they call an 8-D2 Total Organization pack. It's covered with pockets, one of which is insulated and black in color to prevent liquids from freezing. How does that grab you! There are two internal compartments and load-control straps on the outside that not only compress the contents, but can also be used to hold skis, snowshoes, or trail-marking willow wands. Wherever there is space, there are leather-patched tie-ons for hanging other gear. Even if you never use them, they look important. The top pockets are vertically zippered and, they say, extra pockets can be strapped on, although I can't imagine where or why. The price of this elegance is $90.

Just about the same can be said for Sunbird's Condor. It has nine outside pockets (yeah, man!) and three internal compartments. The bag is covered with ice-axe and rope tie-downs. The map compartment is accessible from the outside and a fixed hold-open bar makes the interior readily available. It looks high-mountain all the way, and so is the price—$85.

*Specialized Packs*

Back to reality. In all of the foregoing discussion, I haven't meant to knock rucksacks; they are appropriate when they can do a job. There is a place for a wide variety of these special packs.

For example, there are fanny packs and belt pouches ($5 to $10) that can carry such small items as lunch, tobacco and pipes, glasses, camera, first-aid kit, and so forth. The belt pouch can be worn while carrying a full-sized pack, and I use one to keep my reading glasses, sunglasses, and pipe and tobacco handy.

A whole range of rucksacks is available—from frameless bags with straps ($3 to $17) to beautifully crafted Eiger-type mountaineering bags with internal frames and leather tops and bottoms by such firms as Holubar, La Fuma, and Sierra Designs ($20 to $40). These are also useful for ski tourers. And while we're talking about skiing, it should be noted that the standard Kelty Mountaineer pack can be mounted either at the top or bottom of its frame (with the sleeping bag mounted either above or below) to lower the center of gravity and increase stability when skiing or on difficult climbing pitches.

There are special carriers for toting babies, too. An outstanding one is Himalayan's top of the line that has a small zippered case under the saddle to carry diapers and baby bottles. Gerry has one with a storage compartment, too ($15) and Jonas Bros. of Seattle has a similar baby carrier with side pockets for $17.

For young children who can't yet carry even a small

Packs for special purposes include (clockwise from top left) a rock-climbing knapsack with leather bottom by Class 5, my own Eddie Bauer rucksack and Chris's miniature equivalent, and the baby carrier in which we toted Chris when he was too small to walk far.

regular pack, Kelty has a sleeping-bag carrier that is actually a tiny rucksack capable of holding a lunch, but with large straps underneath for supporting the sleeping bag. It's $5. Chris has a tiny red rucksack of nylon that is just big enough to hold his sleeping bag. If you take a dog camping with you, even your pooch needn't get away free. Gerry has small panniers with leather-reinforced corners for large dogs capable of carrying their own food. It's $20.

The bicycle tourer can get the same CWD as the backpacker from Gerry with compartmented panniers and a compact handlebar pack for $30 and $15, respectively. Morsan's bike panniers are square in construction ($25 and $13). Gerry also makes a horse pack for $28 that lashes behind the saddle, just in case you're interested.

Regardless of what kind of pack you end up with, the first thing to do is to make it waterproof. Nope, just because you bought a urethane-coated nylon pack doesn't make it fully waterproof. You see, each stitched seam creates a path for water to get into the pack. Give these seams a good coating of a standard nylon waterproofing compound, which is made for tents and is available at any outfitter. This treatment should be repeated periodically, usually when you discover that your pack has sprung a leak.

In addition, I believe in a waterproof pack cover. Kelty makes one ($5) that is specially contoured to fit its tapering packs. But Teddy made one for me from vinyl-coated nylon, for about the same price, that fits over my Camp Trails pack and frame and the sleeping bag underneath. It has four short diagonal seams at the top and bottom corners that are easy to waterproof. It is gathered around the edges with a heavy elastic band inside a seamed channel. It is deep enough to fit around the whole pack and gives pretty much total protection, both when I'm carrying the bag or when it is strapped to a tree in camp.

## *How to Pack a Bag*

Once you have your pack, it's time to learn how to load it. The most important thing of all is organization. I don't care where you put things, but put them there all of the time. Make it a habit. It's the only way you can ever lay your hands on anything immediately and also be able to check quickly that you have everything when you break camp.

For example, I always put my first-aid kit in the upper right-hand pocket (when facing the back of the pack). My

Loading diagram shows how to put weighty objects high and toward the front of the pack (against the wearer's back). This is also the location for grills and folding ovens not shown in this drawing.

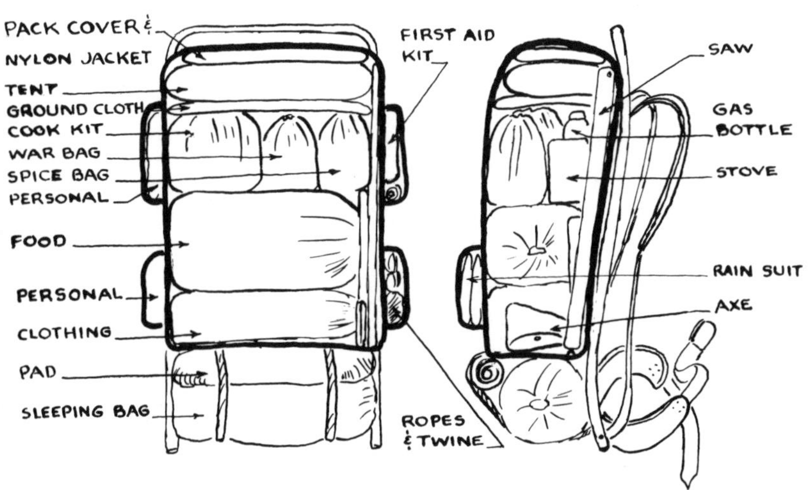

wooden-match container for camp use, spoon, flashlight, cooking foil, sheath knife, and other personal things are always in the upper left-hand pocket. The lower right is reserved for a ball of twine and the lengths of nylon rope that hold up my tarp. The lower left is usually filled with flashbulbs, filters, and other camera gear.

The rear pocket carries my rain suit and maps, since my pack was made, unfortunately, before the Velcro-closed map compartment in the top flap was invented. Pick your own order, but stick to it.

Inside the pack, the theory is that light items should be at the bottom and the heavier gear at the top. Wherever possible, dense gear should be near your back, too, with lighter stuff on the outside. This is one time, at least, when theory pretty much agrees with practice.

You will probably lash your light sleeping bag under the pack. For this, cord is okay, but elastic shock cords with hooks at either end are faster and very secure.

In the bottom of the bag go the spare clothes that are not immediately needed. On top of that is the food, arranged in order of meals—first in, last eaten. Then comes cooking gear. Finally, you put your shelter—tent or tarp—on top with, perhaps, your sleeping pad.

On the very top goes whatever garment you may need when you stop to rest or eat on the trail, a light windproof or a down jacket, depending on the season.

Against your back inside the pack you slide such long and heavy items as your steel cooking grill, collapsible saw, axe, reflector oven, or other frippery. Within each layer as close to your back as possible, you also put such dense items as a stove or gasoline bottles.

Now, everything is arranged in order of need, as we shall see in Chapter 9. You have restricted your selection of gear to only that which matches the kind of trip in prospect, as shown in the equipment and weight chart in Chapter 7. And this gear is positioned most effectively to keep that center of gravity in line with your body, hips, and legs.

Next, let's see how we are going to spend the night.

# 6

# ALL KINDS OF SHELTER

Ever since man crawled out of the cave, he has been terrified of being caught without shelter. It's as instinctive as breathing. Tell me, then, why I like to lie out under the stars when I camp. So do many of my friends. It is breathtakingly beautiful to wake up in the middle of the night at high altitude and see a billion billion stars so close you think you could grab a handful. Or a full moon riding just above a dark cleft in the peaks. Sometimes, such camping is even possible.

More often, however, regardless of whether you are scared to be "outside" or are subhuman enough to revel in total exposure, adequate shelter is essential. I'll repeat what I said in Chapter 2: don't tell me it doesn't rain in your area. If I were to set up camp on the moon, I guarantee you it would rain within twenty-four hours.

Tarps make a versatile shelter, even for an early winter camp such as this one on the Kittatiny Ridge in western New Jersey. This tarp is my own special one, measuring 15 by 15 feet and weighing only 4 pounds. It's made from a polyethylene-coated nylon scrim.

And then, there are the bugs. Oh, boy, are there bugs—in just about every part of the country from early spring to late summer. In some northern areas and southern swamps, insects are so thick and vicious that the only real relief you will get is at night after you have zipped into your bug-proof tent.

On the other hand, in some areas, a tent is not necessary for backpacking. In broad wilderness areas of the South, East, Mountain states, and Pacific slopes, there are great lean-to systems, even huts, spaced out or grouped at key trail junctions or scenic outlooks. Some of the huts in the East and West also serve meals, making it unnecessary for you to carry food. This system is a great tribute to the states and clubs that have made such shelters possible.

But before you shout "Whoopee!" and rush off without either food or shelter, let me warn you. The current boom in backpacking has heavily taxed these facilities and you may hike all day to find your anticipated shelter jammed to the doors. It is first come, first served.

To give you an example of what we will face in this country in the near future, I was climbing recently in Japan on Kitadake in the Southern Alps on a holiday weekend, Autumn Day. There must have been 200 to 300 climbers on the same mountain with me, and more than 120 of them decided to spend the night in a hut near the summit that was built for 80.

We ate in four shifts as fast as we could bolt food with a hut boy yelling at us to hurry, and we slept packed together like sardines. Latecomers lay on planks stretched across the walkways between sleeping platforms. It was an interesting experience, but once was enough. If you are that much of a social animal, stick with it. Most backpackers, including those in Japan, are trying to get away from mobs of people. The only way to do it is to have your own shelter.

Let's dispose right at the start of the romantic notion that you can build your own shelter anywhere in the United States, as described in all of the old camping books. It's against the law—or should be—almost everywhere to cut green wood or plants.

But don't think you're missing something. Makeshift lean-tos take hours to construct and thatch so that they will turn even a moderate shower. Early explorers never built them except for a prolonged stay. In an emergency, you might have to build such a structure, but since this book is about how to avoid such emergencies, let's get on to talking about tents and tarps.

Again, as with other camping gear, the variety of tents and tarps being produced is astounding; the real problem is to select those that fit your types of tripping and your personal outlook on camping. One thing is sure. Despite centuries of development in such gear, there is still no universal shelter that fits all conditions. We have five tents and two types of tarps, and I am still scheming to improve them.

Since the only reason for a shelter is to protect you and your gear from wind, rain, and snow, it doesn't seem on the face of it to be such a difficult problem. The complication is the widely different areas and climates in which you may camp and the number of people who may need to be sheltered.

## *Principles of Shelter*

A backpacking shelter must be light enough for practical toting, big enough to hold the required number of hikers and their gear, small enough to fit into restricted spaces, impervious to wind and water and bugs, and at the same time be capable of transmitting the considerable water vapor exhaled by the people inside and stable in even violent weather. Beginning to get the idea?

Every approach that acknowledges all of these factors necessarily compromises some. You pick a shelter that has the least compromises in those features that are important to you on your kind of trip.

Summer camping in woods at moderate elevations poses the least problems. If there are no bugs, a simple tarp will suffice. If there are bugs, a lightweight tent with a floor and mosquito-netting doors will turn off both storms and insects. Desert and beach camping call for a shelter that blocks the sun but lets plenty of air circulate.

If you are camping at high altitudes in summer or low altitudes in fall or winter, a completely weatherproof tent that is snug and capable of being securely moored is essential. For high-altitude winter mountaineering, only the finest, heavily reinforced expedition equipment should be considered, and it must be coupled with special camping techniques that are beyond the scope of this book. I will discuss some of these tents and techniques, though, since they can be useful even in milder camping conditions.

The number of people who should be accommodated in a single shelter is limited by physical conditions and personal preference. About the biggest tent that can be backpacked with any practicality is a lightweight four-man shelter. Tarps big enough for five or six people can be toted, if they are made from ultra-light materials.

But space is generally limited for pitching shelters. At the shore, in the desert, or in lowland woods with large cleared flat areas between trees, you may be able to fit six men under a tarp. But in canyons, dense woods, and above tree line, you will rarely find enough flat room in a given spot for more than two.

Unless you are intimately acquainted, then, with the places you will camp, it is better to carry two-man shelters and not take a chance. The smaller tents and tarps are easier to backpack anyway and are generally easier to pitch since they involve less hardware.

You can group them as close as is possible for companionship or carry a spare tarp that can be pitched at the campfire in a central place. Much more will be said about setting up a camp in Chapter 9.

So, let's look at the gear, starting at the bottom with simple tarps.

## *Picking and Pitching Tarps*

The bottom, economically though not functionally, is the polyethylene tarp. It is a thoroughly practical shelter for one or two people, maybe three. Any more, though, requires such a big sheet that it is likely to rip in a breeze.

Polyethylene is available in 4-mil gauge at many outfitters and hardware and paint stores. At outdoor stores, in 10-foot widths and any desired length, it runs about 22 cents per foot. Personally, I prefer a 6-mil sheet, which is harder to find and slightly heavier, but a lot stronger and longer lasting. There are also vinyl sheets, which are generally even heavier and more costly, but perhaps even stronger.

The 6-mil polyethylene sheets can be found at Eastern Mountain Sports, for example, at 30 cents per running foot (10 feet wide). This supplier also has an 8- by 6-foot reinforced plastic tarp for $6.

Polyethylene sheets are commonly available in clear, black and white film, sometimes in red or yellow. The white film is supposed to reflect sun heat, which might be an asset if you're going to lie in bed all day. I like it clear so I can see what's going on above and on all sides. And since I'm up and off at first light, its reflective properties are unimportant to me.

Before a sheet is a tarp, though, it needs fastening points for ropes. There are several types. Best known are Visklamps, which are made from wire and look like shower-curtain hangers. To use them, an accompanying rubber ball is pushed into the film near a corner or edge and the large end of the wire is slipped over the film-covered ball from the other side, then is slid to the small end, trapping the film and ball in the hanger.

A similar device, made entirely of plastic, is called a Versa Tie. It is applied in the same way, but instead of a ball, the retainer is a flat toothed disk. Another good device is the Sure-Hold grommet. Here, a real metal grommet is set in folded tape, the inside of which is coated with surely the strongest pressure-sensitive adhesive in the

Fasteners that turn plastic sheets into tarpaulins include (left to right) a Versa Tie made from plastic that works like a garter fastener, Tap-It plastic eyelets that are molded from two pieces of plastic and are hammered or squeezed into place, and the Sure-Hold grommet, which is mounted in a doubled-over pressure-sensitive tape.

world. It lives up to its claims—the plastic will part before the grommet tab lets go. And now there is a two-piece plastic grommet, called Tap-It, that snaps together through the plastic tarp to make a permanent fixture.

But if you get caught in the woods without all of these gimmicks, and need to make a shelter from your tarp or plastic ground cloth, it is easily done. You can tie small knots in the bunched corners of the sheet and tie the ropes behind the knots with slipknots or a series of half hitches. Or you can find some smooth pebbles about an inch or so in diameter and use these to bunch up the film at the corners and edges, tying the ropes behind the film-wrapped rocks.

I've had a great deal of luck in making my own tarps by using the silvery-gray pressure-sensitive "air conditioner" tape for reinforcing and grommeting through this tough material with a low-cost and readily available brass grommeting kit.

Next up the scale are nylon tarps. Some are grommeted around the edges. The more versatile have ties around the edges and in a diagonal pattern across the face, enabling the tarp to be pitched in many different configurations. If you get such a tarp, make sure the grommets or ties are reinforced. The ties inside the tarp should be treated with a waterproofing compound around the reinforced area to prevent leaks through the seams. Unlike cotton, nylon thread doesn't swell when wet to fill the needle holes.

For backpacking, nylon tarps are usually made from material that weighs from 1.1 to 2.2 ounces per square yard. Every supplier has them. But as examples, in the lighter material, a 10- by 10-foot tarp with ties from Morsan will weigh 26 ounces and cost $23. Holubar has a 7- by 10-foot Nylport tarp for $27. Moor and Mountain has a 9- by 9-foot tarp that has grommets around the edges and ties across the face, also for $27.

My own favorite tarp is a 15- by 15-foot monster with edge and diagonal ties made from a fantastic material called Coverall. It's polyethylene-coated nylon scrim, developed by the Lowe Paper Co., Ridgefield, N.J., and weighs 2.6 ounces per square yard—4 pounds for the entire tarp. Furthermore, it can be either sewn or heat sealed—mine is both—and is watertight and extremely strong. I have used it constantly for six years and it is still just as good as the day it was custom made.

Unfortunately, Lowe Paper couldn't interest enough outdoor suppliers in the stuff and has discontinued it.

Since my tarp won't last forever and I have never found another material as good, I hope some manufacturer has better luck with this stuff in the near future.

Once you have your tarp, you have to know how to pitch it. Whatever you do, don't just roll up in the thing. Tarps are impervious to the transfer of water vapor and you will be soaking wet before morning.

The accompanying drawings show some of the usable configurations that can be made from a square (or in some cases, rectangular) tarpaulin. I have used them all for one reason or another.

The simplest method is to lash the tarp at about a 45-degree angle to a deadwood pole that is crotched or lashed between two trees. A separate ground cloth is needed, of course. A better shape uses part of the tarp as a ground sheet with the rest slanting to tent poles or a tree lashing. The back is staked by means of ties. It is great for one person and, if made from a 10- by 10-foot sheet, provides enough overhang at either end and at the open side to protect against all but a driving storm. But both of these patterns are vulnerable to wind. They can be improved a bit in this respect by placing a log or stones on the slanting part where it touches the ground.

The lean-to shape is great for up to six campers. With my tarp, the "roof" can be pitched high enough to stand under. It is wind-vulnerable, but in case of a storm it is only a matter of minutes to drop the roof into a pup-tent shape, which is quite wind resistant. In the latter position, driving storms can be blocked at one or the other end by lashing an extra plastic ground cloth over the open end.

Workable patterns that can be pitched with a tarp. The top two can be made with either a square or rectangular shaped tarp, the rest are best pitched with a square tarpaulin.

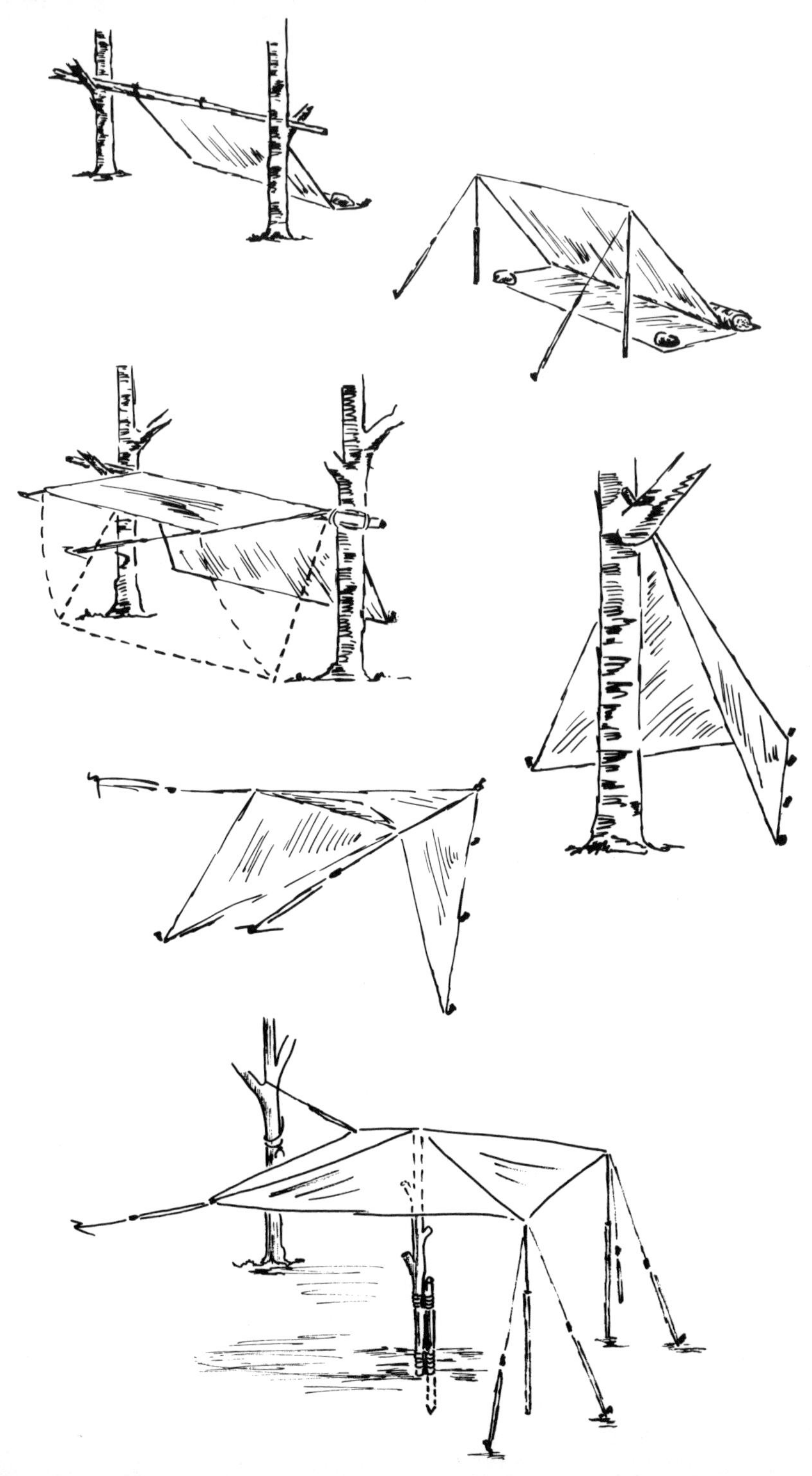

One of the great features of these shelters is that you can lie with your head near the open side and get most of the benefit of being under the stars. Also, a reflector fire in front of any of these shapes significantly increases the temperature inside—as much as 15 degrees Fahrenheit under windless conditions, by my measurement. They do a fair job of sheltering you from wind.

However, even better configurations for warming and much better protection from the wind are the next two shapes shown. These are very wind-vulnerable; they must be pitched with their backs to the breeze. But they shelter four or five people very well when made with a 15- by 15-foot tarp.

For shelter at the campfire, or shade in the desert or at the shore, you may want to pitch a spare tarp as a canopy, as shown. Be sure that the central pole is padded at the top so that it won't punch a hole in the tarp; drive the pole into the ground, or lash it to a shorter stake; to prevent it from falling over if a slight breeze lifts the tarp. Take this canopy down if even a moderate wind springs up or you may never see it again.

Since you can't always count on trees growing exactly where you want them, you may want to carry aluminum poles or use straight 1- or 2-inch-diameter tree branches or trunks (dead ones, please!) to support the tarp. Since suitable wood can really only be found in transitional and climax hardwood forests in the East and Midwest, metal poles are a better bet. The lightweight jointed ones for tents are too light, though. Get the heavier telescoping aluminum poles and lash them to the outside of your pack.

If you use poles to pitch your tarp on the open side or on all four corners in a canopy, you may want to use two ropes per pole, putting them 90 degrees apart, each in line with a line of pull exerted by the tarp. If you have only one rope per pole, put it at 45 degrees to the two lines of pull,

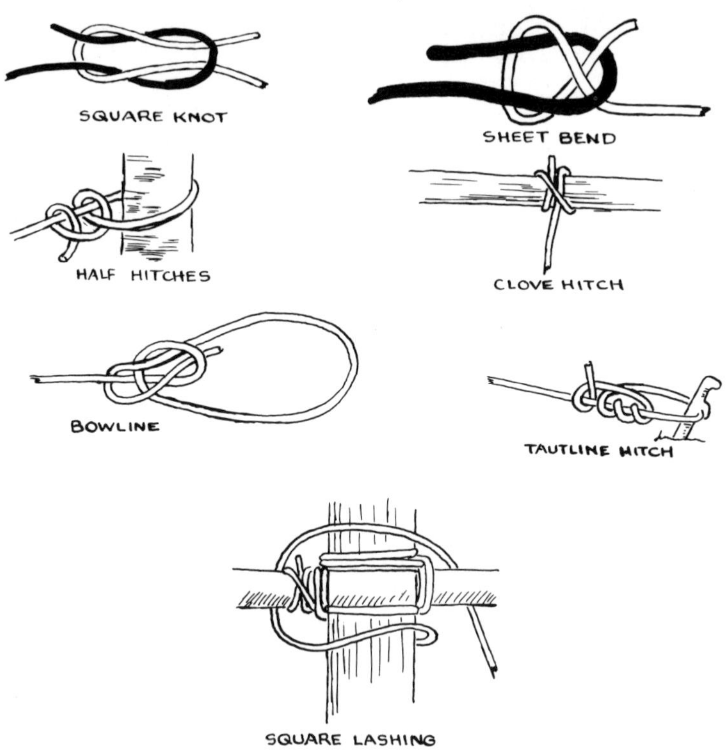


Most-used knots and square lashing for pitching either tarps or tents. A square knot is used to join two ropes of equal diameter, the sheet bend for two ropes of different size. A half hitch and a clove hitch are used to secure rope to trees or poles, and the bowline makes a non-slip loop. A taut-line hitch is adjustable. The square lashing is finished off with "frapping," two turns of the rope between the two poles that are drawn tight to snug up the lash. Clove hitches begin and end this lashing.

and anchor it firmly by putting a heavy rock or log over the line inside the tent stake.

This method of anchoring will be useful to you in pitching all types of shelters in woods where the duff is deep and soft and doesn't offer a strong grip for the ordinary short tent stake. Another alternative is to cut your own stakes from *dead* hardwood in lengths from 15 to

24 inches. Drive them through the duff and into solid soil. There are special long metal stakes of various shapes with a variety of attachments that increase anchoring power, but they are all too big and heavy for backpacking.

You can also tie your ropes to rocks, trees, or firmly anchored bushes. At the shore, dig a trench a foot or more deep and tie your guy line around a deadman—a piece of driftwood at least a foot or two long. Tamp the sand down firmly over this rig and it will hold your tarp against light winds. It is necessary to know several knots and lashings to pitch tents or tarps. These are shown in the accompanying drawing.

The essential knots are a square knot to fasten two ropes of the same size together, a sheet bend for knots of different size, a clove hitch or half hitch or bowline for fastening a rope firmly to a pole or tree, and a taut-line hitch to adjust the tension of a tent cord. Lashings are also useful to attach one pole to another.

### *The Semi-Tents*

There are a couple of shelter constructions that fall between a tarp and a tent that are worth discussing.

The most famous is the Whelen tent, invented by Colonel Townsend Whelen, a noted explorer, hunter, and outdoor writer. Basically, this shelter is still a tarp and is pitched by tying the peak to a pole lashed between two trees. An awning can either be thrown back out of the way or tied to two slanting poles that hold it in position by their weight alone. In a wind, they can be sharpened and driven into the ground. The side panels are a great improvement over standard tarp shelters, since they keep out wind and rain. I'm afraid you'll have to build this shelter yourself, though, since I know of no supplier. Instructions and a diagram are given in Chapter 11.

There is also a tarp/tent combination by Recreational Equipment that is open at one end and has a zip-closed back end. Unzipped, the simple coated-nylon structure opens into a flat tarp. As a tent, it measures 7 by 5½ feet with a 3½-foot peak.

Then, there is the forester, used originally, it is said, by the Hudson Bay trappers. It is a tapered tarp that pitches into a sloping pup tent open at both ends. It is pitched over a slanting pole that is either crotched in a tree or held up by lashed cross poles that form a tripod. Its big advantage is lightness and ease of warming with a campfire. It is also pretty resistant to wind.

Here, again, you'll have to build your own, as described in Chapter 11. I am very high on this tent and I have two that were custom built for me from a vinyl-coated nylon with an added back, mosquito-netting, and storm doors and screened vents in front and back. They work pretty well, although with all of the fancy doodads on them they each weigh a little too much at 12 pounds. Good for canoeing, though.

The nearest thing to this structure in a commercial tent, that I know of, is one by Recreational Equipment. Again, it is made from nylon and slopes from 4 feet in front to 2 feet high in the rear, is 9 feet wide in front and 3 feet at the rear. It's 7 feet long and has an unusual zippered door in front that stops short of the ground. It weighs 2¼ pounds and costs $30 and could be a good tent for beach or desert use, although it is obviously not bug-proof.

At the bottom of any heap is the polyethylene tube tent. This is simply a 3-mil tube of polyethylene film about 9 feet long and 3 feet in diameter. It generally has three grommets at each end, two to stake it down and the third to carry a rope that is threaded through both ends and tied to rocks or trees. It forms a sagging prism that is about 3 feet on a side. It weighs about 1¼ pounds, costs $2 to

$3—and isn't worth a cent in my estimation, because it is cramped and is easily ripped.

An equally incredible shelter is the Inflat-A-Tent, a polyethylene or ethylene vinyl acetate bag with a mouth-inflated tube at one end that creates a triangular opening. It sells for about $8 and I class it as an expensive emergency device that I hope I never have to use.

A better approach to this kind of shelter is a polyethylene tube-tent that you can make for yourself. I'll show you how in Chapter 11.

One final point on plastic tarps and semi-tents. Polyethylene is a marvelously useful material, but not when it is left draped over trees and bushes in tattered shreds. There seems to be a growing belief among some hikers that their torn and discarded tarps will somehow dissolve if they are left in the woods. They won't biodegrade for a long, long time. And in the meantime, they look even more hideous than discarded bottles and cans. So when your tarp finally shreds, *please* tote it back to civilization for disposal. If you don't, people like me will feel compelled to, and we need more help.

## *Tents You Can Live With*

Now, let's get to the subject of true tents. Automatically excluded are all those gorgeous, giant wall and pop-up structures that you see in campgrounds. They are all too big and heavy for backpacking. Hikers' tents are, basically, pup tents. Some of them are pretty fancy with all kinds of attachments and rigging, but most are still fundamentally prism-shaped.

They are made of either nylon or fine cotton, and both materials have their adherents. They come with and without floors or with sod cloths. And each of these styles has its supporters. There are single-layer tents made from coated nylon that are impervious to moisture and there are two-layer tents that breathe. Only the latter *should* have a following, as we shall see.

But let's consider the simplest styles first, the straightforward pup tent without floor or netting. This won't be hard, because there aren't many. Morsan has one for $17 that holds two people, weighs 3 pounds, and measures 7 by 5 by 3½ feet (length, width, and height). Single guy lines on either side help increase inside space.

Morsan also has a cotton double-end pup tent of GI-style for $12 that is 7 by 5 by 3⅓ feet and weighs 6½ pounds. Camp Supply Co. has one for $7 and both the Hirsch-Weis Division of White Stag and Winchester's Trailblazer Division have similar models.

That's about it. Pup tents make a light, inexpensive, and quickly pitched shelter. And if you're up-tight for money, you may have to make them do, but they are not bug-proof and a separate ground cloth must be carried, which destroys some of the weight advantage. Also, since they are single-layer in construction and are not impervious to water, driving rain can come through as a fine mist. Enough said.

You can improve such shelters by adding sod cloths, 6-inch to 12-inch flaps all around the bottom. These are folded in and are covered with a separate ground cloth. If netting doors are also added, the tent will be completely bug-proof. Sod cloths can be useful in other ways, too. Folded outward in winter or at the beach, they can be piled with snow, rocks, or sand to increase the stability of the tent. They work best on larger tents, though, such as the big four-man baker tent I use for canoeing. Applied to small tents, such additions just run up the cost.

So, let's see what a little more tent will do.

The next step up is still a basic pup tent, but it has a

sewn-in floor and both mosquito-netting doors and storm flaps. A few of these are available in cotton poplin that has been "waterproofed" for rain resistance but still retains breathability. Hirsch-Weis, L. L. Bean, and Morsan all make them in two-, three- or four-man models that weigh from 6½ to 15 pounds and cost from $23 to $51.

Problem is that cotton poplin weeps if it is touched on the inside during a storm. And cotton floors tend to get very dirty and to rot, which is why sod cloths are better for cotton tents. If you have a cotton tent, you could improve it immediately by cutting the floor down into sod cloths.

There are some combination tents that try to avoid this problem. Moor and Mountain has a 5¾-pound two-man tent with a vinyl-coated nylon floor that goes 10 inches up the sides to protect your sleeping bag. The top is of 5.5-ounce dry-waterproofed poplin. Herter's also has a two-man job with a top and bottom of vinyl-coated nylon and end walls of poplin. There is a screened rear window to increase ventilation. Weight is 5 pounds and the price is $54. Whereas all of the tents described previously are erected with two central poles, this one sets up with A-frame poles that offer no obstructions.

We're getting better. If you are a nut for cotton, I think either of these last two tents would make you happy. But, as you may have guessed by now, I am not enthusiastic about poplin. It is almost impossible in the cramped confines of these tiny tents to avoid touching the canvas. And in a rainstorm, the resultant trickle of water makes a mess out of your sleeping bag.

Also, nylon is lighter in equal constructions, although admittedly somewhat more expensive. So, let's stop beating around and see what's available in synthetics.

A lot! Starting with the simplest constructions, there are coated-nylon single-layer tents by Himalayan, P&S Sales, and Winchester. The latter two are in both two- and four-man sizes, weigh from 4 to 5 pounds and from 6 to 7 pounds, respectively. Himalayan and Winchester have screened rear vents, while P&S Sales has both rear- and side-screened vents. Both P&S Sales and Winchester tents have side guys to increase inside space and all are pitched with two central poles.

An interesting variation is a Recreational Equipment tent that has broad flaps in the top that roll up to expose huge mosquito-netting panels, and the front is screened, too. It weighs about 6½ pounds and costs $90. The roll-up panels are also grommeted and can be tied out for shade or moderate rain protection. They fasten down tightly with Velcro fasteners. Great for beach or desert.

Now, to be fair, all of these tents are good. They are also uncomplicated and, therefore, very easy and fast to pitch. If you don't have to close them up, you probably wouldn't get too much condensation with one person in them. But I have a similar tent and with two people there is substantial condensation even with vents. With the storm panels closed, it is a veritable rainstorm inside that quickly soaks everything.

Let's try again. I believe that the simplest and most functional tent for backpackers is one made with a coated-nylon floor that extends a short way up the sides and with a plain nylon top and ends. It should have both mosquito-netting and storm doors equipped with three full-opening zippers. Additional side and rear vents don't hurt either. To keep out heavy rains, a thinly coated nylon fly is pitched over the tent. If the tent material is thin enough, it too can be lightly coated on top and still won't stop permeation of water vapor.

Chuck has such a tent, a two-man backpacker made by L. L. Bean. The walls are made of lightly urethane-coated 1.1-ounce ripstop nylon. The floor is 1.7-ounce coated nylon. The fly is of the same material. It has a rear net

Tents that a man can live with are (left to right) Chuck's two-man model from L. L. Bean, another by Gerry, an unusual three-man hexagonal tent by Sierra Designs, and a mountain tent with a tubular entrance by Alpine Designs. Interestingly, these tents were pitched in a 50-mile-per-hour wind. Fastest up was Chuck's tent, which can be staked down first before inserting the poles. Time: five minutes.

window with an inside zippered storm flap and two net side windows with outside flap covers. Netting and storm doors for the front complete the 6-pound structure, which is pitched with two three-piece jointed aluminum poles. There are three side pull-outs to increase inside space, which is a generous 8 by 5 by 3½ feet. Total cost is $57 (a four-man model is 9 pounds and costs $89). Chuck's comment is that it is the best tent he has ever used. And he can pitch it in five minutes flat, alone.

Some of the other suppliers that make tents of this description in two-, three- or four-man models—even

six-man—are Alpine Designs, Blacks, Eddie Bauer, Eastern Mountain Sports, Eureka, Gerry, Jonas Bros. of Seattle, and Recreational Equipment.

These tents are really tents-within-a-tent. The inner one is generally pitched with A-frame jointed aluminum poles. The rain fly usually rests on top of these poles and is staked out with separate guy lines. However, Gerry and Recreational Equipment both have models in which the fly extends beyond the tent at both ends to give more shelter and is pitched with separate center poles.

These constructions not only allow the inner tent to breathe, but permit its construction of a tougher and longer-lasting nylon weave. The lightly coated fly is usually of 1.1-ounce fabric that must be replaced when the coating cracks (but at a lower cost).

These tents are not cheap. A two-man size by Jonas Bros. costs $42, but most run from $70 to $80, and Blacks has two that are $135 and $145. Weights run from 3¾ to

7¼ pounds, except for one of the Black tents, which is 9 pounds. Replacement flies can generally be bought for about $20.

There are endless variations on these basic tents by these and other suppliers. Some have fitted flies with tapered awnings over the front to shield the entrance. An outstanding example of this style is an ultra-light two-man tent from Moor and Mountain that weighs 2.9 pounds. The inner tent is made from a nylon-polypropylene blend. The fly is 1-ounce coated ripstop nylon. The floor and door are of 1½-ounce coated ripstop.

Others have extension flaps on the outer fly that form vestibules in front of the tent for wind protection and also to protect gear. In some, the front door zips down on both sides to form an outer sill, thus preventing the tracking of dirt or water into the tent. Still others have ends that extend in a vee or are slanted outward to increase inside room with little additional weight.

Eastern Mountain Sports has provided an interesting variation on the Kaskawalsh tent replacing the side walls with mosquito netting for full visibility. In bad weather, the tent is covered with a fly that extends beyond the ends. It weighs 5 pounds and costs $70. I really dig this model, since I made one for myself before they were available that weighs only 1 pound, complete. I'll show you how to do it for yourself in Chapter 11.

But tent needs go beyond simple pup configurations. Some people get claustrophobic in these compact shelters. And even the best of them are rather crowded for the number of people they are supposed to be rated for.

There are some new ones in other shapes that seek to offset these disadvantages. In miner-style, or pyramidal construction, there is an 8½-pound hexagonal three-man tent by Sierra Designs that has an external tripod frame and costs $155. My No. 1 son, Rob, fell in love with this tent when we borrowed one for the photo, although he admits that it is a bit difficult to pitch and is hardly big enough for three. Moor and Mountain has a pyramid of permeable nylon, pitched with a waterproof fly, that weighs 7 pounds and costs $170.

A tunnel tent by Blacks, shaped like a Quonset hut, is supported by glass-fiber rods and guys with only two lines. It weighs 8¾ pounds in a "stormproof" model and costs $139. Gander Mountain also supplies a Quonset shape that tapers from front to back and is set up with telescoping aluminum poles. It is available in both 2½-pound two-man single-wall and three-man double-wall models that cost $85 and $135, respectively.

There are also tents with external, bowed aluminum frames that give extra room at the expense of weight. An example are one- and two-man models of waterproofed nylon and poplin by Eureka that weigh 8 and 12½ pounds and cost $53 and $69 (at P&S Sales). A combination of Quonset design and external frame is the Cascade from Recreational Equipment. A three-man tent with high head room, it measures 82 by 70 by 53 inches, is pitched with a waterproof fly, and weighs 9¾ pounds. Cost is $100.

An externally framed tent that is also light is a series by Bishop's Ultimate Outdoor Equipment. The two-man tent with waterproof fly weighs 8⅗ pounds. It costs a whopping $192.

And although wall tents are not usually regarded as compact enough or light enough for backpacking, there is now a 6.6-pound baker tent (called the Forrester after the Moor and Mountain employee who designed it) that is 9 by 7½ feet in floor plan and slopes from 6½ feet at the peak to 1½ feet at the back. It is made entirely of coated nylon and has a full-width screened window at the rear. An advantage of the lean-to-shaped baker has always been that it warms well with a reflector fire and that it is roomy.

But it is a holy terror in a wind if the flap is up. This one costs $150 and has a full front panel that can be thrown back in good weather and zipped closed in a storm.

### *High-Altitude Tents*

The ultimate in tents are the expedition and high-altitude shelters. Most of them are similar in appearance to the prism-shaped or externally framed tents already described. But they have a number of extra features. For one thing, they are generally built from stronger and more-reinforced nylon and are always two-layer in construction. They also usually have tunnel entrances that help brush snow from clothing on entering and can also be used to store gear or to connect two tents. Some have alcove sections that can be added for storing equipment.

Their A-frame aluminum poles slide into pockets in the outside of the tent when erected for better support and to keep the tent from flapping in a wind. There are more guys and tie-downs. These are not bad features to look for in an ordinary tent, either.

Some tents are available with inside frost liners, which are very handy in extremely cold weather. Breath freezes on the first chilled surface it hits—which happens to be the inside of your tent walls. This would be okay if everything stayed cold. But during the day or when cooking, this frost melts and drips all over everything. The tied-in liner can be taken out every morning and shaken off to remove accumulated frost and ice.

Many of these tents also have cooking or toilet holes in the floor, a flap that can be lifted or unzipped. When the tent is erected, you thrust your ice axe down into the snow through this hole and rotate it to create a deep funnel. It doesn't sound attractive, but it beats the hell out of going outside in a raging blizzard. It also permits you to sweep out the tent without opening the door.

To save every ounce of weight possible, these tents are usually made from extra-light but tough nylon and are also tapered in floor plan and elevation toward the rear to save weight and bulk. Because such construction is costly, these tents are usually priced higher than mild-weather tents. About $155 to $175 is a common price range.

In my opinion, they are not for the ordinary backpacker. But if you can afford only a single tent and also propose to go winter mountaineering, it would be wise to make the investment. Then you could use a tarp for the warmest months of the summer.

### *How to Pitch Tents*

Most of the tents described in this chapter can be rolled out on the ground, where the floor is first staked down flat and smooth. Before you do this, though, check the area and remove any sticks and sharp stones that can later damage either you or the tent. (Other considerations in the selection of a campsite will be discussed in Chapter 9.)

Then the aluminum poles are jointed and lifted one by one, starting with the front. The initial staking of the floor holds everything in place and makes tent pitching a quick one-man job. If your tent comes with telescoping or jointed poles that are held together internally with shock cords, so much the better. They just snap into extended position.

In any event, poles for backpacking should be jointed in short sections. If they are to be rolled in the tent, they should be no longer than 14 or 15 inches to fit crosswise in the pack. If they are to be carried separately in a vertical position, about 21 inches fits the height of your pack. Poles should always be bagged to prevent them from cutting or abrading the pack or tent.

Guy lines should be of nylon with a rough twisted or braided surface that holds a taut-line hitch. Also available in this modern day are sliding metal or plastic fasteners that make knots unnecessary. If high winds are expected, elastic shock cords in the guy lines are a good idea to keep everything taut and prevent flapping, which can keep you awake all night. Always close your tent before you leave it during the day in case a wind or storm should spring up.

A nice thing about nylon tents is that they don't shrink when wet. So you don't have to slacken the guy lines or drop the tent poles into a little pit in the ground before a storm, as must be done with cotton tents if you don't want them to pull to pieces or pull the stakes out of the ground and collapse on you in the middle of the night.

One observation we made in pitching new tents for pictures was that some cannot be staked out before the aluminum poles are inserted. Try the latter with a loose tent in a high wind! My two older sons were also shocked at the way some suppliers of expensive tents cut corners with cheap cotton ties instead of using nylon. Some tents didn't even include bags for the poles and stakes. These are details you should check before buying.

There are all kinds of tent stakes and each has its advantages and disadvantages. The lightest are smooth or corkscrew steel stakes, really pins with a loop at the top (1½ ounces each) or U-shaped stakes of aluminum rod (1 ounce) that both have fair holding power, even though they are only about 7 to 10 inches long. The U-shaped pin is the most secure of the two. A trick to improve the holding power of the straight pins is to slip one into the eye of another and drive them into the ground in a diverging vee. You can also put a heavy rock or log behind any stake on the guy line to improve holding power.

Then there are half-tubular or vee-cross-section stakes of aluminum or steel that range from 6½ to 11¾ inches in length and from ¾ to 2½ ounces in weight. They are much stronger, less likely to bend, and give greater security. Finally, the new polycarbonate plastic tent pegs, about 9 inches long and 1½ ounces in weight, are also strong and secure. But these are all a bit bulky.

To save weight and bulk, I usually carry wire stakes for most of the tie-downs and a couple of the bigger, stronger pins to make key tie-downs secure. If you don't want to carry the latter, you can almost always find some dead hardwood with which to make bigger stakes.

On soft forest floors with a thick layer of duff or on sandy beaches or on wet ground anywhere, you may have to use the deadmen described for securing tarps at the beach. Or you can tie into trees, firmly rooted shrubs, or rocks. On mountains above timberline, you may have to use rocks. Make sure they are big enough to hold the tent. Here, a few pitons driven into cracks may also be the answer. If you can't drive a stake at all to hold the floor down, as on rock ledges, then erect the tent and throw two or three lines over the top at either end and in the middle, securing these as best you can to rocks or pitons. At high altitudes it is very dangerous to sleep in a tent that is not firmly secured.

On snow, you can use buried snowshoes or deadmen for an overnight anchor. An ice axe or two also make secure stakes. Pouring water over the buried deadmen at below-freezing temperatures makes a very secure pitch, but they are the very devil to cut out in the morning.

On a glacier, use ice screws to hold the tent. But check them every day, since the sun warms the metal and causes these pins to loosen. You can also have special sod cloths added to the outside of your tent for this kind of camping on which you can pile ice or snow blocks. There are also special shovel- or disk-shaped aluminum deadmen for pitching in snow, but they are really for expeditions and take up too much room in your pack for ordinary hiking.

One last word on tents. Before you go charging off into the woods with your new shelter, set it up in the backyard a few times. This is the place to learn how to do it. Cotton tents should be set up and left for a few days to "condition," to tighten up the seams and stretch into shape. Nylon tents should be set up and all the seams, both in the tent and the fly, given a good coating of a nylon-tent sealer, a treatment that must be repeated periodically *before* you develop a leak.

Cotton tents are subject to mildew if rolled up and left wet. And they should be lifted every few days at permanent camps to have the floor dried out and cleaned or they will rot. Dirt should be sponged off with clean water as soon as possible to prevent staining. When cotton tents start to leak, they can be re-treated by the supplier. Temporary treatment can be made by rubbing the offending spot with a bar of paraffin wax, then melting it in with a warm iron or a clean stone.

Nylon won't rot, but mildew can grow on the surface and discolor the fabric, so these tents should be carefully dried and cleaned after every use, too. Floors can be sponged with soap, both inside and out, and dried with a cloth. All tents should be carried in a stuff bag, but then should be stored loosely at home in a dry spot.

Finally, with floored tents, it's a good idea to carry a little whisk broom and sponge along with you to keep the inside—and also, therefore, your sleeping bag—clean and neat.

# 7

# ESSENTIAL CAMP GEAR

Defining the camp gear a backpacker ought to have is a bit like telling someone where and how he ought to live without knowing what kind of person he is or what his finances are. And every hiker has his own ideas on what gimmick is vital and what isn't.

Therefore, this chapter will simply attempt to define what is essential in the way of camping gear and then discuss those items that might not be quite necessary but nevertheless make life more pleasant.

Strictly speaking, one or two people could get along on a weekend without cooking by taking food that has been precooked or doesn't require cooking in the first place. In this case, the only gear they would need is clothing, sleeping bag, pad, tent, and pack, plus a few safety items.

But part of the fun of backpacking is the evening gathering around a campfire. And as long as you're going to have that, you might as well enjoy hot meals, too. Also, common sense dictates that you carry matches, knife, light, first-aid kit, compass, and insect repellent. So, right away, there are several essentials. First aid will be discussed in Chapter 12 and compass craft will be covered in Chapter 8. Therefore, let's start here with the rest of the gear.

## *Fire Starters*

Matches are the number one essential for any wilderness traveler, so essential that you should have several supplies in various well-remembered places. Your smoking needs should be kept separate from your survival supply, too. I carry three match containers.

My pipe needs are taken care of by several folders of paper matches that I carry in my belt pouch. Under no condition should paper matches be carried as the main or the emergency supply. Damp weather renders them useless. And they aren't much good for starting a fire even under the best of conditions, because they give too little flame for too short a time.

My emergency supply is a container that has not been improved upon in the many years it has been available. It is the Marble match cylinder, which is made from nickel-plated brass with an attached screw-type swiveling cap that is rubber gasketed to make it waterproof. The 2⅝x⅞-inch container holds about fourteen strike-anywhere matches. Even on an afternoon hike in a nearby woods, it is always in my button-down upper left-hand shirt pocket. Some outdoorsmen go so far as to pin the container by its ring into their pocket. It is never touched except in an emergency.

The trouble with disaster is that you never know when it will strike. Even a day hike could end in a savage storm or an accident could leave you stranded in the woods after dark. This little match supply could save your life, or at least make a night-long wait for help more comfortable.

My main supply of cooking matches are also strike-anywhere wooden matches. I carry them in a plastic pill vial, 2 inches in diameter and 3 inches long, that has a tight snap-on plastic cap. This container holds about seventy-five matches and I carry it in the upper left-hand pocket of my pack with the rest of my frequently needed personal supplies. And I always put it right back after use, never leaving the container open or putting it down for a minute. Just a small gripe at this point. Will the do-gooders who have tried to outlaw strike-anywhere matches at least exempt camping supply stores! It's getting so you can't buy any within two hundred miles of a city.

Safety wooden matches are no good for camping. They require the specially prepared surface on the box for lighting, and this scratch surface deteriorates very rapidly when exposed to damp weather, even when it has been cut from the box and stored in a closed match container. Remember, when you need a fire the most, it is likely that your hands will be cold and wet and in your haste you will fumble things. Your matches and their container should reflect this probability.

For this reason, many people prefer waterproofed matches, which have been treated with wax and will light even when soaked in water. They can be bought at any outdoor store, but you can also make them for yourself.

Take as many strike-anywhere matches as will fit comfortably in a paper cup and drop them in, heads up.

Then, in an ordinary double boiler, melt some paraffin wax, the kind used to seal jelly jars, and pour it over the matches until it covers the heads. You may have to push some of the matches down to keep them below the surface.

Set the cup in a pan of cold water and let the wax harden completely. Then, cut away the cup or not, as you wish. That's all there is to it. Anytime you need a match you can dig one out of the wax block, scrape off most of the wax on the head and strike it on any dry surface. One little tip, though. Put these waterproofed matches in an impervious container such as a tightly closed plastic bag before you pack it. Sun heat on the trail can melt the wax, which will run all over everything in your pack.

Then there is the metal match, which is said to replace conventional matches. It's like a super flint and steel, consists of an extruded rod of exotic metals that gives off a shower of sparks when struck with a piece of metal such as a knife blade. The kit comes with a striker and a bag of tinder—all in a pouch for about $3. It is said to be good for about one thousand lights.

Whichever way you go on matches, you may also want to carry some kind of fire starter, even if you think you're the world's greatest fire maker. I've seen times and places when the devil himself would have had trouble striking a blaze, so I sometimes carry three kinds of starter.

The first is a sizable sheet of waxed paper, which is folded repeatedly into a little square that fits under the matches in my kitchen-supply container. A small piece of this will help things get going in ordinary rainy summer weather when the woods have been soaked for a week. You southwesterners don't even know what I'm talking about, of course. But I believe I hear a soft Amen from backpackers who hike the Smokies, Catskills, and Adirondacks and the rain forests of the Northwest.

I also carry a few candle stubs, normally to give a little

light in the evening and so conserve my flashlight. But in a crunch, they are useful also to start a fire. Cut off about an inch of candle or less and put it under your little pyramid of tinder. It will burn long enough to dry out wet slivers and get the fire under way. Wrap candles in plastic or foil to prevent melting and to protect your pack.

For really tough situations in the winter, I carry a small foil-wrapped block of commercial fire starters, which is divided into little squares that you break off one at a time to use. They are made from a brown fibrous material that is soaked in wax. Other starters include a white blocklike starter made from some sort of naphtha compound and a small can of Sterno (a spoonful will do the job). There is also a tubed jelly type of starter that can be smeared on the wood.

Here again, you can also make your own starters. Roll up old newspapers into a tight cylinder about an inch in diameter. Tie the roll tightly with twine and put it in an old pan. Pour melted paraffin over the roll, turning it several times to make sure it is completely coated. To help the wax soak to the core, it is best to put the wax-filled pan in a sink containing hot water that will keep the wax liquid for fifteen minutes or so. Then, replace the hot water with cold water to chill the roll. Finally, cut the cylinder into inch-long sections with a sharp or serrated knife. Store these chunks in a plastic bag.

All of these starters burn with a fierce flame and will start a fire even with ice-filled wood at below-zero temperatures, if you are persistent enough.

I know I said in Chapter 3 to forget fires in the winter time! But there may come a time with you, as it did with me, when you suddenly break through an ice crust into a stream or a hidden swamp pool and have to dry your clothing and thaw your flesh in a hurry. At such a time, the professional niceties of lighting a fire only with tinder and a single match are forgotten and a blaze is much more than a psychological lift.

But these fire-lighting aids should not be used as a crutch all of the time. You should learn how to light a fire under all conditions without them, a subject we will take up in Chapter 9.

## *A Light for Night*

Next on the list is a light. Too many people go into the woods with heavy battery-powered searchlights that are completely unnecessary. Since you will normally go to bed at dark and get up at first light, the only purpose of a flashlight is to guide you to the john and back or to finish up a small task after dark or, in the East perhaps, to spotlight a nosy porcupine in the middle of the night, so you can give him a healthy belt with a chunk of firewood and drive him away from your lean-to, tent, or gear.

For these routine jobs, all that's really needed is a pen-sized flashlight that can be clipped in your pocket. Many hikers swear by the small palm-sized Mallory flashlight with alkaline batteries. I happen to like a very cheap, disposable flashlight that is also hand sized and can be thrown away after the sealed-in battery is exhausted. My first one lasted for over a year, and I think it would have gone a lot longer except that I inadvertently left it out of my sleeping bag on a winter mountaineering trip and it froze. It worked, of course, when I thawed it out, but the zip had gone and it died soon afterward.

And that makes a point. If you have any reason to believe that the temperature will drop below freezing during the night, take your flashlight to bed with you so it will work when you want it to. This is another reason for having a small one. You can keep it in a pocket where you will know where to put your hand on it.

In the summer, I put my flashlight in one of the boots at my head. That puts everything I need in the middle of the night right in one place. At all other times, it is in that upper left-hand pack pocket. That way, I know where to find it.

### *The All-Important Knife*

There is no tool more important around a camp than your knife. When I was a boy, I would rather have been caught naked than without my pocketknife. I still carry one at all times and use it frequently. If you are going to build a fire, it is just as essential as a match.

I'm not going to get embroiled in the controversy over pocket versus sheath knives. If you want to carry a sheath knife, go ahead. It doesn't necessarily mark you as a tenderfoot, as some outdoorsmen claim. But pick a short-bladed knife that you can use—not a Bowie knife, which was designed for fighting and is good for little else.

Select a sheath knife with a 4- or 5-inch straight and reasonably thin blade. Don't worry about blood grooves. They are meaningless and simply weaken a blade. If you are going to use the knife for skinning game, pick one with a rounded point, which is less likely to damage a pelt.

Keep your knife in a fully enclosed sheath that will prevent it from popping out and getting lost. Copper rivets in the sheath are essential, but don't trust them. Wear the knife on your hip where it is out of the way of your pack and won't stab you in the rear or groin if you fall on it.

Personally, I carry my little 4-inch Scout sheath knife in my pack for the occasional camp chore that requires one, and even then only when the planned excursion requires a sheath knife. I carry it in the upper left-hand pack pocket with my other personal gear.

The pocketknife is much more useful, and I carry mine on a clip attached to a belt lanyard. For years, I used a Scout pocketknife that was very satisfactory. Then, Teddy gave me a Swiss Army knife, not the one that has everything on it including a kitchen sink, but the one that has everything but the kitchen sink. There are two blades, a short one and a longer one, a bottle opener/screwdriver, a can opener and corkscrew (indispensable for opening those luncheon and dinner wine bottles), and two types of awls. It also has an ivory toothpick and a pair of tweezers, which I find useful although not essential, and a pair of folding scissors. At first, I sneered at the scissors, but have since found them invaluable for trimming broken fingernails.

Other outdoorsmen prefer large single- or two-bladed folding clasp knives or grind down kitchen knives or files to make custom equipment. Fishermen usually want a thin-bladed filleting knife. Take your choice; just make sure that the blade is of high-quality carbon steel. And make sure you keep your knife in your pocket or on that lanyard. Don't lay it down or stick it into a log. Knife throwing with a good blade is for idiots, of course.

No matter what knife you pick, it is worse than useless unless it is sharp. In fact, a dull knife is quite dangerous. As purchased, no knife has a real edge, so the first thing you should do is sharpen it, a chore that must be repeated frequently. This requires a whetstone. As far as I'm concerned, any good stone will do, whether it is rectangular or round is a matter of personal preference. I have a large rectangular two-sided oilstone at home and carry a small 1- by 3-inch stone in my pack (in that upper

Knife sharpening requires a rotary motion of the blade against the whetstone with the back of the blade raised about ⅛ inch above the surface of the stone.

left-hand pocket) so that I can touch up my knife and axe whenever I think they need it.

There is really no mystery in how to sharpen a blade. It is done with a rotary motion on the smooth side of the stone. Hold thin-bladed knives with the back of the blade about ⅛ inch above the stone, thicker sheath-knife blades angled at ¼ inch above the stone. Keep the angle constant and apply only enough pressure on the forward stroke to feel a light grinding action.

Make sure you cover the entire length of the blade and the rounded tip as well. Then, reverse the knife and repeat the procedure. Now, you will have a slight burr on the first side. Remove this by turning the knife over again and stroking it across the stone in a direction away from the blade edge. To finish up, a truly razor-sharp blade should be stropped on a piece of oiled leather, but this is not essential unless you're a purist.

If stains bother you, clean them from your blade with a soap pad. But make sure water, dirt, and food are cleaned out of the knife handle. Leather-disk handles on sheath knives should be oiled or rubbed with a leather compound occasionally. If you store your knives for any length of time, wipe the blades and other metal parts with an oily rag. If you take care of your knives in this way, they will last a lifetime and become prized possessions.

## *Saws and Sawing*

Before you can cook, you must make a fire, which requires wood. It is thoroughly possible to gather all of the wood you need for cooking with your bare hands (or better, your *gloved* hands). In any deciduous woods, there are plenty of inch-sized and smaller branches of hardwood that can be broken from deadfalls or standing dead trees. And in softwood forests, the lower branches on living evergreen trees die quite conveniently, leaving a quantity of kindling and small wood at hand—even if it does smoke and throw sparks and is inferior for cooking. So, if you want to make a little cooking fire, you need no further equipment.

But I like to cook over a deep bed of hardwood coals and I am a nut for a little bigger campfire in the evening. I also like a log seat, supported by two large rocks, to sit on in front of my fire. Minimum diameter for this seat for comfort is about 6 inches. For the fire, wood from 1 to 3 inches in diameter is about right. To get these comforts requires a saw. The sacrifice in weight is not great and, particularly with a large group or a long stay at a camping site, the saw will greatly speed the wood gathering.

Ordinary carpentry saws with tiny teeth are useless, but today there are available folding saws with big teeth. They take up little space and do a big job. Mine is the 1½-pound Sven, a thin Swedish blade of high temper that pivots into one support arm, which in turn, slides into the other support to make a protective sheath 24 inches long and 1¾ inches wide. Erected in triangular shape and secured with a single wing nut, it will cut through trees of about a foot in diameter with ease. It costs $7 and replacement blades are available for $2.

Wood-cutting tools for backpackers include the Swedish collapsible saw (foreground). My son's all-steel axe (left), my own big-headed Michigan axe (background), and a shingle hatchet are all useful in particular circumstances. Axes should be sheathed in riveted leather cases like the one shown on the stump.

There are also bow saws, but these do not collapse and the blade must be protected with a taped-on length of split hose. Further, they are a bit awkward to stow in the pack, since they measure about 8 inches across the bow and have a 21-inch length. Generally, they are lashed on the outside. Many outdoorsmen think they are stronger and more convenient, though. They cost from $3 to $4 and weigh 1¼ to 2½ pounds.

For the person who worries about ounces above everything, there is a flexible twisted-wire saw with rings on each end that can be pulled back and forth by two people or looped over the ends of a bowed branch and held in place by the stubs of twigs at either end. I class this 1-ounce $2 device as an emergency tool. Same for a folding saw with a 12-inch blade that weighs 10 ounces and costs $5.

Again, you must keep your saw sharp to be useful. But, since these blades come with very sharp teeth, the first sharpening need not come until you have cut a great deal of hardwood. It is easy to do, though, because the teeth are large.

On the Sven, the cutting teeth are grouped in fours, separated by two-tooth groups that simply clear the slot of sawdust. Every other cutting tooth is sharpened on the opposite side. The sharpening of these edges can be accomplished with an ordinary small mill file, if care is used. A saw file that has no serrations on the edges to cut into opposite saw teeth is more convenient, though.

With the blade clamped in a vise, every other tooth is sharpened on the appropriate edge with a couple of smooth strokes of the file, which is held at a diagonal both to the vertical and to the horizontal. Then, the saw blade is turned around in the vise, and the alternate teeth are sharpened in the same way. With a little practice, you can sharpen a blade in less than thirty minutes.

Good sawing practice is very important with these thin, flexible blades. Stroke the saw gently to establish a kerf, or cut, then increase your speed. But let the saw do the work. If you bear down, you will surely bind the blade and it will jump out of the wood—probably to gash your hand. This happened recently to a friend, who then had to make about a 25-mile hike-and-car trip to a hospital to get his thumb re-attached to his hand.

And when you finish with the saw, put it away in the pack if you are sure you are through with it, or hang it up on a stub of a limb over the woodpile. Don't leave it on the ground to get rusty or stepped on. Every now and then, wipe it with an oily rag.

### *Axes: Why and What*

For some reason, the question of an axe is very personal. There are hikers who consider them useless, those who carry only a hand axe, and regular Paul Bunyans who are only happy when hewing mighty logs. I guess I fall somewhere in the middle, except when we are on a high mountain, of course, and carry no axes or saws at all.

But if I'm going to be in a deciduous forest, alone or with one other person, I generally carry a hand axe for splitting firewood. With bigger parties, I carry a gigantic Michigan-style axe with a 29-inch handle and a 4-pound head. It makes short work of the heaviest cutting chores. If I'm going to take a long-handled axe, then I believe in taking a real one that works for me. I'm not too keen on light Hudson Bay axes with short 26-inch handles.

However, Chuck has one that he swears by. It is the size mentioned above, made by Estwing, and is all forged steel. Most of the handle (or helve) is covered with a nylon-vinyl handgrip. It weighs 3¾ pounds, and I must admit it works. Also, there is never a loose head to tighten. Price is $11.

On balance, I would say that the average backpacker who is going to carry a long-handled axe is better off with a lightweight model like Chuck's, a head of about 1½ pounds and a 26- or 28-inch handle. This isn't contradictory. The average camper is not experienced enough to handle heavier axes with safety (and no one but a professional forester should ever carry a double-bitted axe). The amount of wood cut on a camping trip doesn't warrant a big tool.

In my case, I like to keep up my axemanship, which started when I was about seven years old. My 4-pound axe bites deep and I often cut up a downed tree with it instead of using a saw, just for the exercise and to keep my eye sharp. However, normally, an axe is really only for splitting wood on a camping trip. A saw does a much more efficient job of cutting up wood. For this reason, a backpacker really doesn't need a long-handled axe. He can get by very well with a hand axe for splitting larger pieces of wood.

My short axe is called a "shingle hatchet." It has a thin blade with a nail puller and a hammer head instead of a butt, or pall. It was made for splitting and nailing shingles, and it is just great for splitting camp wood.

On big pieces, I simply hold the hatchet in place on the end of the log and swack it on the head with another piece of wood. It weighs just under 2 pounds with a sheath. It is also ideal for repairing lean-tos, which seems to be a sadly growing necessity in these times.

There are other good hand axes. One that is commonly called a "hunter's axe" is an example. It weighs 1¼ pounds, has a sturdy handle and a square-shaped head, and is 15 inches overall. There are also all-steel forged hand axes with cushioned handles.

Before you buy an axe with a wooden handle, check to make sure the handle is of sound, knotless hardwood and is set firmly in the eye of the axe, flush with the face, and properly anchored with either wooden or steel wedges. The handle should be plumb with respect to the axe face and to the front of the axe.

Again, no matter what you opt for, the axe should be taken care of. For the average camper, the bit of an axe is okay as it is, with some sharpening, of course. Axemen usually like to thin the blade down somewhat. This makes it cut faster. To do this, you need a powered grindstone. Draw a chalk line about an inch or so from the bit. Grind the metal flat to within ¼ inch of the bit, then give a slight curve to this last area to keep the blade from binding when cutting.

Now hone the bit with a whetstone, rough side first, followed by a finish with the smooth side of the stone, just like a knife. Stroke off the burr and strop with leather, if you wish.

After this preparation, the axe can be rough-sharpened whenever it gets particularly dull or nicked with a 10- or 12-inch mill file, followed by whetting. A vise is best for this operation, but in the woods you can substitute a small log, against which the axe is braced with your foot while you file first one side and then the other. Work about an inch at a time from the center of the bit to the heel and toe. Follow up with the whetstone. I carry a 6-inch mill file with me (in that upper-left pack pocket, naturally) in case I ever need a touch-up.

However, if you keep and use an axe properly, it will rarely ever be necessary to file it. It should be honed, though, after every use—and in between, too, if you are cutting very old hardwood and feel the axe getting dull.

The handle of your axe should be kept very smooth. Polish rough spots with fine sandpaper and rub the handle with linseed oil every now and then to keep it from drying out. Make sure the head is tight. If it loosens, drive the wedges in further and soak the end in linseed oil. Some axemen drill a 2- or 3-inch hole in the knob end of the handle and fill it with linseed oil, plugging the end neatly with doweling. This will keep a handle in condition for a long time.

Keep in mind that long or short axes are very dangerous tools and are only safe if used with great care. Nothing can stop a backpacking trip faster than a gashed leg.

If you are going to fell a deadhead, first look up at its top to see if there are any heavy, insecure limbs that will drop on your head when you start chopping. You can sometimes bring them down by pounding or shaking the tree. If not, it would be smart to try another tree. These "widow makers" are aptly named.

Decide which way you want the tree to fall. Then take up a position with your legs comfortably apart and well balanced. Place yourself in such a position that if the axe should glance off the work it cannot strike you. Reach out with your axe at full length on all sides and above you. There should be full clearance for the maximum stroke you can take.

On the opposite side of the direction of fall, cut a small notch in the tree that will keep it in line and act as a sort of hinge when the tree falls, preventing it from splitting and the butt from kicking back, which can have disastrous consequences.

Now start your main notch on the other side of the trunk, positioning it slightly below the first notch. Cut at an acute angle to the grain and alternate chips from the top and bottom of the notch. Right-handed people will grip the axe handle with their right hand near the end or knob and grasp the handle near the shoulder with their left hand, holding the axe across their body with the head on

Felling a deadhead tree requires a large notch on the side to which the falling tree is to be directed. First a small guide notch is cut on the opposite side; when the large notch is deep enough, the guide notch is deepened a bit to start the tree on its way. On downed trees, always cut limbs from the underside, not the crotch. Then cut trunk halfway through, using a notch as wide as the tree is thick. Finally, cut through the opposite side.

the left. The swing is from left to right, and as the axe is raised, the left hand is slid down to meet the right. Swing easily and don't try to force it. Let the axe do the work.

If the trunk is very big, cut chips from the center of the notch, then from the far and near sides on both the top and bottom of the notch. When you are past the center of the trunk, step around to the other side and deepen the upper notch until the tree starts to crack. Step smartly out of the way to a previously determined safe spot at the side. Never stand behind a falling tree. If the trunk should kick back for any reason, it could splatter you all over the landscape.

When cutting up a downed tree, first limb it. Cut the branches from their undersides. Do not try to cut limbs from the crotch side. It dulls the bit and can even chip it. Always stand on the opposite side of the trunk from the limbs you are trimming off.

Then cut a notch as wide as the trunk is thick halfway through the trunk. Now change sides and notch the other side to separate the log. Although expert axemen can get away with it, don't stand on the log. It isn't safe for the average camper.

However, as we said before, it is better to fell and cut up trees with a saw. A deadhead can be felled just as easily with your saw and with less danger from widow makers. Make the same two cuts in the same order. When deepening the hinge cut, you may have to hammer in a wedge of hardwood, made on the spot with your axe, to prevent the saw from binding and to help direct the tree in the direction you want it to fall.

For splitting wood, you need a chopping block. It should be a log about 3 feet long and at least 3 or 4 inches in diameter with a notch cut in the center. Pick out a roomy place for your woodyard and stake the chopping block firmly in position with four strong stakes, pounded in one on each side near the two ends of the chopping block. Now it can't shift and embarrass you, or worse, hurt you. Again, reach out in all directions to insure clearance.

Heavy logs are split by placing them in the notch on the opposite side of the block from where you are standing. The top of the log to be split should be level with the top of the chopping block. Stand with legs well apart, raise the axe as when felling a tree, and bring it straight down with

To split wood use a chopping block, a 3- to 4-foot log that is staked in place to prevent it from rolling. A notch in the center steadies the firewood. Strike the chunk near the end, over the chopping block.

an easy swing to strike the log in the center of the end on the chopping block.

Well-seasoned wood will split with a single blow—in below-freezing weather it may even fly apart. But if the log is big and stubborn, reverse the billet and split it from the other end, too, in line with the first split. Don't strike the log below the chopping block or you may dull your axe in the dirt or on a stone. If you extend the billet above the chopping block and hit it there, you may very well catch a hunk of wood in the head.

For splitting smaller wood or cutting kindling to length, use one hand with either a long or a short axe. A short axe, incidentally, should always be used with one hand, never two, which is dangerous with the short tool. Choke up your grip on the long axe to about 15 inches from the shoulder.

Hold the billet of wood at one end in the left hand (if you're right handed). Place the bit of the axe against the billet near the other end and in line with the grain if you are splitting or across the grain at a slight angle if you are cutting off a piece of wood. Bring both axe and wood down together smartly against the top of the chopping block to cut through. This is really the only safe way to split kindling. Never lean a stick against a chopping block and try to cut it on either side of the block or even on top of the block. It's a sure way to get a stick in your head with great force.

This may all seem very fundamental to experienced campers, but it is worth reading carefully. I've seen quite a few supposedly experienced campers handling axes with frightening carelessness. To the newcomer, it may sound very complicated, but it really isn't. After you get some practice, it becomes simple and second nature. Two men with a saw and axe can gather, cut, and split enough wood for two or three days in less than an hour.

When you're through with the axe, either sheath it and put it back in your pack or bury it tightly in the chopping block. The first is the best idea because, for some strange reason, an axe is a temptation for every passer-by who just has to take a few swings. That's how the handle of my big axe was recently broken and the bit badly nicked, after I had kept it safely for ten years. It took me a week to get it back in shape and I've never let another person so much as pick it up since.

Incidentally, when carrying an axe in your hand, keep the sheath on until you are actually going to use it. Hold the axe near the head with the blade turned out away from you. In the pack, I like to store the axe head down with the bit facing toward the rear. Some campers lash the axe on

Chris shows the right way to split kindling. Hold both the stick and axe together while raising them and striking against the chopping block.

the frame with the head up and the bit facing toward the rear. The sheath should be of strong leather that is well riveted.

## *Selecting Pots and Pans*

Okay, now that we have the wood in, let's look at cooking gear. Personally, I believe in simplicity. I like one-dish meals that can be eaten from the pan or from my cup if there are two of us. Another pot heats water for a hot drink and for dishwashing. A spoon to lap your meal up with completes the gear. The cup should be of molded polyethylene, which holds the heat in the food but doesn't scald your lips. I carry a 10-ounce plastic cup with a handle and thick sides. Using a kitchen measuring cup and a hot wire, I have scribed lines on the side of this cup at 2-ounce intervals and have filled the lines with ink to make them more visible. Some hikers feel, however, that a steel cup that can be heated over a flame or just warmed next to the fire is more versatile. Take your pick, but stay away from aluminum, which cools food too rapidly and, before it does so, will raise a blister on your lip.

This minimal equipment is really all that is needed for any number of people. Rob and I survived very well for many years with no more. As the crowd gets bigger, you simply increase the size of the pots a bit. You may want to throw in a frying pan, although it is better to stay away from fried foods, as we shall see in Chapters 10 and 12. But frying pans can also be used for steaming, boiling, and sautéing foods, so they can be useful.

What are the specs? For one or two men, I'm convinced that empty tin cans with wire bails are the best. A 46-ounce tomato-juice can is just about right for water. A large whole-tomato, bean, or shortening can is perfect for the meal. They nest inside each other, too, to save space.

Variety of cooking gear includes the simplest, nested tin cans with wire bails (left). In front of them is a set of nested clip-together utensils. More elaborate are aluminum pots and a frying pan with a detachable handle (right). The plastic bottle is useful for booze or juices, the bota for water. A grill supports utensils over the fire.

Your condiment containers and spoons drop inside and the whole thing slips into a stuff bag. When their appearance begins to offend your sensibilities, you throw them away and get another pair for free. For larger groups, you can get a No. 10 can or two from a restaurant. They make darn good kettles and grand water buckets.

Won't buy it? Okay, spend your money instead. There are excellent nesting cook kits at any outdoor store. Morsan, for example, has small, junior, family, and senior sets—each with three aluminum pots with lids, a detachable handle, a double-boiler ring, and one or two frying pans for $4 to $6. A one-quart aluminum teapot that nests in the family or senior kits is another $3. There are heavier gauge deluxe aluminum kits that cost up to $17. And you can get stainless steel for a lot more, but they are really too heavy for backpacking.

If you are going to buy a ready-made set, get a two-quart and a four-quart kettle with lids that nest. Don't worry about a coffeepot, unless you simply must have boiled coffee. Most people, today, drink instant coffee or tea.

When Teddy is part of the group, we also carry an eight-quart aluminum kettle, because the only condition she has ever made about backpacking is that she have enough hot water to wash in at the end of every day. The big kettle does the trick.

My frying pan with a detachable handle, which is 9¼ inches in diameter, is sized to serve as a lid for this big kettle. In my opinion, this is the minimum size for a frying pan. Stay away from Teflon-lined equipment. In the woods, these non-stick finishes get scratched, and then they actually stick worse than uncoated pans, it seems. If I were going to buy a new frying pan, I would choose one with a clamp-type detachable handle. I have to be careful with my slip-on-handle model for it might easily fall into the fire. Of course, with a frying pan you will also carry a small spatula with which to handle pancakes, fried eggs, fish, and the like.

To cover my frying pan and suit it for sautéing and baking, which will be discussed later, Teddy and I found a recessed lid in a hardware store that just fits the frying pan and the big wash-water kettle. The screwed-on knob can be switched to either side, thus enabling the lid to be reversed with the domed side up for creating a coal-covered baker out of the frying pan.

A steel backpacking grill is useful for holding pans over the coals, particularly if you are where there are no suitable stones. Either the long backpacker grill made from steel rod or a flat, light cooking grate ($6 and $4, respectively) is okay. And a hot mitt is handy, not only to lift pots from the fire but also to hold a pan by the handle when you are doing some fancy bit of work and don't want to fry your hand, too.

Whatever kind of cooking ware you choose, prepare it properly for cooking. That means blackened exteriors! I will brook no argument on this point from spotless-pan paranoids. A pot blackened with good hardwood soot, which is shiny black and sticks to the pan, distributes heat more evenly and does a better cooking job.

Never scour the outside of such a treasure. Simply wipe off any loose soot and spilled food with a damp paper towel. Put each kettle in its own plastic bag and nest them, then put the whole collection into a master cloth bag.

You will still have room in the bag for your condiment kit. I carry small rectangular screw-top plastic drug-tablet bottles for sugar, salt, pepper, and flour. The contents are marked on the outside with a felt pen. I also carry Kodak screw-cap film containers filled with marjoram, thyme, savory, garlic, dried parsley, and chili powder. These containers are also marked with a felt pen. The spices add zip to any meal, particularly dehydrated foods. When the menu requires, I also tote a small plastic bottle of olive oil, salad dressing, and a vial of corn meal. A small piece of foil over the top of the bottle before the cap is screwed on seals these containers and prevents leakage.

In the little nylon bag that contains the foregoing, I also carry an envelope of dehydrated mushroom gravy, a packet or two of onion and some other soup, and several envelopes of chicken and beef bouillon to flavor dishes or to provide a hot drink at night before dinner. This pouch also carries a tiny glass bottle of instant coffee and a number of tea bags wrapped in foil. It is a light, but complete, kitchen. We'll see how this stuff is used in Chapter 10.

Since we often take our dog with us, there are a couple of necessities for her. We take a small metal bowl for water and food; the latter is a dehydrated cake that can be broken up and mixed with water and is compact to carry.

If my No. 10 can for water doesn't grab you, how about a 2½-gallon polyethylene cube with a two-way screw spout. It collapses when empty and costs $2. We have one for large groups and it holds enough water for a full day. There is also a 5-gallon size for $2.50. These are for camp use only, of course, since this much water is far too heavy to carry on the trail. But if you have a lot of people to cook for or are some distance from the water supply, they come in handy.

Ordinarily, I do not carry water on the trail and depend instead on springs for my needs. But in desert areas, high in the mountains, or at the beach, I carry a bota or wineskin in preference to a conventional canteen. Modern botas are lined with vinyl and are very strong and flexible. You can wet the outside of the goatskin, too, and cool the water inside. In winter, they are easier to carry inside your clothes to prevent freezing. They come in a traditional curved shape or a pear configuration, have a carrying cord and a two-piece cap that can be entirely removed for pouring or partially unscrewed for squirt-dispensing, and are sized in pints, quarts, and two quarts for prices from $3 to $4.50.

To quench thirst and provide quick-energy sugar, some hikers carry juices in a semi-rigid plastic bottle. You can get such wide-mouthed bottles with tight-screwing lids for about $1. I don't carry juices, but I do usually carry a flask of cognac for a little nip in the evening before dinner and at bedtime. I carry the stuff in a quart-size coated-polyethylene flask that retains flavor and bouquet. Price is also about $1.

If you are so modern that you can't get along with just a spoon to cook and eat with, then get yourself one of those three-piece sets in a little plastic case. Or the next time you are on an airplane that still uses stainless-steel ware, swipe a set. They are just perfect for backpacking.

Forget about plates. The aluminum ones dent and chill the food very quickly, the plastic ones crack and scratch and then are difficult to clean. If you really don't want to eat from your cup, take along plastic-coated paper plates, or bowls, if you can find them; they're rather scarce in our area. These can be burned after every meal and you can carry enough for a two-week trip with little weight.

One tool is very necessary, both for preparing and tending the fire and for preparing your toilet needs, which will be described in Chapter 9. This is a trowel or shovel.

The trowel is lighter; in fact, today you can get a plastic trowel that is only ounces. But it is not as versatile. I carry a non-folding camp spade that is simply a metal blade about 6 inches long with a 2-foot wooden handle. I have sprayed it with red paint so that it shows up around the campsite. With this, you can clear the fire area, dig up sod if necessary, excavate a "cat-hole" toilet or a larger latrine, shovel coals from the fire to the cooking area—all necessary tasks around a camp.

Admittedly, you can do the same things with the more compact trowel, but the difference in weight is really insignificant and the convenience and ease of use of the shovel are not.

You do need some paper towels for mopping up and for drying both equipment and yourself if you don't want to carry dish and bath towels, which tend to get a bit musty. But don't take the whole roll. Reel off just what you need—I allow five sheets per day for kitchen work, another five per person for personal use—and either roll them or fold them into a compact bundle to be carried in the cooking kit bag. When Teddy is along, we carry a towel and a washcloth as well.

The same with toilet paper. Either remove the central

core or squash the roll flat and it will fit into your upper left-hand pocket with the rest of the personal gear. This pocket is getting pretty full now, but it does have room for one more nicety: a 10- to 15-foot length of heavy-duty foil folded flat into a little packet about 4 inches square. This is very handy stuff to have around. With it, you can construct pot covers or even extra pots. To make a container, just mold a double layer around another pot or the end of a log of proper size and crimp the top over to reinforce the lip. It can be used for cooking or for holding hot food near the coals when you are cooking a multi-course meal.

You can also use foil to make a quick and efficient reflector oven or to wrap leftover food for another meal. You can also make foil packs of food for steaming directly over or in coals, as we shall explain in Chapter 10.

But, *please!* Put that used foil in your garbage bag and haul it out. It looks like hell scattered around your campsite or lying in the fireplace at a lean-to.

Well, that's about all you need for open-fire cooking. But you might get caught in an area that prohibits campfires. Open fires in the dry season are banned in the Sierra, and this safety practice is increasing in the East. Furthermore, in some over-camped areas it is only good conservation practice to avoid open fires, thus eliminating air pollution and conserving downed wood so that the duff on which the woodland thrives can be created. Above tree line you have no choice; all of these situations call for a compact backpacking stove.

## *Backpacking Stoves*

I can only speak from personal experience about one brand of stove, the old reliable Primus Model 71L. I've had two for many years and they have never failed me, even under the most miserable conditions. It is understandable, then, if I speak of this stove as of an old friend.

Its advantages are that it is very light, does not require pumping, holds a half pint of white or unleaded gas that will run for more than an hour at full blast—more than enough to cook a full dinner or melt two quarts of water from snow at sub-zero temperatures.

You simply fill the tank and open the valve. Cupping the tank in your hands causes gas to flow up through the valve and down into a little well around the stem. When this is lighted and the valve is closed, pressure is built up in the tank, which can be lit in a minute after re-opening the valve. The compact case forms a wind shield. An attached key for opening the valve doubles as a wrench for taking apart the brass stem and nozzle. The kit also has a wire cleaner for removing crud from the nozzle, a job that

Camp stoves come in all sizes and shapes. The smallest is the collapsible Gerry unit (left, foreground) that burns propane. The slanted Primus behind it is also a propane unit. With the Bluet (center) the stove is mounted on top of the propane cylinder. The two gasoline stoves (right) are essentially the same in action, but the Optimus is squat, the Primus tall. Gas is carried in a spun aluminum bottle (rear).

should be performed after every two or so lightings, or anytime the stove is not putting out full power. The unit costs $13.

Its only drawback is that its height in relation to the base makes it a bit unstable, particularly on snow; the heat causes the snow to melt unevenly and the stove can easily tip over if it isn't put on a bit of insulation.

There is a new Model 8R that is much lower in profile and cures this problem. It only holds ⅓ pint of fuel, but it has a built-in cleaning device and a detachable valve knob. The gas tank tips forward for filling, too. Price is $14.

Friends of mine have used other stoves that are very similar and report good results. There is one by Optimus ($12), Sigg ($19), and Svea ($11). The Optimus is made by the same company that makes the Primus and the two are almost identical. These stoves all hold slightly different amounts of fuel and, of course, burn for different periods of time on a filling. Weights of all are between 18 and 20 ounces.

Optimus and Primus also have larger models that burn either gas or kerosene. They weigh up to about 2 pounds and cost from $15 to $20.

Of course, with these stoves you must carry fuel bottles. They come in pint and quart sizes and weigh a total of 17½ and 31½ ounces, respectively, when filled with gas. These bottles are of spun aluminum and cost between $2 and $3. A pint will do for a weekend if the stove is filled at the start. Two quarts are adequate for a week.

Then, there are the butane stoves, which work with pressurized cartridges. Bluet has one; so do Gerry and Primus. These cost $8 to $10, the 10-ounce cartridges are under a dollar each (except for the 14- and 16-ounce Primus cylinders, which cost up to $1.50). Burning time for the smaller ones is two hours, up to six hours for the larger Primus.

The Gerry Mini-Stove weighs only 7 ounces, without cartridge, and folds into a small, thin disk. The cartridge can be detached whether full or empty. The Bluet is 16 ounces, but the cartridge cannot be detached until empty. Primus weighs 12 ounces and the 30-ounce cylinder can be removed at will.

Friends who have used these stoves say they work well, although I have heard lately some criticism of the Gerry concerning gas leakage. But they also say that the cartridges for this type of stove are rather bulky to carry on a long trip and do not work well in cold weather. Therefore they advocate propane only for short summer hikes.

For a great table of specifications on many of these stoves, see the chart in the Eastern Mountain Sports catalog. Recreational Equipment's catalog lists some that EMS doesn't carry.

There are miniature cooking sets sized for these stoves. Svea has some pans, for example, that are integrated with Model 123. And, of course, there is always the nesting, clamp-closed Scout cooking kit that contains a cup, pot with lid, frying pan, and metal plate/bowl. It is good for one camper and small enough to fit these stoves. Costs less than $3.

There are also pressure cookers for high-altitude cooking that cost from $15 to $20. They are out of the question unless you are going to spend a lot of time above 15,000 feet of altitude.

What about cleanup gear? If you stick with my tin cans, you only need a small wad of moss, gathered from under a streamside rock where it won't show, and a handful of fine sand from the bottom of the spring pool. It is a perfect scouring pad. If there is a lot of grease in your food (which there shouldn't be), boil it out with water before you scour and pour the residue into the hot coals to dry and burn. Still haven't got you?

Okay, then carry a few soap pads of steel wool. I allow one per day. And, by God, don't you leave them around camp—or worse, in the spring hole along with scraps from your dinner. Haul used pads out with you and burn your garbage! You might try some of the new rough-surfaced synthetic scouring pads, too. I've used them and they work.

If you are going on a long trip and need to wash your clothes along the way, carry cold-water detergent in a double plastic bag. Tote your wash water and rinse water for both dishes and clothes at least a hundred feet from the spring or stream before sousing things and pour out the contaminated water in an area that will not immediately drain back into the water supply.

If you dump your soapy water in the stream, I fervently hope that someday you will be downstream from another slob. The resultant violent case of diarrhea, if you understand where it came from, might cure you of this environmentally murderous habit.

## *Nonessential Fripperies*

Smart backpackers will stop above or even earlier (I'm still buckin' for my tin-can cookers). But there are times when you may have enough people in a group to afford toting luxuries and allow you to show off your abilities at the campfire.

One of the extras that lets you lay it on a bit is a folding reflector oven ($10). This aluminum device measures about 13 inches square when folded and opens into a wedge shape with a shelf in the center that is 13 by 10 inches. The oven is placed in front of a blaze, where it catches the heat and reflects it up and down on the food placed on the shelf. Be sure to get a unit with end panels that regulate heat better and shield the food from wind. With experience, you can bake almost any kind of cake or pie or even roast meat in this cooker.

There are also plastic and metal cases to protect the shells of eggs, plastic bottles and jugs too numerous to count, griddles and aluminum dutch ovens, toasters, fancy utensil kits with cooking forks and spoons and assorted kitchen knives.

I will summarize my opinion of all these civilized devices with this thought: Comfortable backpacking requires the ruthless elimination of excess weight and the substitution of ingenuity for mankind's products, using lightweight substitutes or materials that can be obtained from nature. That's the name of the game, the challenge and the real joy of hitting the trail. Right back to my tin cans, man.

But before leaving the subject, there is one other little thing. Every person has a certain number of treasures that he is going to carry regardless of weight because he wants them with him. Keep such indispensables in a little "war bag."

Teddy carries her personal needs in a belt pouch: a toothbrush and tube of toothpaste, a steel mirror, lipstick, stick rouge and eyebrow pencil, nail brush, hand lotion in a small plastic bottle, and a space-saving roll-on deodorant. She says that women with special skin problems should also carry their own facial soap, wrapped in foil, and that any woman will also have her own ideas on what kind of compact cosmetics she needs to feel feminine.

My war bag is a small nylon bag. I just dumped it out beside the typewriter, and here is what this 16-ounce collection contains and why. In the department of mainte-

Personal gear is carried in a small nylon war bag. From left to right, mine contains: mattress repair kit, tape, screwdriver set, needle-nosed pliers, nails, notebook, sewing kit in little candy can, spare laces and clothesline, flashlight, cards, thermometer, whetstone, match cylinder and fire starters wrapped in foil. On top of the small rock is toothpaste and brush, a nail brush and a small cake of soap in a plastic pouch.

nance, there is an air mattress repair kit of rubberized nylon and a tube of adhesive; a sewing kit of needles, thread, buttons, and pins for repairing clothing, all contained in a flat French pastille tin; a whetstone; fire starters; a bunch of heavy nails for repairing lean-tos; a screwdriver with interchangeable blades for repairing gear, and a pair of needle-nosed pliers for the same or for removing a fishhook from a friend, as I have had to do a number of times.

I also have an extra bootlace and a long, thin nylon cord for a clothesline. I carry a tiny airline tube of toothpaste and a brush, a small nail brush, and a motel cake of soap in a plastic bag.

There is a thermometer in a metal case that is good to −45 degrees Fahrenheit for checking the bragging temperature. And I carry a deck of cards for stormy days.

There is also a tiny notebook and pencil. You can also keep your flashlight and kitchen matches in this pouch, if you don't want them loose in your pack pocket.

Not much, but each has been used many times. This is the key to such stuff—in fact to all your gear. Someone once suggested that when you come back from a hike, you should pile all of your equipment in three heaps: (1) what you used all of the time, (2) what you used only once or twice, and (3) what you used not at all—then discard the last two heaps. Pretty good advice because, as you can see from the accompanying chart, even essentials mount up in weight. This chart is based on the weight of our own gear, so you may have to make some adjustments for your own particular equipment.

## EQUIPMENT CHECKLIST AND WEIGHT CHART

(*One-week two-man loads*)

| | *Tough Trails* | | | | | | *Easy Trails (extra luxuries)* | |
|---|---|---|---|---|---|---|---|---|
| | *Summer/Fall* | | *Winter* | | *Average Trails* | | | |
| *Items* | *lbs.* | *oz.* | *lbs.* | *oz.* | *lbs.* | *oz.* | *lbs.* | *oz.* |
| 2 packs and frames | 4 | 10 | 4 | 10 | 4 | 10 | 4 | 10 |
| 2 sleeping bags | 7 | 8 | 9 | 8 | 7 | 8 | 7 | 8 |
| 4 shock cords | | 10 | | 10 | | 10 | | 10 |
| 2 pads or air mattresses | 1 | | 1 | 8 | 2 | | 3 | 4 |
| 1 mountain tent | 4 | 13 | 7 | | 4 | 13 | 4 | 13 |
| 2 ponchos or rain suits | 2 | 2 | 2 | 2 | 2 | 2 | 2 | 2 |
| 2 pants, shirts, underwear, belt, socks, boots | 13 | 12 | — | | 13 | 12 | 13 | 12 |
| 2 pair sunglasses | | 5 | — | | | 5 | | 5 |

# EQUIPMENT CHECKLIST AND WEIGHT CHART (*Continued*)

| *Items* | *Tough Trails Summer/Fall* lbs. | oz. | *Tough Trails Winter* lbs. | oz. | *Average Trails* lbs. | oz. | *Easy Trails (extra luxuries)* lbs. | oz. |
|---|---|---|---|---|---|---|---|---|
| 2 pair gloves | | 8 | | 8 | | 8 | | 8 |
| 2 hats | | 6 | — | | | 6 | | 6 |
| 2 spare underwear | | 14 | | 14 | | 14 | | 14 |
| 6 handkerchiefs | | 3 | | 3 | | 3 | | 3 |
| 4 spare pairs socks | | 14 | — | | | 14 | | 14 |
| 2 windproof jackets | 1 | 6 | — | | 1 | 6 | 1 | 6 |
| 2 sweatshirts | 2 | 4 | — | | 2 | 4 | 2 | 4 |
| 2 war bags (personals) | 2 | | 2 | | 2 | | 2 | |
| 1 first-aid kit | 1 | 10 | 1 | 10 | 1 | 10 | 1 | 10 |
| 4 insect repellent | | 4 | — | | | 4 | | 4 |
| 2 pocketknives | | 8 | | 8 | | 8 | | 8 |
| 1 sheath knife | — | | — | | | 12 | | 12 |
| 2 compasses | | 3 | | 3 | | 3 | | 3 |
| 1 map and case | | 4 | | 4 | | 4 | | 4 |
| 1 trail guide | | 10 | | 10 | | 10 | | 10 |
| 2 emergency match cases | | 1 | | 1 | | 1 | | 1 |
| 1 regular match case | | 1 | | 1 | | 1 | | 1 |
| 1 packet foil | | 1 | | 1 | | 1 | | 1 |
| 1 roll toilet paper | | 8 | | 8 | | 8 | | 8 |
| 1 roll paper towels | | 12 | | 12 | | 12 | | 12 |
| 1 garbage bag | | 2 | | 2 | | 2 | | 2 |
| 2 belt pouches, pipes, tobacco, glasses | 1 | 4 | 1 | 4 | 1 | 4 | 1 | 4 |
| 1 trowel | | 6 | — | | — | | — | |

| Items | Tough Trails Summer/Fall lbs. | oz. | Tough Trails Winter lbs. | oz. | Average Trails lbs. | oz. | Easy Trails (extra luxuries) lbs. | oz. |
|---|---|---|---|---|---|---|---|---|
| 2 nested pots | 1 | 5 | 1 | 5 | 1 | 5 | 1 | 5 |
| 1 bota | | 4 | | 4 | | 4 | | 4 |
| 2 cups | | 2 | | 2 | | 2 | | 2 |
| 2 plastic plates | — | | — | | | 5 | | 5 |
| 2 spoons | | 2 | | 2 | | 2 | | 2 |
| 1 stove | 1 | 5 | 1 | 5 | — | | — | |
| 2 quarts gasoline | 3 | 15 | 3 | 15 | — | | — | |
| food (dehydrated) | 15 | | 15 | | 17 | | 18 | |
| 1 flask liquor | — | | — | | 2 | 3 | 2 | 3 |
| 2 food bags | | 8 | | 8 | | 8 | | 8 |
| 1 spice bag | — | | — | | 1 | 4 | 1 | 4 |
| 1 camera | 2 | 10 | 2 | 10 | 2 | 10 | 2 | 10 |
| fishing rod and reel | — | | — | | 2 | 8 | 2 | 8 |
| assorted flies and lures | — | | — | | | 3 | | 3 |
| 1 collapsible water jug | — | | — | | | 8 | | 8 |
| 1 axe | — | | — | | 1 | 8 | 2 | 12 |
| 1 saw | — | | — | | 1 | 1 | 1 | 1 |
| 1 file | — | | — | | | 10 | | 10 |
| 1 reflector oven | — | | — | | — | | 2 | 12 |
| 1 hot mitt | — | | — | | | 2 | | 2 |
| 1 grill | — | | — | | | 5 | | 5 |
| 1 frying pan | — | | — | | 1 | | 1 | |
| 1 spatula | — | | — | | | 1 | | 1 |
| 1 spade | — | | — | | 1 | 1 | 1 | 1 |
| Total weight | 75 | | | | 85 | 13 | 92 | 11 |
| Weight per man | 37 | 8 | | | 42 | 14 | 46 | 1 |

## EQUIPMENT CHECKLIST AND WEIGHT CHART (*Continued*)

| *Items* | *Tough Trails Summer/Fall lbs.* | *oz.* | *Winter lbs.* | *oz.* | *Average Trails lbs.* | *oz.* | *Easy Trails (extra luxuries) lbs.* | *oz.* |
|---|---|---|---|---|---|---|---|---|
| *Extra for fall/winter* | | | | | | | | |
| 2 insulated jackets or vests | 2 | | 2 | | | | | |
| *Extra for winter* | | | | | | | | |
| 4 pairs mittens | | | 1 | 8 | | | | |
| 2 heavy parkas | | | 6 | | | | | |
| 2 pairs snow goggles | | | | 8 | | | | |
| 2 sets wool pants, shirts, long johns, socks, insulated boots | | | 21 | 12 | | | | |
| 2 balaclavas | | | | 8 | | | | |
| 6 spare pairs heavy socks | | | 1 | 6 | | | | |
| 2 pairs nylon gaiters | | | | 11 | | | | |
| 2 pairs snowshoes | | | 4 | | | | | |
| 2 pairs ski poles | | | 2 | | | | | |
| 2 ice axes | | | 5 | | | | | |
| 2 pairs crampons | | | 2 | | | | | |
| emergency extra food | | | 4 | | | | | |
| Total fall weight | 77 | | | | | | | |
| Fall weight per man | 38 | 8 | | | | | | |
| Total winter weight | | | 111 | 7 | | | | |
| Winter weight per man | | | 55 | 11 | | | | |

### *Storing Gear at Home*

You will have to find a place at home for these heaps of gear when you are not on the trail. As you broaden your experience and start collecting a lot of different gear for many types of camping, this can become a bit of a problem. But don't just give up and throw it into a corner of the attic or into a heap in the damp corner of a garage. You paid a lot for the stuff, and it will last you a long time and be ready whenever you are if you take care of it.

Where you store it depends on how you live. I have an apartment-dwelling friend who makes a conversation piece out of his backpacking gear by hanging it up in full view inside an antique glass-doored cabinet. Somehow, I don't think Teddy, or your wife, is going to buy that.

But if you are a homeowner, you probably have at least one dry and secure spot; the garage, the basement, a full attic, or a spare room. Pick the best bet and set it up to serve you properly. Here are some basics.

All the gear that can be hung up should be—separately, so that when you come with your check-off list to pack for a trip you can pick out the necessities like a clerk pulling packages off a store shelf. Provide also for the storing of leftover nonperishable foods. And there must also be a place for equipment that won't hang up.

The best thing I can do is describe our setup. We use one side of the basement, which is reasonably dry. Packs are hung below the floor joists on hooks; so are boots, waders, ponchos, hats, life jackets, and other miscellany. All of the other hangable gear is mounted on a large pegboard from hooks of appropriate size. This includes ropes, ice axes, wood axes, saws, cooking gear, food bags, gas bottles, canteens, water jugs, and botas. An old table in front of this board holds all of the non-hanging stuff—cartons of plastic bags and steel-wool pads, cans of fire starters and spoons, gas stoves, foil, rolls of paper towels and toilet paper, and so forth. A shelf under the table holds tents, ground cloths, pads, and air mattresses. Leaning next to the table are the fishing rods in cases and on the floor beside them are the tackle boxes.

There are no sleeping bags here, however, because everyone is too concerned about these expensive items to trust them to a dusty basement. We each keep our own on a shelf in our own clothes closet.

We use an old plastic-foam picnic cooler for the spare food, each kind bagged separately in plastic. We keep the paper plates and bowls here, too. When we make up a shopping list for a trip, the first step is to see what's already in the larder.

Now I know what comes next is going to sound like a real drag, but there is only one way I have found to keep this wealth of gear in shape with efficiency and that is to take care of it the minute we get home from a trip. We try to make it back by midafternoon. Then we take an hour or so to check everything out as we put it away.

This is the time to pound out a dent in the cooking ware and to give it a thorough washing, if necessary, sew up a rip in fabric, or wash a dirty spot on the tent or sleeping bag. Sharpen the axe with a few passes of the stone or a touch-up with both file and stone. It only takes about a half hour to sharpen the blade of the saw, if you found it pulling a little hard in the woods.

We always string a line in the basement and hang out tents and sleeping bags for at least a day to air and dry. If it was a wet trip, we hang them out in the sun for a day. The last thing I do is hand-wash my wool hiking socks and put them on sock stretchers. The whole thing can be done in just about the time it takes for that martini glass to chill properly in the freezer.

Why at this time? Because you are still up from the trip, you remember more clearly just what needs to be done and it goes faster. Just before a trip is not the time for this because you will have enough to do just checking out your gear and packing it and making arrangements with your companions. This is not the time to remember that the clevis pin that holds your saw blade in its holder is broken and that the only camping store where you can get another one is closed.

On this score, I try to keep such expendable components in stock. I have spare clevis pins for packs and saws, wedges for axes, nozzles for stoves, and so on. They are all plastic bagged and hung on the pegboard near the equipment they go with. It is no real trouble or expense and it does help to maintain sanity.

# 8

# HITTING THE TRAIL

Before you throw your pack on your back and go racing off to the woods, hold up for just a minute. A backpacking trip—whether it's just for a weekend or for a month-long expedition—takes some planning to be successful. Where are you going? Can you make the desired mileage comfortably in the time available? What are the alternative routes? How much equipment and food will you need, and what kind? What is the size of the party? And who is the leader?

That's right—*leader!* I'm going to be a big bore, but a bunch of hikers in the woods without a leader is an undisciplined mob. No matter how friendly you are with each other, there will be bickering over routes, mealtimes, and tasks unless someone is clearly in charge.

So get together long before you go and pick a person to

lead. It should be the most experienced trail person in the group, and one who also possesses tact and an ability to persuade the independent spirits to comply with what is best for the group. Let's suppose that this paragon is *you.*

Okay, you now have the responsibility for the welfare, comfort, and safety of your party—a large responsibility. That doesn't mean that you have to do all the work, but it does mean you have to see that it is done. And a good leader takes the initiative in working. Right?

### *Before You Go*

First, you must get agreement on where you are going and how you are going to get there, which is not always as easy as it sounds.

Where to go can mean almost anything—from a weekend jaunt in your nearby woods to a three-month expedition covering the entire 2,313 miles of the Pacific Crest Trail from Canada to Mexico or the more than 2,000 miles of the Appalachian Trail from Maine to Georgia. Generally, though, you will start with a moderate weekend trip, build up to tougher week-long hikes, and, finally, plan for a two-week or longer trip into a deep mountain wilderness somewhere in the United States or Canada. You may hike continuously or with breaks every few days, or you may establish a central base camp and take day hikes out of it.

Many states and Canadian Provinces have guides and maps and other helpful information on their outdoor recreation areas. Some clubs also have developed detailed guides. See the book list at the end for a list of common sources from clubs. Many catalogs from outfitters not only list club guides but also numerous guides by commercial publishers (particularly for the Sierra and Rocky mountains).

Proper trail procedure is to space hikers far enough apart so they won't step on each other's heels. Chuck, who is familiar with the trail, leads as second in command. The hike leader brings up the rear (when he isn't taking photos) to keep an eye on the column. The bulky appearance of the packs is caused by draped jackets, which are hung over pack and frame to be ready at rest stops.

When you have made this decision, there is transportation. If you are going by car, who will drive to the trailhead and how will he be reimbursed by the others? If the trail trip is not a circular route, there is a car drop-off to arrange at the far end. Generally, in a small party, one or two cars will carry the group with everyone chipping in to pay the owners for gas and tolls.

Sometimes public transportation must be arranged by the leader. Reservations may have to be made at a base camp or lodge. And substantial sums of money collected by the leader for tickets and advance payments must be budgeted and accounted for.

If a car drop is needed, make sure that time is allowed for shuttling one car to the end of the trail. And make sure, too, that everyone understands when you are leaving and when you plan to return. If someone plans to travel separately and to meet you at the trailhead, make the time of meeting very clear. Nothing is more irritating than being all psyched up to go and then having to wait for a latecomer. Make sure that the cars you will use are mechanically sound so that you can all arrive at the same time.

In such vast wilderness areas as Canada and Alaska, you will have to arrange for charter planes to drop you off and pick you up again at a prearranged time and place. On very long wilderness trips, you may even have to plan for one or more air-drops of supplies. These latter arrangements make a detailed schedule a real necessity.

In many areas, permission must be obtained for campfires or for camping in other than authorized spots.

Write well in advance to the ranger headquarters in the area of your interest for such permits. It generally takes several weeks for a reply. And if you want to do something out of the ordinary, explain why and describe the qualifications of your party, its experience and its consideration for the environment. Rangers are understandably nervous about allowing tenderfeet to leave the beaten track, both because they have to rescue so many and because of the mess neophytes can make of a wilderness. But I have almost never had a problem doing anything reasonable, after I satisfied the rangers as to my ability. At the ranger station, sign your party in, indicating where you are going, the route, and when you expect to be back. Then, at the end of your trip, *come back* and sign out so that the authorities are not left wondering if you ever made it.

Just a word about hiking alone. Anyone who goes on a mountain trip alone without at least one companion is an idiot. Everyone knows that, right? Okay, meet one. I readily acknowledge that lone backpacking is foolish and should be avoided if there is any possible alternative. But I also feel that backpacking alone is better than not backpacking at all.

If you are out of your normal territory, as I am when I go to California every year on a two-week business trip and want to backpack on the middle weekend in the Sierra, you may not find anyone who is very enthusiastic about climbing with a stranger. It's either go alone or not at all.

But if you go, make sure your experience is up to the challenge, keep to sensible routes, and be prepared for some active hostility on the part of rangers when you sign in. Finding one injured person in the middle of a big wilderness area is not their idea of fun and games. John Muir I'm not, but so far the rangers haven't had to come looking for me, and a good track record and the appearance of a solid citizen will go a long way toward reassuring them.

Another point, alone or in a group, let someone at home know in writing where you will be, by what route, and when you are going in and coming out. If you put your itinerary in writing, your at-home contact won't have to remember complicated routes or Indian place names. Telephone your at-home contact when you return to civilization, particularly if it is a difficult or dangerous trip. If you don't check in within a reasonable time, they can urge the authorities into action and avoid delays caused by uncertainty.

Of course, in some areas and at some times—such as in the desolate and vast wilderness areas of Canada or other foreign areas or in winter mountaineering in many U.S. mountains—you are entirely on your own. You constitute your own rescue party and you should be prepared for it, both psychologically and physically.

Okay, back to the group effort. Have a meeting well before the trip to discuss routes, food, and equipment. As the leader, you will have to know the abilities of everyone in your party and be able tactfully to veto routes that are beyond someone's physical capabilities or experience. Then, for long trips, make sure that everyone has a marked copy of the trail map and give them a briefing on the area and trails. When this is settled, you are now ready to take up the very personal matter of provender. Nothing can ruin a trip faster than forcing someone to eat food he detests.

The way I get around this is with the system devised by Sir John Hunt in planning the first successful assault of Everest. I have a list of food that can be backpacked. It's longer than you might think, as you will see in Chapter 10. It also includes some goodies, which are essential to prevent monotony on long trips.

I read down the list with the group, and if even one person objects to an item, it is crossed out. From the types of food that are left, I can construct a menu that is generally approved by everyone with no further objections. I also ask every participant what his favorite treat is. If someone is passionately fond of sardines in mustard sauce, he should be able to have at least one small can per week. A choice tidbit provides something to look forward to, planning when to eat it and so on.

The menu and the nature of the trip will determine to a great extent the equipment that is needed. Everyone will probably contribute, and his contribution should be noted and checked off on a written list, so that you will have a complete accounting of what is needed and where it is. The gear—everything, including clothing, sleeping bags, and packs—should be gathered together in one spot a few days before the trip to be checked out. At this time, food can be repacked from its commercial containers into smaller and lighter plastic bags and, in turn, into meal portions in larger bags, which are marked with a felt pen. These are further overpacked in larger plastic bags by day and are also marked with a felt pen.

These master bags are distributed to all hikers and a note is made of who has what days. The best way is to give each person, in succession, a day's rations. Then, as food is consumed, everyone's pack is lightened in turn without having to repack constantly to even up weight distribution. Cooking and camp-making gear can be kept in one pack, of course, and shelters in others. These people get proportionately less food to carry. The only way to do it equitably is to have a bathroom scale on hand. One person weighs all packs, deducts his own weight and shifts gear until equality is established.

But equality doesn't necessarily mean equal weight. If there are women or children in the party, their load must be scaled to their abilities. A husky man should be able to carry a 40-pound load without strain. Women and young teen-agers will probably be comfortable with about 20 pounds and very young children should carry no more than 5 pounds. With experience and *need,* these weights can be doubled. It should be stressed, however, that the lighter the weight, the more enjoyment a person can take from the trail. This is why every unimportant element should be eliminated. The division of the loads should be discussed as they are made up so that everyone is in agreement with the arrangements.

Now the leader pores over maps and trail descriptions to familiarize himself with the route and to plot the length of each day's hike and the camping spots. If possible, enough flexibility should be built into this schedule to account for bad weather. One way is to build in a rest day for every four or five days on the trail. If there are children along, it should be every three days. Children need a rest from the push, push, push.

A rest day has been described as a day on which you do nothing but climb a few nearby mountains—and that's one purpose, certainly. If you can stop at a strategically located spot, the gung-ho types can do some rock climbing or scrambling unencumbered by heavy packs. Others can fish, swim, photograph, rock-hound, repair gear, or just lounge around. This break in the routine allows you to enjoy the outdoors fully. And if ferocious weather delays the trip, a rest day can be canceled without throwing your schedule out of whack. Most people have to be back at work or classes at a given time and get rather nervous about delays.

In my youth I went on several trips where a lack of planning caused essential gear to be left behind ("I thought you had the axe!") and where misunderstandings created hard feelings ("He hasn't carried his weight the whole time!"). So, I strongly urge these pre-trip procedures for any backpacking group of any age or size.

### *Physical Conditioning*

There's another important step in preparing for a backpacking trip and that's to get yourself in shape. I guess I have a knee-jerk reaction to this subject because of some unfortunate experiences in the past with under-trained partners.

It seems you always run into this type at a party. In the warmth and comfort of someone's living room, he says, "Hey, I understand you backpack. I've always wanted to do that. How about taking me on your next trip. I'm in great condition—I ski all winter." Fortunately, they usually forget about it by the next day. But occasionally they don't and put you on the spot the next time they see you.

Now I'm not going to claim that backpacking is the ruggedest sport in the world or that every trip is equal to an Everest climb. But a run-of-the-mill weekend jaunt of twenty or thirty miles, say in the Catskills, requires more physical conditioning than most people acquire with the lazy type of downhill skiing that is now common at resorts. Stiff climbs of a week or two in the Sierra, Rockies, Smokies, Adirondack, or Green or White Mountains require deliberate and extensive preconditioning. And winter mountaineering in any mountains should be attempted only by those in the very peak of shape and stamina.

The degree of conditioning isn't a matter of age. Any healthy and strong person from the late teens to at least the fifties can qualify for tough backpacking expeditions. But age definitely has a bearing on how long it takes to get in shape and how long you stay there.

Since such training is highly dependent on the individual, I can only describe how we train and hope that you can relate this to your own physique and methods. I make the assumption that you are in school or business and, therefore, are normally sedentary. If you are a professional athlete or guide, skip this section. You don't need it.

First, I try to get in a local hike every week or two. Just about everyone lives near some area where this is possible. We have a number of spots, but our favorite is Bear Mountain State Park, actually the Harriman Section, where there are countless trails and small hills with steep sides to add variety and pull for the muscles. I go flat out for ten miles and over at least three hills. If I can't make it in three hours without too much huffing and puffing, then I know I'm not in very good shape. And it should take at least six miles before I feel the stretch in my leg and stomach muscles.

Personally, I prefer this type of conditioning to calisthenics, which I abhor. I think that day hiking exercises most of the muscles that are needed for backpacking; it is a more specific training. However, I also travel a good deal and spend a lot of time in city motels where there aren't very many opportunities for hiking. So, on the road, I do get up early in the morning and do a half hour of vigorous exercises, mostly deep-knee bends, sit-ups, push-ups, jogging in place, and climbing over the bed (I figure fifty times up and over the bed is equal to a small hill, but pick your motels for their cast concrete floors or you'll drive the guy under you bananas!).

Before a long expedition or a winter trip, I spend at least a month with the above conditioning routine and also running—not jogging—about three miles every night. Chuck does the same thing, but, being only seventeen, he gets in shape in about half the time it takes me and he keeps his conditioning twice as long. If I stop, I'm as flabby as a jellyfish in about three weeks. It is the only real penalty I can think of in the process of aging.

## *On the Trail*

Okay, you're in shape and you've made the trailhead with all of your gear neatly and methodically stowed *inside* your pack. Each hiker helps another on with his pack and the waist belts are cinched up to distribute the loads properly.

To do this, hunch up your shoulders to raise the pack and then tighten the belt. As you relax, the pack should settle snugly on top of your hips. You know it will because you made the necessary strap adjustments at home before you came so that your friends would not have to wait while you tinker with or repair your gear. Now you're ready to go.

The order of hiking is subject to variation. Normally, if a second in command who knows the trail thoroughly is on hand, he goes first and the leader goes last so that he can keep an eye on the whole party. If not, then the leader is in front and he has a trustworthy type sweep up the rear.

The reason for this is that hiking parties should stay together. I am unalterably opposed to everyone doing his own thing on the trail. No matter how carefully matched a backpacking group may be, there are always stronger and weaker people. Unfortunately, the weaker hiker is also the one who is most likely to be weak in experience and technique, too—just the person who should *not* be left to struggle on alone while the stronger ones forge far ahead. On high mountains where fog or rain or snow can descend suddenly, leaving someone behind to find his own way can be fatal.

But under any conditions, you came as a group, so stay

one. If it becomes obvious that someone doesn't fit in, then leave him at home the next time. For this trip, though, you have a responsibility for both his safety and his enjoyment.

I can always determine a person's experience by how he starts out on the trail. The tyro plunges off up the path like a frightened rabbit. He quickly zaps out, though, and in a couple of hours is tired and sore. The expert starts off with a purposeful but slow step that is easier to demonstrate than to describe. It is almost a deliberate amble—about two miles an hour on level or slightly sloping ground, about one mile an hour on steep grades. He can keep up this pace all day without stopping and passes the "hare" a short way up the trail, never to see him again.

Some backpackers do not believe in stopping at all, except for a look at the view or a call of nature. When I am alone, I generally hike this way. A couple of years ago, I did more than twenty miles in a ten-hour day in the Cathedral Mountains, in the Tuolumne area of Yosemite. I never sat down and wasn't particularly tired when I stopped to camp. John Muir, the great naturalist and explorer of the Sierra, regularly made that sort of mileage seem like a Sunday afternoon stroll, but he was a man of solid iron.

For the average backpacker, it is a good idea to take a rest every now and then. After a short time on the trail, a leader can judge the abilities of his party and rest accordingly. Once an hour is a good average, and for young people and those not in top condition, every thirty minutes is better. With children from four to seven years old, you may have to take it even easier for the first few tries until they get trail hardened. If you're not willing to do this, then you shouldn't be in the parent business, right? Don't rest too long or heated muscles will get cold and have to be re-warmed all over again. In my experience, a three-minute breather is just right.

The rest stop is another reason for keeping the group together, for if someone is straggling, just about the time he catches up is when the leader is ready to say, "Okay, let's go!" There is no more brutal rejection for a person who already feels that he is holding people back.

Don't take that first rest for at least the first thirty minutes of a hike. It takes at least that long for everyone to get his "second wind" and to start hiking easily. And never take a rest at the bottom of a steep pitch. Tackle the toughie while you are warmed to it and then rest at the top. You don't have to sit down to rest, either, if you don't want to. Lean against a rock or tree that will support your pack. On steep grades, use a "rest step" as often as necessary to avoid extra rest stops.

In the rest step, you advance a step, locking the knee on your rear leg, which carries your weight. Hesitate a moment before taking the next step. This rests the leg muscles. In high mountains, you may want to shift to this step at every so many strides, or you may have to use it continuously at very high altitudes.

Also, in all hiking, try to breathe in rhythm with your stride; in and out at every other step on moderate slopes or with every step on steep grades or at high altitudes. It helps to establish a whole body pace that defies fatigue.

The leader should always walk with consideration for both his own resilience and for that of the people behind him. You may be able to step up a three-foot ledge, but it isn't smart and others may not be able to without a struggle. Never climb over anything that you can walk around. And avoid mud wallows and rock-strewn areas whenever possible. If those following you start treading a different path from the one you are walking, it is probably because they are dissatisfied with the trail you are making.

In winter hiking, the lead is something else. Breaking trail in deep snow on snowshoes or skis is very arduous and the lead should be rotated among all members of the party to even out the strain. Presumably, on winter climbs you will not have weak or inexperienced members in the party.

Coming downhill, try to keep your legs flexed and avoid locking your knees, which throws a great strain on these fragile joints. The only exception is on steep, deep snow slopes, where you can descend with a stiff-legged sliding step. In the summer, watch the trail constantly to avoid stepping on a loose stone that can throw you. On scree slopes, descend in diagonals with sliding steps, keeping your weight over your feet like a skier. On talus, step on the inside of rocks, which are likely to be more firmly braced. The outsides can pivot on you.

There are also courtesies to be observed toward other hikers on the trail. If you meet someone, it is only common manners to say "Hi!" Lately, it seems that half the people you meet on trails in the United States simply glower at you. Foreign backpackers always smile and sometimes will even stop for a brief word. It is also good trail manners to let climbing hikers have the right of way over a descending group so that they don't have to break stride. The same goes for people overtaking you. The rule is to step aside and invite them to hike through. Let's put humanism back in backpacking, shall we?

At least once a day you might stop for a prolonged break, perhaps a half hour. Not necessarily for lunch, although this might be the time for it, but just for a break in the routine and for a friendly gathering to compare notes and chat about your experiences.

If you have planned a luncheon stop, pick a sunny spot with a view and a spring for water. If it is cool, have everyone put on an appropriate garment to avoid chilling. Some time before the stop, the leader starts looking for a good spot. It should have resting places for everyone, preferably not on the ground, which is usually damp. A long fallen log or some flat rocks are good. A needle-strewn patch under a pine tree is often okay. And on a rainy day, a giant overhanging ledge can be great if there are no water seepages.

If no suitable natural spot can be found in rain or snow, then tarps or ground cloths should be at hand in the tops of packs so that a temporary shelter can be constructed.

Some backpackers do not eat a single lunch at all; instead, they snack almost continuously throughout the day whenever they feel the need for energy. I belong to this group. A single, large lunch leaves me feeling logy and it takes an hour afterward to get back in stride and wind for the climb. So I carry a bag of "gorp," the composition of which will be described in glowing detail in Chapter 10. I munch on this mixture whenever I feel the need. But when I'm with a group I also usually have some fruit and a cup of tea or soup at the long stop just to be sociable.

How far is a good day's hike? It all depends on the nature of the trail, the weather, and the physical condition of the party. In summer on moderate trails with adults in good physical condition and with an early start, a party should be able to get in from eight to twelve hours of hiking, which could translate into from fifteen to twenty-five miles, if you have the stamina. I would say that the average hiker, though, ought to shoot for eight miles or less at first.

On very steep trails or bushwhacking off trail or on winter expeditions in deep snow, you may make only a mile an hour or less. And in the winter, you will have less daylight, particularly in the northern latitudes. Under these conditions, you might be lucky to make a day-long trip of only five or six miles.

With children, pace your hiking to their limited stamina. Before they get their full growth in the late teens, kids have

Pace on the trail is one that all of the hikers in the group can match. When youngsters such as Chris are along this may mean a slow amble with a short stop every thirty minutes to rest up—or even more often for the first few trips. A tot's load should match his ability, too. Here on Balsam Lake Mountain in the Catskills, when he was four, Chris carried only his light sleeping bag in a tiny nylon pack.

seemingly great strength, but they actually have very little lasting power. Also, they may be more gung-ho than their ability warrants. When they were young, Chuck and my daughter, Pat, were so determined that they would hike themselves into the ground without admitting they were bushed. When they have exhausted their immediate strength, children are finished—indeed, they may even get sick to their stomachs. For this reason, you must watch them carefully and stop before they are exhausted. This means that even with experienced youngsters a day's hike should be made at about one mile an hour and a total of six or eight miles is the limit.

The problem is usually parental egotism (or ignorance). I recall one evening just before dark during a storm in the Adirondacks when a family burst from the brush dragging a little seven-year-old boy who was shaking and pale with fatigue. The father proudly announced that they had made seven mountain peaks since dawn (and they still had four miles to go to camp). I almost had to forcibly restrain Teddy from assaulting him. We did insist on giving the tad some hot cocoa at the fire and a half-hour rest. Then they were off without flashlight to negotiate a rough and muddy trail in the dark. I can guarantee that that boy did not grow up to love the outdoors and backpacking.

Camp should be made about two hours before sunset to give ample time for setting up, dinner, and a chance to enjoy the outdoors. That's how nature-loving Japanese play the game as they gather, here, outside the hut and tents on Kitadake in the Southern Alps to watch a spectacular sunset over the Central Alps.

Plan to stop at least two hours before sundown. This allows plenty of time to make a good camp in the daylight and to have a relaxed dinner. The night meal is generally the only leisurely time of the day and it should be relished.

Under no circumstances should you hike after dark. It's better to camp in an unexpected and unsatisfactory place rather than risk stumbling around in the dark looking for the trail and your planned camp. This is how people get hurt; a broken arm or leg, a branch in the eye, even a sprained ankle is a disaster in the wilderness that will require termination of the trip and a tiring evacuation of someone incapable of walking.

The answer to good mileage is an early start. Most backpackers shift their life-styles to sun time in the woods. That means getting up at dawn and going to bed at dark. In the North during the summer, you will rise at about five or six in the morning and go to bed about nine at night. In the winter, dark comes about six in the North and you lose a good three hours of the day. The early start is particularly important if you are climbing on ice or snow. It's almost always firmer and safer in the early hours; it generally becomes sloppy and prone to avalanche in the afternoon after being warmed by the sun.

You don't have to go to sleep at dark, although you will probably be tired enough to drop off almost at once. We sometimes lie in our bags for an hour or so discussing the day and the coming trail, occasionally playing cards or drinking a last coffee royale. But pretty soon the conversation lags and then everyone is "gone."

### *How to Follow Trails*

Thanks to state and federal rangers and to the work of many outdoor clubs, most trails in the wilderness areas of the United States are pretty well marked today. Wooden or metal trail signs are erected at the start of trails and at important intersections to show you the way and the mileage to prominent mountains, lakes, and campsites. They will also usually tell you the color and design of the markings for each trail, which is then nailed or painted on trees and rocks along the way. Usually these marks are close enough together so that the next one can be seen from the one you are passing.

Above tree line, trail markers are painted on rocks and are often located more closely together. Sometimes these markers are supplemented by painted arrows and by stacked rock cairns that show the way over trackless scree or talus. On well-traveled trails, of course, the way is worn deeply into the ground and can be traveled by a child.

A few states publish excellent trail guides with maps that show the symbol and color of the trail mark and also contain a written description of the trail, the location of shelters, and interesting features along the way. New York is outstanding in this regard. Some clubs print complete guides, too. Exceptionally good are those by the Adirondack Mountain Club for the Adirondacks and by the Appalachian Mountain Club for the White Mountains of New Hampshire and the mountains of Maine. The Green Mountain Club covers the Long Trail in Vermont and the Appalachian Trail Conference publishes a series of guides for the Maine-to-Georgia heritage enjoyed by easterners. The Sierra Club covers the West Coast, and other guides cover many of the other areas between East and West. These specialized guides also usually include club trails and shelters that are not always indicated on state or federal maps.

The appropriate guide should be obtained and read thoroughly before you start on your trip, not only so you can learn the names of the features you will pass, but also so you can check on possible hazards that you might encounter as well as areas of special interest that you may want to see.

Even if you don't need a map to find your way on heavily traveled trails, use your compass anyway as a matter of practice and to make sure you are still headed in the right direction. Sometimes a key directional sign will get turned around or destroyed and you can veer off onto another trail without even knowing it if you are not alert.

This brings up another important point. In heavily

traveled areas, stay with the trails. Don't take short cuts across switchbacks or meadows and create new "herd paths" that not only disfigure the landscape but also cause serious erosions. In fact, go an extra step toward helping to take care of the wilderness and its trails. If you see a trail sign that has been knocked down or is leaning precariously, take a moment to nail it up or brace it with rocks.

If a steep trail section has started to erode because a water-diversion channel is missing or has been damaged, take a few minutes to repair the damage by implanting a new log or by banking the channel with rocks. Fill in a small swampy section with a corduroy walkway of cut logs, nail back the railing of a bridge over a stream that some careless person has torn loose.

For economic reasons, most states have had to cut back on the personnel who formerly maintained trails. Growing crowds of campers have pinned down more of the rangers in the maintenance and overseeing of central camping areas. Unfortunately, there are also more careless backpackers on the trails now and even a few deliberately destructive types. This makes trail maintenance extremely difficult. So every good hiker has a responsibility to help out in every way he can if we are to maintain the marvelous trail system that has been created in this country.

One of the ways you can help is to join one of the major outdoor clubs. They all have trail committees and some have officially taken up the responsibility for maintaining a certain section of a major trail or of the trails in a certain geographical area. They usually sponsor a cleanup week or several weekends in the spring, when club members turn out to repair winter damage or construct new facilities. Whether you get involved as a loner or with a group, be a builder not a destroyer. It's the only way we will be able to save our wilderness.

*Getting Lost and Unlost*

If you wander far from civilization, sooner or later you will be lost, although professionals don't like to call it that. When Daniel Boone was asked once if he had ever been lost, he was reported to have replied, "No, but I was a mite confused once for three days."

Perhaps the difference between being lost and just confused is what you do about it. Now this is not a book about long-term wilderness survival, which would indeed require a whole book. But everyone should be prepared to survive for a limited time if he gets "confused" on a hunting or backpacking trip. If you have your gear, there's no need to panic. After all, everything you need for your health and welfare is right on your back. If you don't have your gear when you get separated from your party, there are well-established rules to follow.

First, don't flap. In fact, sit down. In this position you can't go running madly through the woods. Chances are, when you first realize that you are off the track, you probably aren't very far off. Think. If you have a mental map of the area or, better, the trail map the leader gave you, get it out and try to orient yourself with visible landmarks.

Even as a follower in a party, you should always keep yourself aware as to where you are and not leave it all up to the leader. Be conscious of direction of travel, by the sun, by a knowledge of terrain and water drainage—"instincts" that are acquired by experience. This is how all guides find their way. There is no such thing as inherent ability to know the way, even for professional outdoorsmen or aborigines.

Chances are that, after some calm reflection, you will realize where you went wrong and be able to retrace your steps. But before you go, mark where you are—after all, this is the one place on earth that you are really sure about. Blaze your trail from this spot with some simple and, hopefully, nonpermanent means. Avoid slashes in trees. Knots in tufts of grass or shrubs, scrape marks in the leaves or dirt, little piles of stones, scraps of foil twisted around bushes (the inner lining of your pack of cigarettes, remember?), little shreds of a handkerchief—all are satisfactory and will enable you to find your way back to "the spot" if the first cast is wrong.

You can shout a few times if it makes you feel better, although in dense woods, deep canyons, or heavy snow cover, voices carry only a short distance.

If you are high on a mountain—perhaps in fog or rain or a snowstorm—be careful how you move around. It's easy to walk off an edge. The best thing, here, is to sit tight in as deep a crevice as you can find until it clears.

If the afternoon shadows deepen, and you still haven't found your way, then you might as well resign yourself to a night out. Start well before dark to prepare camp so that you will be comfortable. If you don't have your pack, you will have to improvise. Here, certain practices are permissible that would be frowned on normally.

If it is a warm, clear summer night, a camping spot is simple. Find a big boulder or downed log; or better, a big rock with a log in front of it or two logs a short distance apart. Clear the ground between them down to mineral dirt for your fire and gather a quantity of wood and kindling that you can break up by hand, enough so you can keep the fire going all night if you must or want to. A campfire is a psychological lift at a time like this. It makes your bivouac seem more like home. Now you know what the emergency supply of matches in your shirt pocket is for.

You build the fire between two reflecting surfaces, one

Where rain is unlikely, a snug bivouac can be made against a fallen tree. On this ridge near 10,000 feet, high above the Kings Canyon in California's Sierra wilderness, I was lucky enough to find two ancient spruce that had fallen at right angles to each other. A pile of branches reflected the fire heat to keep me warm on an icy evening in early summer, while a flowered tablecloth kept drafts from blowing under the log.

behind the fire and one behind you so that you are surrounded by reflected heat. If you can only find one reflector, put your back to it and then build another one behind the fire with rocks or logs. But again, be sure the fire is built on mineral earth in a cleared space sufficiently large (10 feet in diameter) so that you won't set the woods on fire and add to your embarrassment. And read Chapter 9 before you get lost in order to learn how to light a fire under adverse conditions.

Now rake together enough dry leaves or break off the ends of evergreen boughs (in an emergency only!) to make a bed that is deep enough to be heaped over you if it gets chilly. If you only have a bit of a snack with you, eat it slowly, savoring every bite, after you have made camp and are relaxed. Some sugar at bedtime always helps to keep you warmer. Then, go to sleep to get maximum rest and to forget your empty stomach.

You won't need any water for a single night, but a nearby supply will make you feel better and less hungry. It might not be the best night's rest you ever had; you will wake up when the fire dies down and you get chilly, and then you can build up the blaze again. In the morning, everything will look brighter and you can try for that trail again. By this time, you may be sure, your friends will be looking for you, too.

If you take children into even a small park with wild areas, equip them with a loud whistle on a lanyard in addition to the emergency matches, and train them in the survival techniques just described (you can make a game out of it by suddenly asking them where they are and what they would do if they were to discover at that very moment that they were lost). Make them understand the importance of staying with you and not wandering away from camp. And then never let them out of your sight. Every year there are needless tragedies caused by neglect of these rules.

In bad or cold weather, survival when lost is a more serious matter. You need a shelter from the elements as well as a good fire. A deadfall may provide some shelter, which can be improved by interlacing the downed branches with live evergreen boughs or grass or large leaves. The low-hanging branches of a young evergreen may also provide the start of a shelter. Break off just enough limbs on the downwind side so that you can crawl underneath and use these branches to close the space on the windward side. An overhanging ledge or a cave or the space between two rocks roofed over or closed in with branches can also give you protection.

The tiniest fire in such confined spaces provides an amazing amount of warmth. You can usually find some dry wood and tinder under evergreens, deadfalls, or even under ledges and rocks. After you get a blaze going, wet

Colder weather requires more preparations for an emergency camp. Either logs or branches stacked against a downed tree or rock make a lean-to that can be heated with a reflector fire. An alternative is a low-branched evergreen. The windward side can be blocked with sticks or branches and a tiny fire, reflected by rocks, will keep a lost hiker warm for the night.

wood can be dried over or near the fire until it will burn. This will give you something to do, believe me, and you may become so engrossed in the struggle to get dry and warm that you almost forget your broader predicament.

Deep winter is something else again, but not necessarily fatal if you keep your head. First of all, you should be able to retrace your tracks in the snow until you regain the trail and your friends. If you can't for some reason, then shelter and a fire become critical.

You can look for the same kinds of bivouacs mentioned before or dig yourself one in the snow. A good spot is under that young fir tree. Knock the snow off the lower branches and hollow out a trench under them with a snowshoe. Taper the hole from a small end in the open to

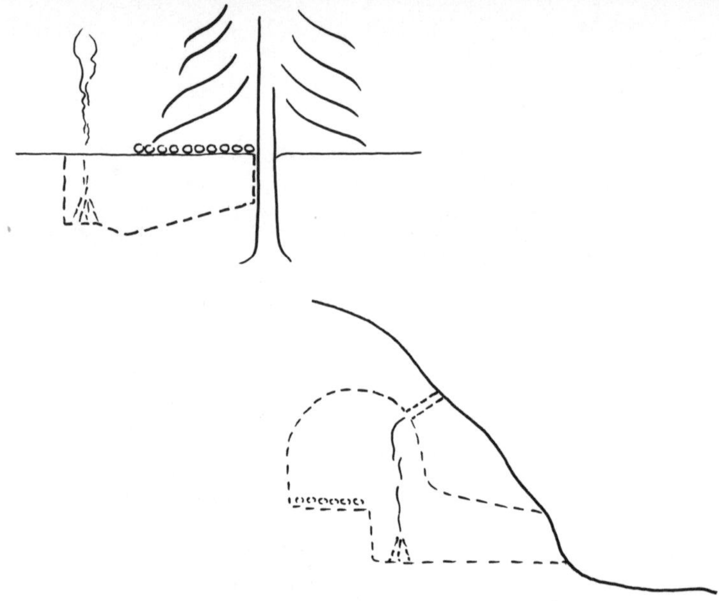

Deep winter bivouacs can be dug in the snow to keep off wind and weather. A trench camp under an evergreen should be sloped and floored with branches to insulate the sleeper from snow and wet. It can also be roofed with branches to improve heat retention from a small fire. A cave in a snowbank should be tunneled upward and curved at the roof to prevent collapse. The sleeping platform is floored with branches. A tiny fire can improve warmth, but a vent hole near the top is essential.

a larger space under the branches. Dig the trench on the cross-wind side of the tree to prevent drifting snow from burying you.

The fire goes at the small end of the trench; you go at the large end. Put branches under you to insulate you from the snow. Slope the trench downward from you and from the fire and build the fire on top of wet or green wood so that the melting snow will not put it out.

Any clean melted snow water that collects in the pit will give you a welcome drink, which is even more essential in winter than summer, since the lower humidity and high body respiration rate necessary to keep you warm promotes dehydration and exhaustion.

You can also dig your trench under a deadfall or roof a trench over at your sleeping end with branches (make sure they are big enough to hold a load of snow). You can improve a rock overhang by heaping up snow on the open sides or by stacking snow blocks, if the snow is compact enough to be cut into blocks with your knife or saw. Regular igloos made of snow blocks will probably be beyond your ability and should not be necessary.

Another survival technique is to tunnel into the snow itself. Snow is a good insulator, believe it or not. But watch this one! It is not as simple as some accounts would make it appear. You need a big drift of compact snow located cross-wise to the wind. Then, dig in and up, creating a short tunnel and an elevated platform on which to rest. Make sure the roof is domed to increase its strength or it is liable to collapse. Pad the platform with as many boughs as you can gather. Punch a hole near the top front of your little cave for ventilation. Then, if you want to, you can start a tiny fire on the floor below your platform. It must be tiny, first because a big blaze will asphyxiate you and, second, because such a fire will soften the snowbank and cause it to melt all over you or collapse. With a small blaze, the interior snow melts slowly and refreezes into an ice sheath that actually strengthens your shelter.

With your winter clothes, you can survive a night or so in any of these shelters. Keep your spirits up, keep as dry as possible, and rest. It is not true that you have to keep moving. Quite the opposite. Continued activity without food, water, and rest will exhaust you and promote freezing. So get your rest and go about finding your way the next morning with renewed determination. People have survived incredible experiences in winter by following these simple rules. And many others have died of "exposure" in relatively mild weather by running themselves ragged.

The best advice, though, is not to get lost in the first place. To achieve this goal, you must know how to find your way in the wilderness.

### *Map and Compass Technique*

It's amazing how many people can't read a map—even a road map—but are afraid to admit it. They seem to feel that maps are a mystery totally beyond their ability to comprehend, so they don't try. Well, there is nothing mysterious about a map, even hiking maps, which are a bit different from road maps.

This section will not make you an expert in orienteering. There are whole books on the subject (see the book list). But you don't need to be an authority on map and compass reading before it is safe for you to go into the woods, at least on average trails. So, let's dispel the mystery about maps and compasses right now.

A map is a symbolic representation of a piece of countryside. Once you understand the symbols, you can visualize what the country looks like and what features it contains. Most hiking maps are topographical in nature—that is, they employ lines that connect every point of the same elevation and create in two dimensions a top or plan view that can be visualized in three dimensions. A topo map is like a series of thin slabs of different and diminishing size stacked on top of each other and viewed directly from above. Since there is usually less ground at higher elevations, the slabs get smaller in size as you go up in elevation. They are irregular in shape because the ground is irregular in height, being cut up by gullies and ridges.

On a topo map, the edges of these imaginary slabs of equal height are shown as brown lines. Different maps have different intervals between these elevation lines and this distance in feet (or meters) is marked at the bottom of the map as the contour interval. Often, it is 20 feet. At regular intervals—such as 100, 500, or 1,000 feet—the appropriate line is a darker brown and has the elevation in feet printed along it wherever there is room.

This enables you to figure out the exact elevation of any spot, if you know the contour interval, by adding the number of intervals between this spot and the next numbered line below your spot (or subtracting from the next heavy brown line above).

Obviously, where these lines are rather far apart, the ground slopes less steeply and as they get closer together, the rise in the terrain is steeper. When they are almost on top of each other, it marks a cliff. When the lines sweep in

Topographic maps use a series of lines to represent all areas of similar altitude. The lower drawing shows a mountain that falls away in a cliff to a river, then rises to a low hill (right to left). The horizontal lines, numbered from 1 to 8, represent slices of altitude. These are shown and numbered on a topo representation above.

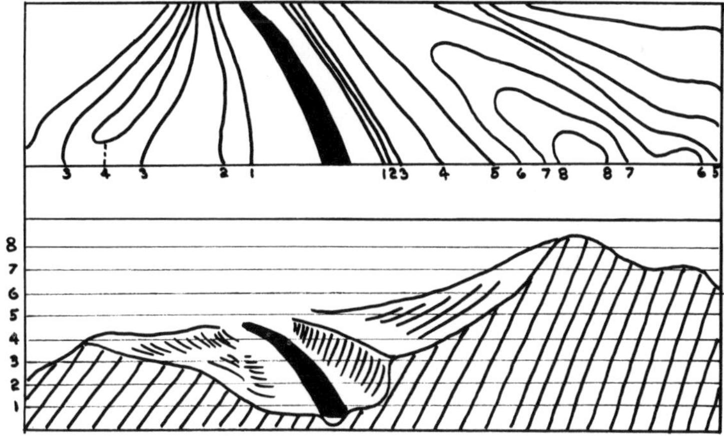

a vee, it marks either a ridge or a canyon, depending on whether the lines go up or down in elevation as they close in the vee. Prominent features, such as lakes and mountains, are generally marked with a little X or a triangle, which signifies a surveying point or bench mark. It has the elevation in feet printed beside it.

But topos give you a great deal more information. Water features are always shown in blue—oceans, rivers, canals, streams, springs, and swamps. Streams are shown as thin blue lines, springs as a little blue circle with a tiny tail like a polliwog; swamps are dashed lines interspersed with a tufted symbol that represents marsh grass. Larger rivers, streams, and canals have two blue lines with a blue tint between them and, of course, oceans and lakes and ponds are outlined in blue and are filled in with a solid blue tint. Permanent snowfields and glaciers are shown with dashed-line edges.

Man-made features—houses, roads, railroads, power lines, and mines—are in black. Most important, trails are shown as dashed or dotted black lines. Some structures, such as churches and schools and cemeteries, have special black symbols. Often, a major highway is shown in red, as on a road map. Towns are a dense collection of little black squares, which represent individual houses.

If you ask for a woodland map, the newer topos from the government also indicate vegetation in green. There are different tints for orchards, vineyards, and scrub, while woodland is indicated in general extent by a solid green tint.

These symbols are often explained in the margin of a topo map, which also shows the date it was drawn or last checked and how this map relates to other maps on all four sides of it and to the rest of the world. This is done by putting the names of the adjoining maps at the appropriate edges of your map (or on a little map symbol at the bottom) and by latitude and longitude numbers in degrees, feet, and minutes at the four corners. The name of your map is prominently printed at either the top or bottom. In addition, the map has a scale, which is important to you.

There are three common topo scales in which an inch on the map variously represents 24,000, 62,500, or 250,000 inches of actual territory—or to put it a more useful way, a map inch can represent about 4/10, 1, or 4 miles, respectively. This fact is shown, for example, as 1:24,000 on the map right above a ruler scale that represents inches and fractions of an inch as feet. Now the larger scale—that is, where an inch represents less area—obviously shows more detail and is, therefore, more useful to you on the trail. The smaller-scale maps are sometimes useful in getting a perspective of a larger area or in planning an entire trip.

Personally, I prefer to get all of the larger-scale 1:24,000 maps I need to cover a trip area and lay them all out on a floor to get a detailed look at the broad scheme.

To get these maps, you first need an index map of the state you are interested in. This index is available at many book, map, or outdoor stores, or can be obtained free from the U.S. Geological Survey in Washington, D.C. (for eastern maps) or in Denver, Colorado (for maps west of the Mississippi River). You locate the specific quadrangle map you want on this master index, which then can be purchased for a nominal fee. In some park areas, there are also special shaded topos that enhance the three-dimensional effect.

Your topo has another feature. The top of the map is always true north. That is, if you point the map at the North Pole, it will automatically be in relation to the ground around you. But, you say, how the hell do I know where the North Pole is? Glad you asked. That's what a compass is for. A compass, however, doesn't often point to the North Pole. It points to the magnetic pole, which is somewhere west of true north in the eastern United States and is directly in line on a wavy diagonal running from Lake Michigan through Indiana, Kentucky, Tennessee, and eastern Georgia to Florida; it lies east of true north everywhere west of that line in this country.

The angle between magnetic and true north is called the declination. You can get special maps showing these various declination lines, but you don't need it. There are two arrows printed on the bottom of your topo that show true north and magnetic north and the declination angle between them.

To orient your map, you simply center your compass on the point where these two arrows converge and rotate the map and compass together until the north end of your compass needle lines up with the line representing magnetic north. The map now is oriented with the terrain. You can also orient your map without a compass by lining it up with a prominent landmark, such as a mountain peak. To do this, you must know where you are. Then, sight across the map from the point that represents your position, turning the map until the actual mountain is viewed across its map representation.

Conversely, if you don't know where you are, you can determine this rather interesting piece of information by triangulating your position from two prominent and well-separated landmarks, such as two mountains. Triangulation simply means that you take compass bearings on the landmarks and transfer them to the map as lines that cross the landmark in the direction of the compass reading. Where these lines cross should be where you are. To double-check, pick a third landmark and draw in another bearing. If all three cross at exactly the same spot the first time, you are either very good or damned lucky. To make compass sightings and map orientation so precise

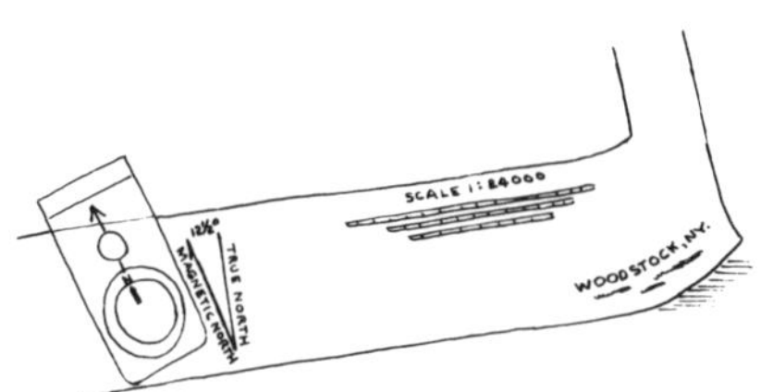


Orienting a topo map with the countryside is easy. The compass needle is simply aligned with the magnetic north line printed at the bottom of the map by placing the compass parallel to this line and turning the map until the north end of the needle is also parallel.

that you can pinpoint a tiny location takes practice. And the only way you can practice is with a good compass.

Now there are many kinds of compasses, but the ones generally used for backpacking are all constructed the same way. They have a magnetized needle or pointer that is free to rotate on a pivot and, thus, lines up with the magnetic lines of force that envelop the earth. In other words, the needle always points north and south toward the respective north and south magnetic poles. The north-pointing end of a good compass needle is always painted a distinctive color, usually red or black or phosphorescent, or is marked with an N.

Compass performance can be fouled up by strong local magnetic fields that may be created by a motor or generator or magnetic ore or large masses of manufactured steel or iron products. Exposure of the compass needle to strong artificial magnetic fields can even reverse the polarity of the compass, causing the ends to reverse direction. So keep your compass away from motors, batteries, and other electrical fields. When you use it, hold it away from your body or pack where there may be a concentration of iron or steel objects. It is a good idea to carry three compasses on deep wilderness trips to make sure that the "working" compass is really pointing true (if two out of three compasses show the same direction, you can be assured that the two are accurate).

The simplest compass is a metal cup with a glass window over the top and a card or compass rose inside under the rotating needle that indicates the cardinal directions of north, south, east, and west. Such a compass card is also usually subdivided between each of these points into three other directions, such as north-northeast, northeast, and east-northeast. But these sixteen simple directions are not enough for fine direction finding.

Modern compasses also have the entire 360-degree circle indicated either by individual degree marks or by marks that represent 2 or 5 degrees. North is both 0 and 360 degrees; east is 90 degrees; south, 180 degrees, and west is 270 degrees. Some compasses have a snap lid with a sighting notch or slot for fine determination of direction. There are others that are enclosed in a watch-type pocket or wrist case. They may have a free-swinging needle or a liquid-filled interior to damp the action of the nervous needle.

My workaday compass is a Voyager by Silva, which has a liquid-damped needle and is mounted on a plastic baseplate, which has a direction-of-travel arrow engraved in it. The baseplate also has inch and millimeter rules engraved along the sides. The compass case has degree

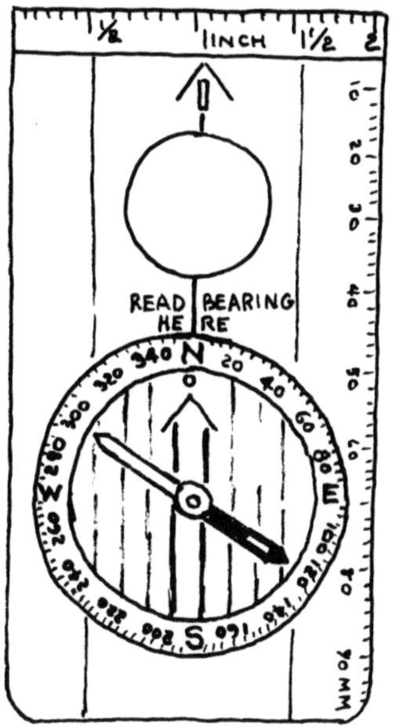


The important parts of a good compass are shown on a drawing of a Silva Voyager, a liquid-damped compass that slows oscillations of the needle.

marks engraved around its edge and an orienting arrow engraved inside under the needle. This case is free to rotate so that the desired direction of travel can be aligned with the directional arrow on the baseplate. I hang this compass on a lanyard around my neck and carry it in my upper right-hand shirt pocket, ready for instant use.

The compass is used to (1) orient the map, (2) take a bearing or direction from a location, (3) follow a bearing, and (4) return to a specific place after traveling away from it on a given bearing.

Map orientation has already been discussed. To take a bearing with a Silva compass, face the object that you wish to locate. Hold the compass in one or both hands (to steady it) with the direction arrow on the base pointing directly at the object. Then, rotate the housing so that the orienting arrow aligns with the compass needle. The "true" reading of the landmark is now indicated by the degree reading on the outside of the case that is over the direction arrow.

If you can't see your objective for a bearing, then determine its direction from the map. Orient the map with the terrain, then place your compass with the center of the needle directly over the spot where you are located. Point the direction arrow toward your objective on the map and turn the case until the needle and the orienting arrow are aligned. The degree reading over the direction arrow is your bearing.

You will note in all of this that after you have aligned your map with the terrain by means of the magnetic reading, all further bearings can be made on a magnetic basis without concern for magnetic variation, if you wish. It is simpler, because it is easier to align your compass needle directly on the orienting arrow than it is with a few-degree variation to one side or the other.

As long as you don't touch the housing, you can follow your bearing by holding the direction arrow pointed straight in front of you and turning your body until the compass needle aligns with the orienting arrow inside the case. Your direction of travel is the direction-of-travel arrow on the baseplate.

To return to your original location, you simply point the direction-of-travel arrow toward yourself and follow the reverse end of the baseplate, which is 180 degrees from your original bearing (with the compass needle on the orienting arrow, of course). If this reverse method doesn't satisfy you, add 180 degrees (or subtract it) from your outward-bound bearing and rotate the housing until this new number is over the direction arrow, then follow the arrow as before.

To get to an objective, measure the distance on your map and calculate the approximate hiking time in minutes or hours, using your normal hiking speed for the particular type of terrain, say 2 miles an hour. At the end of that time period, you should be very close to your objective.

Now it is seldom possible to walk in a straight line in the woods or mountains for very long. There are deadfalls and swamps and rocks and cliffs that cause you to veer from a straight line. To avoid these obstacles, you must detour. This variation is usually accounted for by time and direction.

Say, for example, that you are traveling a north bearing to a distant mountain and on the way you come to a swamp that must be bypassed. You walk in an easterly direction by the compass for one hour and then find that you have cleared the side of the swampy area. Now turn north and walk until you have cleared the other end of the swamp, then turn west and walk for another hour. Now, when you turn north once again, you should be back on your original line and can follow it to your objective. The additional two hours of lateral travel must, of course, be subtracted from your watch accounting of the hiking time to your objective.

A trick that will help you follow your bearing is to sight along the direction arrow at the start and pick out several prominent objects—distinctive trees, rocks, or the like—that are in line with each other and with your bearing. Now walk forward, keeping them in line. Before you reach the last one, take out your compass again and select another group of reference objects.

The more practiced you are, the closer you will come to your objective without having to cast about at the end of the estimated hiking time to find it. But suppose your goal is a tiny campsite in a large wilderness area with no prominent local features to help you pinpoint it. You can still find it with some common sense.

Suppose, for example, your camp is on the bank of a large river in northern Canada. You have hiked away from camp in this flat land on a bearing of 0 (or 360 degrees) for two hours, hunting or exploring. Now, you want to go home. You know the bearing for camp is 180 degrees (south), but when you reach the river you see no camp. Is it upstream or down? By trying to pinpoint it, you don't know. However, if on your return trip you had hiked slightly east of south until you reached the river you would know that your camp was on your right, or west, along the riverbank because you had deliberately diverged in the other direction. This method is particularly useful in flat prairies, deserts, and featureless forests.

Where no such prominent feature as a river occurs and your camp is in the middle of a forest, you may have to take other measures. In a truly trackless wilderness—and *only* in such a location—it is useful to blaze four trails to the cardinal points of the compass for a mile or two from your camp. Use a different blaze for each direction and put this blaze on both sides of the trees at right angles to the direction of the trail. Then, put another blaze on the camp side of the tree. No matter which way you travel from your permanent camp in hunting or exploring, when you return you are sure to catch one of your radiating trails and can follow it back to camp. But, please! Such trails are only for such trackless wildernesses as northern Canada or Alaska or the jungles of Central and South America—*not* for wilderness areas in the United States. And it is usually possible to avoid this last resort anywhere you might be camping because the land *does* generally have distinctive features—valleys, ridges, mountains, lakes—that you can memorize or orient with your map.

Practice with your map and compass—it is worth the effort. It is not safe for you to leave the beaten path until you are an expert. Get a good book (see book list) and familiarize yourself with different orienteering techniques. At the same time you are practicing orienteering techniques on the trail, develop your sense of direction, so that, at least under normal circumstances, you will have an awareness of where you are, where you have come from, and where you are going to.

But never trust your senses over the unerring compass needle. There are times when you will swear it has gone crazy and that your campsite lies in a different direction from that indicated by the needle. Curiously enough, this is particularly true when clouds or fog have blotted out familiar landmarks on a familiar trail. It also happens in tricky watersheds where the crossing of a ridge puts you in a canyon that points in a different direction from that of the canyon you have been following. Here, sometimes, a twist of trail or terrain will make you think the new gully runs in the same direction as the last when, in truth, it is very different.

In such cases, trust your compass and map implicitly. Steel your mind to ignore your "instincts." They are invariably wrong.

Once you have achieved expertise in orienteering, you are ready for new adventures off trail.

### *Leaving the Path*

As trails and conventional campsites get increasingly crowded, the only way to achieve peace and solitude is to get away from the marked paths and to bushwhack into backcountry. In many mountainous areas of the East and West, in fact, it is the only way to explore because trails to many summits have not been blazed. Often you can proceed visually in such country with reference only to the map. But always take compass bearings anyway and write them down either in a notebook or on the margin of your map. Before you decide to return, a storm or fog may roll in and blot out all of the landmarks.

Also make it a practice on trails or when bushwhacking

to look behind you frequently as you go. Try to memorize the appearance of prominent landmarks and trail features, especially significant canyons, ponds, streams, cliffs, and the like. They look very different from the other direction —the one you will have to follow when you return.

Before bushwhacking, study your topo maps carefully and pick a route that avoids dead ends, such as impassable cliffs or swamps. The route should also follow the least difficult terrain. This is not always easy to choose, since a topo map won't show deadfalls, rock fields, or every small swamp. But from experience, you will know that wooded canyons or slopes that face in the direction of prevailing storms are likely to be encumbered by windrows of

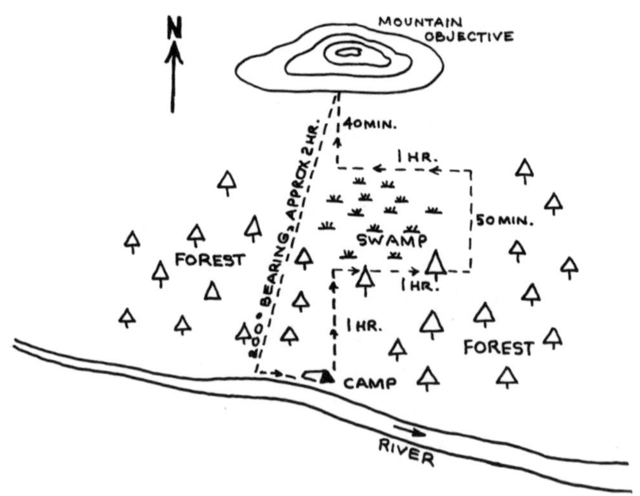


Finding the way to an objective and back to camp on a bushwhack is simply diagramed. The correct line to the objective is maintained, despite a long detour around a big swamp, by walking for an equal time both east and west. A deliberate line west of south is taken on the return trip to reach the riverbank to the west of camp. At this point, the hiker knows he must turn downriver to reach his tent.

downed trees and that the area below cliffs of rotted rock is also likely to be a scree or talus slope. It is almost always easier to follow a longer route on ridges than to follow a stream or cut across a valley.

Bushwhacking requires a knowledge of the geology and the environment of the area you will travel as well as the ability to interpret topo maps.

Your rate of speed will not be the same as for trail travel. If the ground is difficult, you may achieve only 1 mile an hour, and 1½ miles an hour is probably the best you can maintain through heavy woods or over rocky or snow-covered ground. Plot your entire route with compass bearings before you go and be prepared to make many adjustments.

To choose a good campsite, identify map areas that look suitable—near water or springs in a gently sloping or flat area that also shows woodland nearby where you can collect firewood, and a hill or mountain to windward for weather protection. When you get to this area—well before dark—cast around for the most suitable camping location. This will take some time to find and prepare, particularly if you are in the high mountains.

Finally, once again, let someone at home know where you will be, by what route, and for how long. Take every possible precaution and be prepared to serve as your own rescue party if somebody in the party suffers a minor injury. Try to involve the authorities in a rescue effort only if it is a matter of life or death. Continued freedom to travel where we will is a responsibility that may be taken from us if careless backpackers and climbers continue to get into needless trouble and to require massive, expensive, and dangerous rescue efforts.

# 9

# SETTING UP CAMP

It's late afternoon. You've done your mileage for the day—whatever it may be—and you're looking forward to a comfortable camp with old friends. If you've planned well, it just could be a camp that will stay in your memory for life, long after the hard trail and even the personal climbing triumphs have been half forgotten.

Such is my recollection of Indian Falls in the Adirondacks at many times of the year and with a number of old buddies, of a lone camp in a grove of trees under Mount Lyell in the Tuolumne area of Yosemite, of a one-night stop with my family by a little wilderness stream in the Smokies, and of a week-long base camp with a group of boys in the Great Gulf of the White Mountains in New Hampshire.

If you choose unwisely, you may remember clouds of insects, deep mud and wet firewood, a rocky outcropping that was the only available flat ledge on which to throw your bag, or a half-mile walk to the nearest water. Sometimes the choice is not yours; more often, however, it is.

It starts with map planning, as we said in the last chapter. But the final crunch is at the scene when you cast about for the best place to put your tent or tarp. Let's take things in order. The prime requisites for any campsite are potable water, a wood supply (if you propose to have a fire), protection from wind, weather, and insects, and a flat open ground for your shelter. Another consideration is whether you are simply making an overnight stop or are establishing a base camp from which to take side trips. If you are going to stay at an established lean-to or hut, these factors have already been decided for you (although some lean-tos are in dry locations requiring considerable trips for water and others can be swampy in wet weather). But, if you are on your own, then it is up to you to pick the right spot.

### *The Water Supply*

The first thing to do is to locate the water supply, either a pond, stream, or, preferably, a spring. Flatly stated, it is always unsafe to drink untreated water from a source that cannot be completely inspected for contamination. The only source that really qualifies is a small spring that you can scan completely for dead animals and for either animal or human fecal contamination. Some of these springs are a joy forever, delivering ice-cold water of a purity and flavor that you will remember for life. There is a fountain that gushes out from under a big rock near the

The way to leave a campsite is shown as Rob and I set up camp in one of our favorite secret spots (left) and as we were ready to leave later (right). The fireplace has been dismantled and the stones returned to their original location. The ashes are buried and the leaves have been scattered over the site. The barked tree in background of both pictures is porcupine damage.

top of Balsam Lake Mountain in the Catskills that is just about the best water I have ever tasted.

Now, I take a chance on streams in truly wilderness areas and on high-altitude ponds where I know that few animals abound and that it is unlikely anyone is camping above me. The risk is slight, in my view, for me and my family. But when I take groups of other people out, I always take a more conservative view.

Water that cannot be proved safe should be treated with fresh halazone tablets or chlorine bleach or iodine. All are effective. So is boiling. However, halazone tablets deteriorate in an opened bottle and, therefore, should be obtained fresh each season from an outfitter or drugstore. They are added according to the instructions on the bottle, one tablet per pint for ordinary water and two tablets per pint if the water is turbid or suspected of heavy pollution.

Common household bleach can be used for purification at the rate of about two to three drops per quart of water,

depending on turbidity. Iodine is added at the rate of three drops per quart, six drops for highly turbid water.

With any of these compounds, close the water container and shake vigorously to soak all parts of the interior. After loosening the cap, slosh some of the contents over the lip and neck of the container to sterilize that too. Then let the tightly recapped container stand for thirty minutes. Open and sniff. If you can smell chlorine or iodine, it is safe to drink. If not, add another tablet, two drops of bleach, or a drop of iodine and let it stand for another thirty minutes, sniffing again for the presence of free chlorine or iodine. Such water tastes foul and makes rotten tea or coffee—but it's safe.

Because of the taste, many people prefer to boil the water. To be safe, water should be brought to an active boil in your cooking pot and be held at the boil for five minutes at sea level. Add another minute for every 1,000 feet of elevation. To regain some of the flavor of natural water, the boiled liquid must be re-aerated by pouring it, after cooling, back and forth with considerable splashing between two sterile containers or by shaking it in a partially filled jug. Store sterile water in a sterile container, such as a jug, bota, or canteen. Never put contaminated water in these containers; if they should become accidentally contaminated, sterilize them with chlorine or iodine.

Remember, the same precautions must be observed in washing cooking and eating equipment. Use only sterilized water for washing dirty pots, pans, plates, cups, and utensils. If you should forget and wash them in water suspected of contamination, boil them in a pot of water for five minutes. There are several dread diseases, a few that can be fatal, that are contracted from contaminated water, so it isn't smart to take a chance where contamination—particularly fecal contamination—is a distinct possibility. This is not just true in foreign areas that are noted for epidemic diseases. It applies anywhere in the world where man has set foot.

How do you find a water supply? In mountain areas, finding water is generally not a problem. Melting snowfields or glaciers create streams—or you can melt ice or snow directly. Mountains also tend to spawn springs. Many will be marked on your topo map. Desert oases are also marked on the maps.

If you can't find water in this way, look for clumps or lines of dense or darker vegetation. Such patches often mark surface or buried water. The latter can be obtained by digging a shallow pit in the ground and letting moisture seep in to form a pool. But don't count on this unless the ground or sand is damp. In desert arroyos water may be many feet deep, if there at all.

Sometimes there are natural catch basins in rock that hold rainfall, which is always pure. The catch basin itself, however, if frequented by animals or man, may not be clean. If in doubt, treat this water as contaminated.

On a beach, you may be able to get water by digging a pit at low tide just below the high-tide line. If subsurface fresh water is draining to the sea, it is lighter than salt water and floats on top, seeping into the pit before the salt water.

In game country, you can often find water by following deeply worn game trails, trod through the forest by animals that year after year take the same track to a spring or pond.

Be careful of turbid streams from glaciers and of desert pools. The former may contain minute but sharp crystals of rock silicate, worn from the cliffs by the ice stream, which can cut your insides to ribbons. And while "poisoned" pools of the desert are so much fiction, there are some areas where the mineral content is either loathsome to the taste or could make you sick if you drank it in quantity. If there is little vegetation around a pool where there is the soil to support growth, taste the water with caution.

In normal woodlands, it is often possible to spot springs along the sides of streams. Sometimes a basin must be excavated and the downhill side lined with rocks to form a pool from which water can be dipped with a cup. Sometimes a little waterfall can be created with rocks so that the water container can be filled directly. After such re-engineering, the muddy water will settle in ten to thirty minutes and will remain clear if you are careful not to touch the bottom of the little pool.

On high mountains, it is wise to carry at least a little water with you if you don't know the territory well. Sometimes springs that are marked on topos or described in guides have either dried up (particularly in mid-summer) or can be very difficult to find. A canteen or bota of water can carry you through dinner and breakfast, if you are thrifty.

### *Spotting the Right Wood*

If you are going to have a fire, it helps to have the right kind of wood. Not all wood burns well and some is downright disastrous for cooking and warming your shelter.

Most soft or evergreen woods are in the latter category because they contain considerable quantities of resin, burn fast with a sooty flame, and throw off showers of sparks, which can, of course, damage tents and sleeping bags and are a general fire hazard. Softwoods also do not supply the long-lasting coals needed for cooking.

If you are in an area where pine, spruce, fir, or hemlock are the only available woods, then confine your cooking to the boiling of water for dehydrated foods over a small and carefully guarded fire and forget about the evening blaze. Softwoods are useful, though, as tinder and kindling to get harder woods ablaze. This is particularly true of the resinous knots from an old, decayed pine. If you can find one, its shavings will burn like a fire starter and coax even wet wood into a blaze.

For real cooking and for a pleasant and long-lasting evening campfire, hardwoods are the thing. Trees that have grown on high, dry ground make better fires than the same kinds of trees that have grown in swampy areas. The best woods for hot fires, in my opinion, are oak, maple, hickory, ash, ironwood (or hornbeam), and dogwood—in that order, although other outdoorsmen have their own favorite order. The birches burn well but fast and have short-lived coals. They are good, though, to get harder woods to burn. And both birch and poplar are fine for a quick luncheon fire.

The rest of the hardwoods are pretty indifferent stuff for campfires. However, brush and scrub in the desert burn pretty well and well-dried driftwood along the shore almost always makes a good fire.

Learn to recognize the good woods by their bark or grain pattern because this is all you will see in deadfalls or in standing dead trees. Then look for these woods when you are selecting a campsite. It helps to have your wood supply near at hand.

## *Protection for the Camp*

Next in importance is the protection of your camp from weather and insects. In the United States, wind and weather generally flow from the northwest, although local conditions can produce variations and an occasional storm can blow up from just about any direction.

But, in general, you will want your camp guarded on the northwest side by some natural barrier to break the force of a storm. A mountain range, hills, or a sizable forest will all diminish the impact of a gale. Failing these large obstacles, pick a site with a cliff or large bank to the northwest for protection.

Bugs are something that you cannot completely avoid. If they are in season, they will be everywhere. But not equally. Obviously, low and swampy areas will have more insects, as do damp, heavily wooded, and shrubby or grassy spots. Pick a campsite that is high and dry and in a clearing, if at all possible. At a lake, a high and gravelly peninsula is better than a low cove. Breezy locations tend to discourage bugs from hanging around.

Camp sanitation is also critical during high-insect seasons. Be sure to put your food away, avoid scattering scraps, and cover latrine contents with dirt or sand after every use.

Check your proposed site for wasp or hornet nests.

You'll never forget it if you stumble into one of these hot spots—and if you should happen to be allergic to the stings, it could be fatal. Nests are located from the tops of trees to the undersides of shrubs and even in holes in the ground. In the desert, avoid pitching your tent over holes in the ground. They could harbor snakes, which usually come out for a night's hunting just about the time you settle in for the evening.

Most of all, in the woods, look up. Do not pitch camp under deadheads or large dead branches on living trees. If their time has come, these silent killers can fall even in the absence of wind. Naturally, you will also avoid the downwind side of a dead tree too.

Also avoid camping under very tall trees in a forest or single trees of any height in the open. In barren spots, put your tent in a depression to avoid making it the highest object around and, thus, the target for lightning during storms. Try not to camp on the peak of a mountain for the same reason. And in the Southwest, stay out of dry washes, which can turn in minutes into raging torrents from cloudbursts many miles away in the mountains.

In short, the ideal campsite is a high, dry, flat area in a clearing in a hardwood forest with a spring or stream a short distance away. The tent site should be as flat as possible so you won't slide downhill all night.

On a mountain, try to find a sheltered gully or ledge that is protected from the wind and has a flat area big enough for your tent. Anchor your shelter firmly as described in Chapter 6. If you are above tree line, you will have to use a stove or backpack wood up from timberline. The latter is rarely satisfactory, except in an emergency, since high-altitude growth is generally dwarf spruce that burns poorly.

But, one way or another, you will finally select a camping spot by considering—and probably compromising—these basic needs. Now, you must set up camp.

*Establishing a Camp*

How do you go about it and in what order? Get your shelter up first. Then, get wood and water. Build your fireplace. And finally, cook your dinner, eat, and do your chores. Then relax.

The mechanics of pitching a shelter were covered in Chapter 6, but there is more to it than that. The direction in which you face your tent or tarp may determine how comfortable a night you will spend.

You have already taken into account the probable direction of the prevailing wind. But there are purely local considerations, too. For example, in a canyon, even without a general wind, the flow of air varies with the time of day. During the sunny hours, heated air in the valley at the foot of the canyon causes an upward flow through the gully. But at night, air at the top of the canyon on the mountain ridge chills off and becomes heavier, causing it to flow downward.

At the shore, there are day and night breezes that blow in from or out to sea, depending on locality. Large lakes also create consistent wind patterns. Some mountain chains breed their own weather patterns—often a violent string of thunderstorms.

Pitch your tent crosswise or with its back to the calculated direction of wind flow. This will not only keep you warmer at night by preventing wind chill, but will keep sparks and smoke from the fire from blowing in your face or onto your fragile nylon gear. Be prepared to shift your camp immediately if the wind takes an unexpected turn and blows up into a storm. It is better to take a few moments in the first dark to shift a tent than to spend all night in wet misery. If you become completely familiar with how to pitch your tent before going camping, this will be easy.

Select a site that will drain naturally in the event of a storm. No trenching! This old-fashioned practice disfigures a campsite and leads to gullying.

Immediately after pitching the shelter, get out your sleeping bag. Spread out the foam pad or blow up the air mattress and shake out the sleeping bag, fluffing it up to get maximum loft. Place them in the shelter on top of the floor or ground cloth to air and be ready when you are for a night's rest.

Next bring in a container of water so you can slake your thirst while gathering wood and completing the chores. Now clear a spot for the campfire. Scour an area 10 feet in diameter free of leaves and other vegetable matter down to mineral soil. There is no exception to this requirement. Do not build your fire against either a downed log or stump, either. Fire can travel underground through rotting vegetation or through roots or can lie hidden in the punk of a rotten back log for a long time, ready to burst into a raging forest fire at a favorable opportunity. So scrape that ground! Leave the vegetation in a neat heap at the edge of your camp. You will need it when you break camp.

If there is live grass in the fire area, cut it out in squares with your spade or trowel, digging deep enough to clear the roots. Stack this sod in a shady spot to be replanted when you break camp.

If you are camping in snow and insist on using a fire, either stamp down the white stuff in a compact circle or scrape it away down to the ground so it won't turn to water later and drown out your fire and wet your feet.

Now gather your firewood and stack it near the center of the cleared area, bigger pieces to the outside, kindling next to where you will build the fireplace. To hold it in a neat pile, you may want to drive four stakes at either end of the stack. But it is usually possible to make a neat stack just with bigger pieces of wood holding things together at each end. Have a poncho or spare ground cloth handy to cover the woodpile at night or in the event of rain.

## *Various Fireplaces*

Now you are ready to build your fireplace. The kind you use depends on locality, wind conditions, and the type of cooking or heating you need.

Personally, I like a keyhole fireplace with a reflector back. It provides just about everything. It is called a keyhole because it's shaped like one. The round upper part contains a continuous blaze of hardwood that reflects off a back wall of rock to warm you and your shelter. The key slot in front is made with low, flat rocks that support a grill or, directly, the pots and pans. Cooking is accomplished here by raking coals forward from the blaze.

A keyhole fireplace with a reflector stone back has everything. The fire burns in the main portion, heating the water kettle, which is suspended over the blaze on a dingle stick. The grill on low rocks in the front is for cooking over coals. Note the neat stack of firewood and kindling alongside the fireplace. The hot mitt is over the handle of a short-handled spade.

If you want to bake, a few stones are removed from the side of the fire area and are replaced with the reflector oven, which faces both the blaze and the reflected heat from the stones on the other side of the fireplace. I also hang my water pot over the blaze or to one side of it on a "dingle stick," which will be described a little later, so that I always have hot water for tea or coffee without cluttering up my cooking area.

The keyhole is about 2 feet in diameter, enough space to permit the stacking of a log-cabin style fire in the evening or when you want to quickly produce a lot of coals for cooking. The key slot is from 6 inches to a foot or so wide, depending on whether you have a grill or are using stones to support the pans.

Be careful when you build your fireplace not to use shale-type rocks or stones from stream beds, both of which are likely to contain moisture. The amount of heat generated by a hardwood fire is intense and can turn entrapped moisture in rocks into steam. If that happens, your fireplace becomes a circle of hand grenades. Exploding rocks are no joking matter.

I recall once in the Catskills when the ground was soaking wet and we wanted to bake potatoes in a pit. The only rock readily available was slate. So we dug a pit and lined it with the flat slabs to keep out the moisture, then built a small fire in the hole. When it was reduced to ashes and coals, we put the foil-wrapped potatoes in and covered them with about 2 feet of ashes, coals, and dirt and built another fire on top.

Shortly thereafter, a series of muffled explosions shattered the calm evening. The new fire heaved into the air and rock fragments started whistling around our ears—from under two feet of soil! About an hour later, after everything had calmed down, we dug up the potatoes and found them done—but shot through and through with

A hunter's fire is fed by Teddy at the wide end. The coals are then raked under the grill at the narrow end for cooking. The pots hang on a stick over the fire suspended between two forked stakes. The birch side logs used here would last for no more than a meal or two. Cured hardwood or green wood is longer lasting.

slivers of slate, probably what would have happened to us if we hadn't ducked for cover.

If there is no suitable rock, or no rock at all, then my second choice is the hunter's fire, which is made from logs. The ideal wood for the base of this fireplace is green hardwood. Now you don't have to chop down a living tree to get such logs. You damned sure better not! But green trees are often downed by storms or heavy winds and can supply your needs. If not, then use well-cured hardwood logs; they'll just have to be replaced a little oftener.

In either case, obtain two logs about 4 feet long and 4 to 6 inches in diameter. Lay them in the cleared fire area with one end of each log about 3 to 6 inches apart and the opposite ends about a foot or more apart. The spread should be to windward. The active fire goes in the broad end and coals are raked to the narrow end for cooking.

To keep the logs from rolling either apart or together while you are cooking, square them off with an axe, stake them, or brace them with small rocks. You can put the grill across the narrow end to hold the pots or put the pots directly on the logs.

To keep dry logs from burning, it helps to soak them in water or to smear the inside edges with mud. Even banking up dirt or sand inside will help. This is a particularly good fire for the beach and can be built from driftwood that is banked inside with wet sand to keep the main logs from burning up. Keep the fire small and under control with this fireplace.

If you can find a straight green branch from a windfall that is about 4 or 5 feet long, you can make another cooking aid. Get two forked sticks about 3 feet long, preferably green but at least hardwood, and drive them into the ground at either end of the fireplace. The straight stick goes from fork to fork to form a support. Then get two more crotched green sticks and cut them for pot hangers. The crotch hangs over the supporting pole and the pots are held over the blaze by hooking the bails into deep notches cut in the downward-hanging portion of the limb. You can cut several notches at different heights, if you wish, so that the pot can be adjusted to receive different degrees of heat.

Personally, I am a devotee of the dingle stick—over any kind of fire. This handy pot holder is simply a green stick about 1 inch in diameter and from 3 to 5 feet long, depending upon the construction of the fireplace. One end is sharpened and stuck in the ground behind the fireplace or, better, is weighted with a heavy stone. The stick leans over the rear rock and hangs over the blaze. A notch, or notches, permits one or more pots to be hung over the blaze and to be moved backward and forward so that they can boil away or just simmer.

If a rock ballast is used on the rear, the stick can be swung from side to side to further increase versatility. My water pot always hangs on this stick and I often cook stews and other one-pot meals in this way. For quick lunch or hunter's fires, a dingle stick can be set up in the same way or can be supported over a tiny blaze by a forked stick thrust into the ground.

In deserts and in very windy locations, where large wood may be scarce or where there is a danger of sparks spreading the fire, then a trench fire is the only answer. Dig the trench about a foot deep and taper it from a

Special-purpose fires include a dingle-stick blaze for lunch, a trench blaze for windy areas, and a closely grouped rock support with coals for boiling water.

narrow to a wide end in the direction of wind flow. Make the wide end shallow to further improve ventilation. Build a small fire in the big end of the trench and cook over either the direct flames or over coals in the small end. Here, a grill is handy to support pots, but if the trench walls are cut narrow and vertically, you can also bridge the sides directly with the pots. In sandy areas, a combination of the trench and hunter's fires can be constructed with logs holding the soft walls in place.

For simply boiling a kettle of water for either a one-pot meal or for a lunch-break cup of soup or tea, an even simpler fire is possible. Put some flat-topped rocks about 6 inches high in a tight circle about 4 to 6 inches in diameter. Leave some air spaces between rocks on the windward side. Then build a tiny blaze in the center from hardwood sticks no more than ½ inch in diameter.

Place your pot on the rocks as soon as the fire is well under way; the fire will have died down to coals at about the time the water comes to a boil, enabling you to simmer the soup or meal until it is done. Because such a fire concentrates the heat, the whole operation may take no more than fifteen minutes. An effective cooker fueled with charcoal briquets can also be made in this way; it will hold the heat long enough to cook a stew. This is valuable in those occasional places that ban open fires but permit charcoal.

These basic fireplaces will accommodate anyone's needs, really. There are other types of fires: towering log-cabin council fires that are lit at the top and gradually burn down through the stacked wood, elevated cooking fires that are built on top of stone or dirt-covered log-cabin platforms. But these are not usually used by backpackers just stopping for a night.

Even without a reflector oven, baking can be accomplished in a number of ways. A reflector can be con-

Homemade reflector for baking in a frying pan is formed from heavy foil that is bent in a U-shape below and above the pan to reflect heat evenly from the fire at other end of a hunter's blaze.

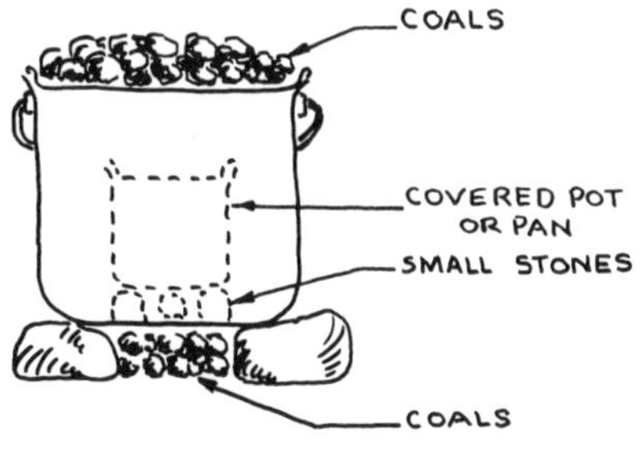


Pot-within-a-pot baker. A small pot containing the food is placed on three small stones inside a larger pot. Coals are placed on top and underneath the larger pot to raise the interior temperature.

Frying-pan baking can also be accomplished by covering the pan with a high domed lid and piling coals on top. Just the right amount of coals should also be put underneath to provide even heating.

structed from heavy foil in exactly the same shape as a regular reflector oven, or, more usually, in the shape of a rounded hood that focuses heat down on the pan (which is also supported on stones or sticks and has foil underneath to reflect the heat upward). A large covered pot can be used as an oven. Put three small pebbles in the pot. Place a smaller pot on the pebbles. Put the food in the smaller pot. The rig is placed on your grill over coals, and coals are heaped on top of the lid. It works very well. I even get the same effect for non-critical baking, such as corn bread and biscuits, by covering the dough in my frying pan with a domed lid and piling coals on top. The pan, of course, sits on the grill over coals. With a little practice, you can judge how many coals to have underneath (the critical area) so that the breads cook evenly above and below, without scorching, in the allotted twenty minutes.

Fancy ovens can be dug in claybanks by hollowing out a cave and punching a chimney in the top. A fire is built inside and when it has died down, the food is put in, the chimney and front are sealed up, and the business is left to cook—all day, if you want. Personally, I tried it once and it seemed like an awful lot of work.

A pit baker starts with a hole in which a fire is built. The pot containing food is covered with foil and placed in the hole on the coals. It is then covered with ashes and coals and sealed with dirt.

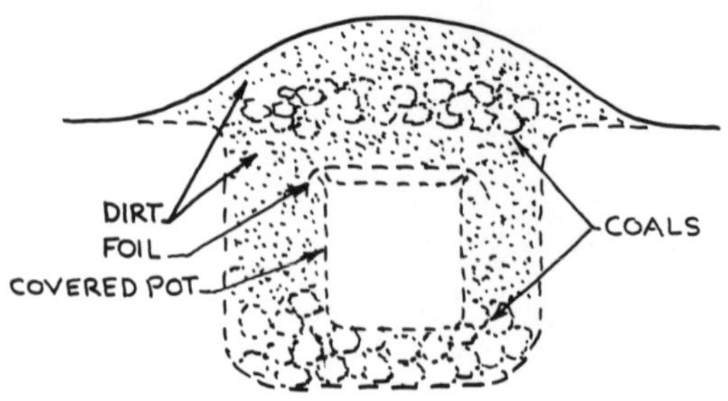

An easier way to get the same results is the baking pit described earlier (without the exploding rocks). This pit can also be used with a large or small kettle with a tight-fitting lid. After the fire in the pit has died down, put the kettle full of food in the hole and cover it with ashes and coals. Then, seal up the whole pit with dirt. You have now created a Dutch cooker or oven that can be left all day and will turn out a hot meal for you when you stagger back into camp in the evening, tired from a long haul on the trail.

This device is particularly good for baked beans and stews, or even foil-wrapped chickens or meat roasts. For shorter periods, it is also useful for baking potatoes or fresh corn-on-the-cob. You can also cook entire seafood dinners in such a pit at the shore. Here, a huge fire is built in the bottom of a large pit. When it has died down, potatoes, corn, lobsters, crabs, clams, oysters, and fish—or any combination of these—are layered in the pit over the coals, separated from the heat and from each other with layers of fresh seaweed. The top is covered with seaweed and a large tarp, which is weighted down all around the edges with sand. This is left for several hours until done, occasionally lifting an edge of the tarp and poking for tenderness (the potatoes are usually used as a measure).

With such pits, though, make sure you have them deeply covered with dirt or sand before you leave them unattended. And they must also be dug in mineral earth or sand to prevent the spread of fire.

### *How to Start a Fire*

To cook all of these goodies, though, you have to be able to start a fire. So, back to reality. A fire needs three things: oxygen, fuel, and a temperature high enough to cause combustion. It sounds easy and generally is. But sometimes the last two are difficult to attain.

The availability of oxygen is created by the design of your fireplace and the way in which you stack your tinder and wood. The fuel is, obviously, dry wood. The combustion temperature is provided, initially, by a single wooden match and, later, by successively larger pieces of wood until a point of "self-combustion" is reached in which the temperature of the bed of coals and of the air in the immediate vicinity of the fire is so high as to cause almost any wood placed in the fire to catch fire immediately. This is the delightful goal toward which the procedure is aimed. Let's start at the beginning.

And at the beginning, all ingredients should be at hand. First in order of importance is an adequate supply of tinder and small kindling. Tinder can be oily birch bark, the bark of wild grape vines or hemlock trees, the shavings

How to start a fire. Small shavings and twigs are piled against a back log and lit (below). Larger twigs are added as blaze grows (right, above), and still larger wood is gradually added in crisscross fashion to make coals (right).

from an old pine knot, globs of exuded resin from a spruce interspersed with fine hardwood shavings—all are good. Fuzz sticks are a combination of tinder and kindling created by shaving down very dry and straight-grained woods such as ash, hickory, and birch, leaving the shavings attached at one end of the twig or split. The curly ends are placed downward in a teepee arrangement that is lit at the bottom.

I prefer fine shavings of dry hardwood or birchbark. They take less time to prepare. The tinder is stacked either in the teepee or against a back log of about 3 inches in diameter. I prefer the latter, since it gives support against which larger kindling can be propped and will not collapse after burning as does the teepee. Another prop is a green stick thrust into the ground at a 45-degree angle.

If the ground is very wet or snow covered, build a substantial base of logs to protcct the blaze until it is big enough to dry things out underneath. If it is raining, shield the fire area with a poncho or a large piece of bark until the fire is well established.

I believe in lighting the tinder before piling on kindling and firewood, because I think it allows more oxygen to get to the fire and also allows the subsequent exact placement of kindling, as needed. Hold the lighted match under the windward side of the tinder until it is ignited. Then lean very fine kindling over the blazing tinder and against the back log. Add only a few sticks at a time so as not to smother the flame. The initial kindling should be ⅛ to ¼ inch in diameter. If you only need a simple fire for cooking a quick lunch, continue to add sticks up to ½ inch in diameter.

If a longer-lasting blaze is desired, continue to lean kindling against the back log in the blaze until unsplit wood of ½ inch in diameter is afire. Then place two logs, 2 or 3 inches in diameter, about a foot apart, along both sides of the blazing kindling, touching the back log and extending toward the front of the fireplace. Crisscross 1-inch-diameter wood on top of these logs, first one way and then the other in log-cabin style over the blaze. These sticks should now readily catch fire.

Soon the fire will be roaring and you can add bigger wood in crisscross fashion at the top. As the logs burn down, it will be necessary to rearrange them every now and then, tossing unburnt ends into the center, with a couple of "tong" sticks that you keep handy beside the woodpile. Occasionally, you may have to raise the blazing wood on one side or both and slide fresh side logs underneath. These hold the fire up a bit and allow the free circulation of air. They also permit you to rake coals out from under the front, with your shovel or a long stick, for cooking.

In dry weather, such a fire takes no more than ten minutes to start and perhaps twenty minutes to become self-sustaining. You can, of course, be boiling water while it is abuilding.

In wet weather or in winter, when the woods have been soaked for a long time, fire starting is a challenge that takes experience to master.

Well-cured hardwood that has been supported off the ground in a deadhead or deadfall will usually be dry at the core. This wood can be obtained by splitting it out with your axe or hatchet after sawing the wood to length. Dry kindling can also be obtained from dead evergreen branches that are attached to a living tree and kept dry by an overhead canopy of branches. I have never been very successful in finding those pockets of tinder that are supposed to exist in hollowed tree trunks and rock crevices. These sources always seem to be rotted or wet or both when I get there.

However, birchbark will burn even when wet and birch,

maple, cottonwood, and quaking aspen will burn even when green, particularly in the winter when the sap is down and when the tree is located on high, dry ground. Or you can use one of the fire starters described in Chapter 7. Place this aid under a small teepee of the driest shavings you can produce.

In the wettest or coldest weather, you may have to work your way up from fine shavings to light kindling very slowly, gradually increasing the temperature of the fire environment and building up coals that will ignite larger wood. If you are patient, though, it is possible—even with poor spruce that has been soaked with fall rains and then frozen to the core. But a fire under these circumstances is not recommended except in an emergency.

When you get a fire going, dry out enough tinder, kindling, and wood for the next day. Put the tinder in a plastic bag and store it under cover or in your sleeping bag where the heat of your body will keep it dry. Store the dry tinder and wood under a ground cloth. The best way to dry wood is to stack it loosely on a grill that is supported over or near the fire. You will congratulate yourself on your advance planning the next morning.

## *Camp Practices and Chores*

Everyone has certain habits and gimmicks that they believe make a camp more homey. For a simple overnight stop, you probably won't bother with frills. But if you are on a layover day or have established a base camp and are hiking out and returning every day, you may wish to make your camp more homelike. I like a log seat in front of the fire, for example. I get a length of downed timber at least 6 feet long and prop it securely in front of the blaze on two or more large stones or crisscrossed logs so that my companions and I can sit comfortably while cooking and talking. I usually place this log just under the edge of the tarp or canopy so that it is shielded from possible rain. And I plane off the top with my axe just enough to remove rotten bark and stubs.

The woodpile of course, is located next to the fireplace. I generally arrange the kindling, used only rarely, into a smooth platform closest to the fireplace, a sort of kitchen side table on which I can rest pots and pans and food during cooking. If I'm carrying my short spade, I drive it into the ground behind the woodpile and drop my hot mitt over the top, ready at hand. My pack is strapped to the nearest handy tree, with the waist belt holding the bottom in place and the top secured by a short cord slipped through the frame bars and tied around the tree. The pack is lashed about 4 feet from the ground, which seems to discourage small animals that might pry. The waterproof pack cover is put over the pack every night in case of rain.

I often suspend my food bags, cooking-kit bag, war bag, thermometer, and towel from a short line tied between two nearby trees about 4 feet from the ground. This is also the location of my trash bag, a plastic garbage-can liner into which I put all non-burnable trash, which should *always* be lugged out of the woods by any good camper. See Chapter 11 for other handy devices you can whittle or make with an axe and saw to improve a long-term camp.

In setting up camp and maintaining it, everyone in the party should share in the chores. Generally, one person pitches the tent or tarp while another prepares the fire area and fireplace. Both partners haul in the wood and cut it up together.

While one person cooks dinner, the other tends the fire to keep a constant blaze and supply of coals and also does the dirty dishes afterward. Larger groups should be divided into smaller parties with a chore assigned to each.

For a long trip, it is best for the leader to write out a chore list, rotating the tasks so that everyone gets an even shake and each person knows what is expected. Of course, each person takes care of his own sleeping and personal gear.

Making a complete camp sounds like a lot of work—and at first it is. But with experience, the whole thing comes as easy as breathing and can be accomplished in less time than it takes to read this chapter. But things can be simplified even more, particularly in cold weather, if you elect to use a stove and forget the fire. After the tent is pitched, the gear stowed away, and the water (or snow and ice for water) obtained, just fire up your little camp stove and cook away.

There is an old rule about not ever having an open fire in a tent. And it's still a good one. I know that high-mountain expeditioners do, but for them to remain outside in freezing temperatures is even riskier. For ordinary campers, I strongly suggest cooking outdoors. Even a small gasoline flare-up in the stove will damage tents and sleeping bags, which are made of fairly flammable, meltable stuff.

In winter camping, stamp down the snow or scrape it aside with your snowshoes before pitching your tent. If you have and want to use the toilet hole in the tent, prepare it as described in Chapter 6 as soon as the tent is pitched and before the snow underneath has packed into ice.

Even in winter I would suggest cooking outside, if possible. Shield the stove under the tent canopy or with a triangular shield created with a poncho or packs. Stoves do not burn well—or at all—in the wind. If you must cook inside, use either the cooking/toilet hole or support the stove on a piece of fireproof material such as a square of asbestos. Carefully fill the stove with fuel to make sure there are no spills. Do it outside, and if possible get the stove going outside before bringing it in. Keep the gas bottle tightly capped and far away from the burning stove. Let the stove cool after turning it off before you put it away. And make very sure you have adequate ventilation in the tent while the stove is burning. Camp stoves generate carbon monoxide and can kill you in a tightly closed tent.

Prepare and serve the food on paper towels or a square of plastic so that you don't slop up your sleeping bag or tent floor. If you cook on snow, be sure to support the stove on insulating material or on a slab of wood. These stoves generate such a lot of heat that they melt their way into the snow—but not evenly. It is very discouraging to spend an hour melting snow for water and then have the rig tip over just as success is at hand. I have not only had it happen but snarled at Chuck for not watching the pot while I was getting the food ready—and then found Chuck sound asleep leaning on one elbow. Score one for how to lose friends.

### *Animals Around Camp*

The first thing that any non-camper always asks us is, "But what about the bears or snakes or whatever." Actually, small animals are of little concern to the camper, but they can create havoc with your gear or with your dog, if it is along. The pack-lashing arrangement described earlier is satisfactory protection from such small animals as raccoons, porcupines, and skunks.

But in bear country, I keep the food in my pack and suspend the pack at least 8 to 10 feet from the ground. To do this, I lash the pack to one end of a rope and toss the free end of the rope over an extended tree branch. Then I hoist the pack and secure the rope to the same tree or a different tree as high as I can reach. My trash bag is hoisted, too. Bears in the wilderness are rarely troublesome unless they can smell the food, which is unlikely with dehydrates in tightly sealed pouches. But "tame" bears that are accustomed to campers are hell-on-wheels. They know that packs and bags contain food and they'll tear a whole camp to pieces looking for it.

In such areas as the Appalachian Trail in the Smokies, which is loaded with knowledgeable black bears, remove from your pack only the food you are going to prepare and keep your pack high and secured at all times. If a bear wanders near and makes it obvious that he wants your dinner, let him have it and retreat promptly but deliberately to a safe distance. Some people have been able to scare bears off by banging pot lids and cans and shouting. I wouldn't like to take the risk myself. It might just make the bear mad and when a bear gets aroused, it is just about the fastest, strongest, and meanest critter in the world. This is true of *all* bears, not just the western brown bears, which have received most of the bad publicity.

Remember, bears may look cuddly and friendly; but they are *all* wild and, furthermore, they will not tolerate anyone getting between them and their cubs or the food they have decided to have. A number of injuries are caused every year by stupid people who just won't recognize this basic truth. Because some dogs can never learn this fact either, they are banned from some park areas where bears are prevalent—the Smokies, for example.

You can almost forget about snakes. I know, you've heard all kinds of horror stories about snakes crawling into bed with people. The guy usually dies of fright, right? I've heard the same stories, but never firsthand, so I'm skeptical. As a matter of fact, unless you really search for them, you will rarely see a snake even in so-called snake country.

Naturally, you are not going to stick your hands under ledges or into holes. Even a harmless large snake will bite you if it is frightened. And it isn't wise in poisonous-snake country to go thrashing around in the brush or to jump over a log or rock without first looking to see if a snake is sunning or shading itself on the other side. In the South, you will watch how you walk along riverbanks and in ditches or next to an overgrown cutbank that might shelter moccasins or copperheads. If you take these sensible precautions, you don't need to worry about snakes. You are too big to eat, so they leave you alone if you give them a chance.

Your biggest problem—if you have one at all—will be with small animals. In the East, raccoons, porcupines, and skunks can be pests. They are curious and love to poke into anything that is left within reach. The cure is to hang up not only your food packs but your pots and pans, too.

One very rainy night on Hunter Mountain in the Catskills, after a very long and very rainy week, we finally achieved a fire and dinner and our very last pot of boiled coffee. We left the pot on the fireplace with just enough coffee for breakfast. We didn't think any wild animal would be addicted to caffeine. In the middle of the night, however, we heard a mighty crash and awoke to see our remaining coffee spilling down the hill and a very large and scared raccoon going hell-bent for election in the opposite direction. It had just wanted to see what was in the pot.

Porcupines are worse. They crave anything salty, and can make a pile of splinters out of your axe handle or canoe paddles or just about any other stained object. They are also so stupid that they have little fear and must often be driven away from camp by a good belt with a stone or a chunk of firewood. The best solution is to put everything that can be chewed out of reach and to burn food cans and papers after every meal. The cans are then crushed underfoot after cooling and are put in your trash bag.

To protect your dog, keep him either tied up at night at a lean-to or inside a tent. Many dogs never learn to leave porcupines alone.

Every lean-to has its family of mice. And these can be the peskiest of all. They will climb anywhere to get food and will even crawl into your pack and gnaw their way into food bags or envelopes. Since they are kinda cute little fellas, and I can't beat them anyway, I stoop to bribery to keep them under control. I leave some crackers or bread or cereal in a wrapped packet on the lean-to shelf so they will think they are getting away with something. By the time they get inside and get the food, they are satisfied.

Of course, if you are just dying to see one of these animals in the "wild," don't take any precautions. Leave a noisy, tasty tidbit by the fireplace. You will undoubtedly be awakened by a bump in the night and if you move quickly and quietly, you'll get your reward.

I don't know what to say about the following. One bitterly cold dawn on a shoulder of Mount Marcy in the Adirondacks, I awoke to a yell from Chuck that some animal was on his head. I clawed my way out of dreamland in time to see a very scared mink racing out of the shelter while an equally scared white-tailed mouse, which had been munching carelessly on our breakfast cereal, dove for its hole in the corner. Apparently extreme hunger had overcome the mink's fear of humans (which doesn't run very deep in these fierce little predators, anyway), and it had tried to catch the mouse by jumping over Chuck. You'll probably never have the same thrill, but if you do, it will give you a tale to tell for life.

*Dealing with Insects*

Bugs are something else again. They are never satisfied. A good tightly screened tent is the best defense, but you can't spend your life in it; and in the far North and Northeast there is a special little brand of midge called a no-seeum that laughs at mosquito netting. With these nearly invisible little monsters, only a strong repellent—applied continuously—will work whether you are outside or inside the tent.

Body chemistries, however, are not identical and not all repellents are effective, or at least are not equally effective, on everybody. And some people attract insects more than others. I'm a natural magnet, it seems. But even people who claim never to be bothered by bugs nevertheless attract them occasionally. To be as bug-free as possible, there are some principles you can follow.

A clean camp attracts fewer bugs than a littered one. Light-colored clothing is less attractive to bugs than dark hues, particularly dark blue, which seems to have an especially strong fascination. Ointments and oil-based liquid repellents are more effective, in my experience, than are solid-stick or aerosol-spray compounds.

My favorite gunk is an old-fashioned repellent called Woodsman, obtainable apparently only in the north country of upstate New York and New England. It is formulated from pine tar and citronella in a kerosene-type base, just like the stuff that old woodsmen brewed up in their cabins when I was a boy. Liberally applied every two hours or so, by the end of the first day it will repel every living thing, including any human who happens to get downwind from you. But man, it works!

Nearly as effective for me, and a whole lot less smelly, is Union Carbide's 612, either the lotion or the oil. Cutter has a good one, too. The others don't work too well on me. But everyone should experiment to find out his own best combination. With any repellent, the secret is to keep applying the stuff and never ever wash it off, except from the palms of your hands (repellent makes a lousy food condiment). I know this means an end to bathing, but at the height of the black fly–deer fly–mosquito–no-seeum season in the northern states and Canada, you wouldn't stay alive long enough after removing your clothes to take a bath. I feel the same lack of affection for the giant snow mosquitoes that inhabit upper elevations in the Sierra. I swear they can stab you through a down sleeping bag.

After I apply the repellent to my face, neck, hands, arms, and the tops of my socks and calves, I wipe my hands off—this time through my hair, the next time over my shirt sleeves, and again over my pants at the thighs. Gradually, I build up enough repellency all over to keep insects hovering a few inches away. When they start to zero in, it's time for another application.

Some people favor a net draped over their hat and tucked into the neck of their shirt. For me, a net just seems to obscure the view. I find that a white handkerchief tied over my nose and mouth and a white sweatband on my forehead does repel bugs. The light color, I guess. In camp, you can also try a smudge fire, which is made by piling wet grass or leaves on a briskly burning campfire. It works, but you can't cook that way and asphyxiation is almost as bad as insects. Better off to eat fast and retreat to your tent, I say.

### *Toilet Facilities*

A disagreeable subject to many people is the question of personal sanitation. But with the crowds of people now inhabiting trails and shelter areas, it is a matter of the utmost importance that must be faced bluntly.

In lean-to and hut areas, there are usually outhouses. Today they are often not very pleasant, particularly on a hot summer day. Trail maintenance crews no longer make regular rounds with lime, either because the staffs have been whittled down or because the men are needed to maintain the larger campgrounds, where there is now more work than they can keep up with.

As a result, many hikers refuse to use the outhouses; instead, they use the woods around the shelter. Or, they use the outhouse but leave the doors open, giving access to rodents that chew the interior and scatter excrement and toilet paper through the woods. This, in turn, attracts insects, creating a distinct health hazard and also the possible pollution of nearby water sources. Such practices must stop.

One way to help preserve attractive and healthy woodlands is to carry a bag of lime with you. It doesn't take much lime to do the job. Even a couple of pounds will sweeten an outhouse. If everyone did it, the odor problem would be minimized. If two pounds of lime puts your pack in the overweight category, your next best bet is to scatter some dead campfire ashes in the pit—that is nearly as good.

Another wilderness preservation rule to follow is: don't throw trash and garbage into the outhouse pit. There is very little space for these accommodations in woodland and mountain areas, most of which is rocky ledge that is unsuitable for digging pits. Yet, I have seen several outhouse pits completely filled with camp trash and garbage in less than a season. Rangers tell me this problem is widespread. The answer: burn your garbage or tote it out.

If there is no outhouse, pick your toilet spot with care. It should be far away from streams and springs, so that no immediate drainage can cause pollution, and well away from the trail. Dig a small pit with your spade or trowel about a foot deep at the base of a fallen log or rock that is out of the way of hikers. After you are through, replace the soil and tamp it down. I am not in favor of burning the toilet paper after use, since such "cat holes" are often in duff that could retain sparks and cause a fire. Toilet paper rots fairly rapidly, anyway. Needless to say, no one should urinate in the immediate area of the camp or near a stream or spring.

If you are camping in the wilderness with a gang, individual cat holes are inadequate for sanitation. Only a

A wilderness latrine for large groups is dug in a secluded spot well away from camp and water courses. Dirt is piled behind hole to be scattered back in after every use. A limb lashed between two trees makes the set-up more comfortable. Toilet paper can be hung on a stub and covered either with a plastic bag or a tin can.

regular latrine will do. Pick a suitable spot away from the water supply, downwind from camp, and suitably screened by bushes or trees. You can often find deep soil between two trees that are close together. Dig a trench 6 inches wide, 36 inches long, and, preferably, 18 inches deep if there is enough soil. Dig it right between the two trees. Now, lash a pole between the trees about 2 feet above the ground. Some people lash two poles, one on each side of the trees, to make a more comfortable seat for long-term camps.

Pile the dirt on the rear side of the trench and leave a shovel or trowel nearby so that dirt can be scattered in the pit after every use. Put the toilet paper over a stub of limb and cover it with a plastic bag to keep it dry. Needless to say, when you break camp, you will fill in the hole completely, tread the dirt to pack it down, rescatter leaves, and take down your lashed poles.

### *Breaking Camp*

Of the utmost importance is how you leave your campsite. If it is a recognized camping area, such as a lean-to or a hut, you will simply pack up your gear, making sure you haven't forgotten anything. A place for everything and everything in its place—generally in the pack—is a habit pattern that will help you keep your gear together.

Put the fire out dead. I am amazed at the number of lean-tos I have arrived at and found the coals still hot. The previous campers had just walked away, assuming that ordinary fire-prevention practices didn't apply because it was a constructed fireplace. That's how lean-tos get burned down! Sprinkle water over the coals in every corner of the fireplace while stirring the ashes with a stick. Then pour in some more water until you have a soup. Make sure there are no sparks remaining on charred logs by soaking them and turning them over in the soup.

Take another last look around for stray gear (remember that thermometer you hung up behind the lean-to, and the saw hanging from a tree stub). Pack up the trash bag last. Don't leave your trash or abandoned gear for someone else to tote out.

And don't tell me there is a trash pit behind the lean-to. I don't care. The woods are getting so full of trash pits that rangers have given up digging new ones in many areas. The only solution is for people to take out what they took in—and that means hauling *all* of your non-burnable trash home.

In fact, do us all a favor. Haul out as much of everyone else's trash as you can carry. I do. Others do. If everyone did, the woods would be spotless. The Scout troop for which I am an outdoor advisor is a gung-ho backpacking bunch that has an inflexible rule about cleaning up every camping area, trail, and canoe stream along which they travel. In one case, on a canoe trip up the Rancocas River in New Jersey, we brought out almost 100 bushels of junk from six miles of river and left the stretch spotless. This regular chore has won us a great number of friends and has helped to change the somewhat jaundiced opinion that many rangers and outdoorsmen have of Scouts and other youth groups. It has also improved the environment wherever we have traveled.

The last thing is to leave a supply of firewood and kindling in the shelter as a courtesy to the next camper. I don't care if you didn't find any when you arrived. You don't want to be a slob, too, do you? If you judged your needs correctly originally, you will have some left over. It is one of the few ways in which we can put some courtesy back into backpacking—and it sure makes you feel kindly toward your fellow man when you arrive late in a driving rainstorm and see that someone you don't even know was concerned about your welfare.

If you are in a wilderness area where there is no permanent camp, you are obligated as an outdoorsman to restore the camping area to its original appearance. Remember, you were attracted to this spot because of its pristine appearance. You may wish to see it that way again, and anyone else coming along has an equal right. It's not hard to accomplish and takes little time.

After you have struck your tent or tarp and packed it away, destroy your fireplace; put the rocks back where you got them from, blackened sides down so that no one can tell there has been a fire. Then soak the coals thoroughly as already described. Scatter any unburned wood widely, preferably in the bushes. It will decay.

Then dig your fire ashes into the soil or cover them with dirt if you excavated a trench. Rake back all of the duff into place over the 10-foot circle and finally scatter leaves over the entire site. Or, if you removed squares of sod, replant them. Press them firmly into place and water them.

It shouldn't take you more than fifteen or twenty minutes, and when you are through, it will be impossible to tell that anyone has camped there. Pressed-down grass and leaves will spring back in a few hours and your camp will be invisible.

Check the area to make sure you haven't left any gear around or ropes or twine tied up in trees. You are now ready to pull out with a clear conscience and the knowledge that you have done your part to keep virgin woods or a heavily used campsite clean and attractive for the next group coming through.

### *Pursuing Your Hobbies*

During those layover days, you will have time to follow up a few special interests: photography, rock hunting, botany, wildlife observation, or fishing.

Photography is probably the most popular hobby among outdoorsmen. I always carry at least one camera with color film and usually a second one loaded with black-and-white. While adequate snapshots can be taken with an Instamatic or Polaroid, I believe that a good 35-mm. camera is necessary for the flexibility required in shooting in the wide variety of lighting and visual conditions that you run into in the outdoors. Personally, I have standardized on Minolta. I use a Hi-Matic for color and an SLR T-101 for either color or black-and-white. But any other good camera is probably just as suitable.

Although I guess I have to qualify as a professional, since I sell my pictures, I feel like a very modest amateur, so this will not be a learned discussion of photography. Here are some tips I have picked up that will help to improve your pictures.

First, equipment. A wide-angle lens is very useful to capture broad mountain panoramas or to take in a whole camp from a short enough range so that people can be recognized. I use a 28-mm. 76-degree lens. A telephoto lens is essential for wildlife studies. A 135-mm. unit is just about the biggest that you can hand-hold and is good for getting a close-up of that beautiful flower in the middle of a swamp. For more serious wildlife pictures, you need equipment in the order of 200 to 400 mm. or more. Not only is this expensive, but it also necessitates a steady tripod and a great deal of patient stalking and waiting. In short, it is not really for ordinary backpacking trips.

I have always carried a flashgun and a handful of bulbs

for those nighttime pictures around the campfire; but now I have a compact and rechargeable Bauer E161 electronic flash that I prefer. It is good for about forty shots on a full charge. Close-up lenses are a must for the serious flower photographer who wants to crawl right into the stamens.

Your ordinary camp gear can serve as an aid in photography. A sheet of foil, crinkled to diffuse light, can be used as a reflector to soften shadows. Cloth or paper towels, a light-colored sleeping bag liner, or a windproof jacket can make a background, if you want to cut out distracting elements.

For carrying your camera, there is nothing like a camera and binocular harness ($7 to $9), obtainable at many outdoor stores. It is an elasticized sling, designed originally for climbers to prevent the camera from swinging, that replaces the leather strap on the camera. The sling passes around the chest and neck, holding the camera close to the chest. The camera can be instantly disengaged from the restraining chest straps, and the elasticized neck straps actually help by tension to steady picture-taking. The same rig will also hold binoculars at the ready for ardent bird and wildlife watchers or hunters.

Since you will always want the entire party in some pictures, you should have a self-timer, preferably one built into the camera. You can perch the camera on a rock for such pictures, but a light tripod is more versatile. I found a tiny little tripod under a foot long in Japan that is just the thing. It is perched on a rock, too, but it holds the camera at any angle. It is rugged and adjustable. There are small tripods and clamps available at camera and outdoor stores in the United States, too. However, a conventional tripod that is both light and sturdy (if there is such an animal) is okay.

The rock hound needs a hammer, which is a bit of weight. And then he always wants to bring out samples, which can be very heavy. But if that's your thing, go to it. I must confess that I always bring home a distinctive mineral sample from the top of every major mountain I climb and I would lug the two or three pound thing through hell to get it back. Carry a few cloth bags with you to keep the samples intact in your pack.

I don't feel particularly friendly toward self-styled botanists who collect live samples. They always seem to prefer rare species that should be left for everyone to enjoy. For such plants and flowers, please use your camera. But if you want to collect samples from plentiful varieties, gather them away from trails where the scars will not show and only where permitted.

Flowers should be preserved in a proper press. You can make one at home with a stack of uniformly cut plywood or hardwood sheets, each separated by two sheets of blotting paper. The samples are carefully placed between the blotting paper sheets, arranged in the desired position, and the entire stack is kept together with powerful rubber bands. An emergency press can be made with two large sheets of birchbark lined with paper towels. The birchbark is held in place by lashing several sticks together on either side beyond the edges of the bark. But, please, only loose bark. Don't peel and kill birches.

You can also collect wildlife tracks in the woods. It's done with plaster of paris and a few collars of paper. Cut a flattened paper tube into strips about an inch deep and about eight inches long. This can be done by cutting on an angle from the edge of the tube. When straightened out and formed into a circle, the strip should be two to three inches in diameter. Carry your plaster in a tightly closed plastic bag inside another tightly closed plastic bag. The stuff can be mixed in your cup. A soft camel's hair brush is useful to remove traces of dirt or mud from the track. The circular paper-tube strip is placed around the print, and the plaster, mixed rather thin, is poured in and allowed to set.

The safest spot to store the result is in one of your cooking pots, padded with paper towels or toilet paper. It will also infuriate your insensitive partner when he attempts to cook dinner.

If you are winter camping, snow need not deter your wildlife track collecting. Look for good tracks in the snow near springs or along muddy spots in the trail. When you locate a frequently traveled trail, prepare a surface by removing the snow to ground level or by digging up the dirt, crushing any lumps, and smoothing the dirt out. Examine the spot in the morning for tracks.

The backpacking fisherman is truly a happy angler. Many of the remote alpine lakes and streamlets get very little fishing pressure and, therefore, can provide a lot of action. The best gear is a telescoping combination fly and spinning rod with two appropriate reels. You can carry two small plastic boxes with assorted flies and spinners.

I carry a conventional 2-ounce 6½-foot fly rod in an aluminum case that I strap to my pack frame. I carry one reel with a floating fly line and another one with a sinking line. I use them for flies and for tiny lures, respectively, as conditions require.

The rest of the fishing gear you had better leave at home. Waders and vests are too heavy to tote very far and you can usually fish from the bank anyway, particularly above timberline. But, if you have to wade, take off your boots—even your pants—and jump in. You'll never know the thrill of taking a trout while your feet and legs are losing all feeling in a glacier-fed stream until you've tried it. However, I would advise wearing a pair of stockings while you wade. They give a better grip on slippery rocks and help prevent cuts from sharp fragments that could cripple you for a long hike.

If your children are backpackers, you can use a hiking trip as a novel birthday party, too. Twice Pat asked me, when she was thirteen and fifteen years old, if I would lead her and a group of friends on a weekend trip for her party. So, I took six teen-age girls into the Catskills, once on a bitterly cold weekend with snow flurries (Pat's birthday is in October). Despite the dire predictions of various non-backpacking parents, we all had a great time.

We took small gift-wrapped prizes, cosmetics and such, and planned a number of crazy woodland games that filled in the time and gave everyone a chance to win something. For example, one game was a fire-building contest, starting from scratch with each girl gathering her own wood. The fires had to become self-sustaining and a five-minute penalty was assessed for every match used after the initial freebie. Before the girls started, we explained the basics of fire building. Believe it or not, one such contest was won in eleven minutes by a girl who had never camped before in her life or ever built a fire.

We have also had woodland scavenger hunts for various nuts, leaves, barks, types of moss, and so on. And there is the woodland sculpture contest, the creation of figures or tableaux with only what the woods provide, using an axe, saw, or knife for tools. It's amazing what those kids could come up with. On another trip to a lakeside area, we took a spool of fishing line and hooks with bread for bait. Each girl was provided with a straight pole scavenged from the woods, to which was attached a length of line and a hook. The bread was formed into dough balls for the sunnies and perch with which the lake was filled. The contest was to see who could catch the most and the biggest, with a fish fry as the ultimate prize. A flapjack cooking contest to see who can make the most perfect giant pancake is a Sunday-morning tradition.

There are a million games one can think of. And the girls also have fun setting up camp and fooling around. So do boys. Both Rob and Chuck also elected such parties when they were younger. The only requirement is to make sure that everyone has enough warm clothing and good sleeping bags. You can probably borrow extra packs. Don't hike too far, either. About five or six miles is enough.

Whatever you do, though, hobby or party, have fun. It's part of backpacking and of the enjoyment of the outdoors.

# 10

# A GUIDE TO CAMP FOODS

Now we come to my favorite subject—eating. I have been an amateur cook since I was seven and a full-time eater for even longer. So, when I go camping I like to eat from the very "top of the hog." But even if you are not a cook, it is not necessary for you to eat any less well when camping today. It only takes money and the ability to boil water with modern camping foods.

But since the special camping foods are costly, and because a vast variety of dehydrates are also available at lower prices in every supermarket, let's start the discussion from the bottom by exploring the many ways to eat well at the lowest cost. Then we can look at ways to supplement this chow with the foil-packed camping dehydrates.

At the outset I will state that I have no intention of

including recipes or many cooking instructions. Packaged foods include exhaustively complete cooking instructions and even supplementary suggestions if you aren't satisfied with the basic recipe. Furthermore, there are a jillion good cookbooks—both the outdoor and indoor variety—some of which are listed in the book list.

What I am going to do is outline basic nutritive needs and suggest a wide variety of specific prepared foods that can satisfy both these needs and the stringent weight requirements of backpacking. If you want to learn how to cook (a noble objective), then start by reading some good cookbooks and do your learning in a kitchen, transferring your knowledge to the outdoors only after you know what you are doing. Some special tips on campfire cooking have already been given in Chapter 9. More will be given here.

Before talking about individual dishes, though, does everyone know the basic objective of eating? Right, to fuel the body. Every day, you need a balanced proportion of carbohydrates for quick energy and roughage, fats for long-term energy, and proteins for rebuilding body tissue. The fats and proteins, which are the most difficult to obtain in a backpacking diet, are very important.

Also important are a scattering of minerals and vitamins that serve as building blocks and catalysts in body action. Most are automatically obtained from food, but essential salt and vitamin C must be specially provided for—salt because so much is lost through sweat and vitamin C because ascorbic acid is not stored in the body.

Vigorous activity such as backpacking burns up from 3,000 to 4,000 calories per day or even more under severe climbing conditions or in very cold weather. Young people can burn somewhat more because their fires burn brighter and because they are not quite as careful as adults in the conservation of energy.

Now it is not necessary to calculate every blasted calorie

Food stokes the furnaces, but most backpackers keep it simple and fast. High in the Cathedral Mountains of California's Yosemite near Vogelsang High Camp, I prepare a cup of Bircher müsli, a nutritious cereal made with four or five grains, dehydrated fruits, and nuts. This and a cup of tea launches the day.

that you eat. A general knowledge of the values and contents of basic foods will enable you to roughly calculate the correct intake. Every day, about a fifth of the calories you eat should be protein, about a third from vegetable sources and two-thirds from meats. Another fifth should be fats. And three-fifths of your diet, then, are carboyhydrates.

According to basic dietary guides, these proportions can be supplied by two servings of milk, cheese, or butter; one or more servings of meat, eggs, or legumes; two portions of green or yellow vegetables and fruits, one of which should be a citrus fruit or drink; and two servings of cereals, grain products, or rice.

It's as simple as that and does not require the use of nutrition tables unless you are a statistical nut. If you are, the work has already been done for you by the Sierra Club in *Food for Knapsackers* (see the book list), or the U.S. Department of Agriculture's Bulletin No. 72, "Nutritive Value of Foods," where the nutritive value per unit of weight has been worked out for just about any food you could want.

For the ordinary camper, it is better to plan on the generous side, so that you have enough food for the heartiest appetites, which usually increase after the second or third day on the trail. But I should also point out that a backpacking trip is a great time for the average slob to lose some weight. With the unusual amount of exercise, all you have to do is decrease the caloric intake and off comes the lard. But do it carefully. Don't try a starvation diet while you are putting out maximum energy. It will just make you weak. And don't come home from a one-week trip and expect to count the lost pounds immediately. In fact, you may not have lost an ounce. That's because the body pulls fat out of storage slowly, burning carbohydrates and proteins first. But if you stay on a sensible diet, about four or five days after you get home you will suddenly notice that you have dropped five to ten pounds.

A major thing that's needed in all backpacking menus is variety. You *could* get along on a trip with the kind of rations carried long ago by Hudson Bay trappers and by our Army until well into this century. It consisted of flour, dried split peas, beans, rice or hominy; fat salt pork or bacon; salt and soda with which to flavor and leaven the bread, and brown sugar when any was available. But nobody ever pretended to enjoy these vittles, and they are inexcusable in the light of today's wealth of choice.

Just take a look at the master list of goodies on pages 274–281, which are all available at large eastern supermarkets. An even broader variety of prepared foods is available in western supers. Until a few years ago, even a king couldn't eat as well. Therefore, the problem is really one of choice, not necessity. Three basic rules should govern the selection.

First, as we mentioned in Chapter 8, only those foods that everyone likes should be taken. And the time to find this out is before you go, not after dishing up a meal on the trail.

Second, certain laxative foods should be included in the diet to keep your system in order. A steady diet of dehydrates is a bit hard on the digestion unless you lubricate the way. First in importance for this purpose is plenty of fluids, so fruit drinks and soups should be high on your list of provender. Stewed fruit is real dynamite, with stewed prunes ranking in the atomic class. You should plan on serving such fruits at least every other day.

Third, and related to rule number 2, is the choice of cooking techniques. Most foods should be boiled, baked, or roasted, or, occasionally, sautéed. Frying should be regarded with the darkest suspicion because fried foods are hard to digest and a heavy diet of such gunk will inevitably cause a stomach upset.

I recall a recent TV program that purported to show how a Dutch oven could be used on a pack trip, and I settled back to learn something. But the opening shot was of a mess of eggs being deep fried in at least an inch of bacon grease. I almost went into a coma, not just because this is a hideous way to treat eggs, but because any trip that started on this note was bound to end in personal disaster for everyone along.

For this reason, some outdoorsmen refuse even to carry a frying pan. I admit it is not essential, but if not abused, it is a useful tool that can be used in other ways than for frying. In any event, the food you select should be basically light in nature, packed with nutrients, and easy to prepare, and its method of preparation should require a minimum of utensils.

That means one-pot dishes that come as near to a balanced diet as you can achieve. Most backpackers are more interested in the trail than they are in the kitchen, and elaborate menus take time and equipment, which means lost trail time and a heavy load. So save the occasional fancy dishes for the layover days.

The final basic is how you construct the menu. There are two approaches: by weight and by meal. Stand by for a personal prejudice. I don't buy the ounces- or pounds-per-man-per-day concept. Maybe it is convenient on major expeditions involving large groups of people (although I doubt it). And maybe it does provide more flexibility by freeing the cook from fixed menus. But I regard the latter as a disadvantage because it puts a premium on the accurate measuring of ingredients for each meal and on a continuous evaluation of the remaining supplies. Otherwise, as the trip progresses, it is inevitable that certain supplies will be depleted, and the final days will be spent eating a hodgepodge of sugarless tea and cereal and a monotony of beans and rice and biscuits that have been postponed from earlier meals.

I feel that each day's meals should be planned in detail, as in the sample meals shown here. And the food should be prepackaged by meal and by day—complete with every ingredient. It insures that nothing is forgotten and that there is an adequate supply of everything. You can still switch meals around or even a whole day's menu, if you want. And as a matter of fact, if you have been slightly generous in amounts, there will gradually develop a small inventory of extras that make meals increasingly versatile. This can give you a real psychological lift toward the end of a long trip.

So that's the way we are going to plan things here. Once the menus are selected, individual foods must be translated into gross amounts, anyway. If you favor the man-day-ounces approach, you can pick it up from that point. Let's look at things on a meal-by-meal basis.

### *What to Eat for Breakfast*

There are two theories about the first meal of the day. One group advocates the biggie—bacon and eggs and biscuits or pancakes, perhaps hot cereal as well—on the grounds that such a foundation is necessary for hard work. I call such thinking the logging-camp syndrome. It may be okay for a layover day when you have the time to lie around and let such a mass digest. But most of the time, backpackers arise at dawn and hit the trail as soon as they can see. A heavy breakfast puts you in a torpor and makes hiking a chore.

Obviously, I belong to the second school that believes breakfast should be high in quick energy and low in bulk. For this reason, I favor the simplest foods: hot or cold instant cereals, a serving of fruit or juice, and a cup of hot tea or coffee to give you that feeling of ease and warmth while you talk over the coming day's trip.

High on my list of cereals is Bircher müsli, a health food invented by a Swiss doctor. It contains a variety of grains, nuts, dehydrated fruits, and sugars and is high in both carbohydrates and proteins. Sold under a variety of brand names, such as Familia, this cereal is almost a complete food, especially after you mix in some powdered milk. One

10-ounce cup of this cereal, either hot or cold, will keep you going for many miles. With cold water, it is a bit on the crunchy side, but pleasant. Hot water helps soften the dehydrates and turns it into a very acceptable cooked cereal.

Also good are the instant and flavored oatmeals by Quaker Oats that come in unit pouches. They are available in a number of flavors (see the master list). But, if these don't give you enough change of pace, you might also try Cream of Wheat, Farina, Wheatena, grits, or cornmeal mush. You can add wheat germ to any of these cereals to boost its nutritional level and add your own dried fruits, too. When you cook bulk cereals in a pot, add a dab of butter to the water. It reduces sticking.

Then there are the traditional cold cereals such as Rice Krispies, Wheat and Rice and Corn Chex, Raisin Bran, Corn Flakes, and Grape Nuts. As a substitute for, or an addition to, either hot or cold cereals, high-protein breakfast drinks are good. Carnation and Pillsbury both make these products; Carnation, in fact, has a Special Morning drink that is said to have 33 percent more protein and is fortified with vitamins and minerals. A friend mixes this stuff with cereal, and he continues to look pretty healthy.

I generally take my stewed fruit at breakfast, prepared the night before by simmering the fruit with a little water until it is soft and then hanging it up overnight to chill. Because the stuff works so fast, you can get the consequences out of the way before you hit the trail.

My absolute favorite is dried pears, which I can eat dried or stewed at any time. The action of prunes is too violent for me in stewed form, and I can only eat a few in the dried state. But I like the tart flavor of dried apricots and peaches. You can buy these fruits either separate or mixed. Don't forget the possibility of mixing in some raisins. In addition to their laxative action, stewed dried fruits are a valuable source of vitamins, minerals, and simple sugars. But try to get the fruit that has not been treated with sulfur dioxide (put in to prevent molding). You don't need this chemical.

If you aren't eating fruit, a drink fortified with vitamin C is the ticket. There are a number of commercial synthetic orange drinks, such as Tang or lemonade mixes, that are okay. Later we will find a better pure-fruit drink.

For a fast hot drink, it's tea or instant coffee or cocoa. Cocoa now comes in unit pouches by Nestlé, complete with milk and sugar. I favor Tasters Choice freeze-dried coffee for its flavor, but there are a lot of other good ones. However, I save coffee drinking for night. In the morning, I am a tea man.

The only trouble with tea bags is that almost all of them contain poor tea. The alternative is to carry your own bulk tea and brew it. It takes a few moments longer, but, boy, is it worth the effort. There are two approaches. You can throw the tea into a pot of boiling water and let it steep off the fire to the desired degree of strength. Or you can use a tea strainer or ball for each individual cup. With the strainer, you put the tea in and pour the boiling water through it. It helps if you fill the cup full enough to cover the tea in the bottom of the strainer and let it steep a few minutes. A metal tea ball is dunked in a cup full of hot water and is left to steep for a moment. These procedures make a much better cup of tea, if you are passionate about the stuff. If not, then use the tea bags.

One trick I learned in Japan is to combine tea with fresh vitamin C. On one trip, my companion carried fresh lemons, which we sliced into our tea. Then he squeezed the rest of the juice out of the lemon and we drank it with the last sip of tea. Very refreshing. On long backpacking trips, I intend to substitute lemon crystals for fresh fruit.

One important advantage of the quick breakfasts we

have just described is that they require only hot or cold water—they can be prepared while you remain in your sleeping bag. You'll never know how comforting this can be until you try it on a cold and dark morning.

On layover days, you have a wide choice of foods with which to show off a bit. Since pancakes are like motherhood to American campers, you will probably want them at least once. Now, most pre-mixes call for the addition of an egg and milk. The latter is no problem with powdered milk. But you may not be able to rustle up a fresh egg. You can use powdered eggs or ignore the egg altogether. In either case, the result will be flapjacks that are only a little on the heavy side. However, if you can find them, there are a couple of mixes in the supermarket that are complete and require nothing but water. Flap Stax is one, and it turns out good pancakes.

If you don't want to carry liquid syrup in a plastic bottle or buy a maple-flavored dry mix that is specially made for campers, then just take some brown sugar, mix it with a little water, and bring it to a simmer. It makes very acceptable syrup.

As a variation on the ubiquitous flapjack, try some alternatives occasionally: fried mush or hot cornbread with syrup or ham gravy, biscuits with syrup or pork gravy, or French toast. You can also mix a package of biscuit mix with a package of French toast batter and fry the resultant dough. It makes a delicious treat, something like a fritter. The gravies, available in unit pouches that each make a cupful, are produced by McCormick, French's, and Durkee. Go slow on all of these fried foods though. Not more than once in three days, I say.

There are other breakfast dishes available in supermarkets. Bacon will keep very well, particularly if it is unsliced. And it is a valuable source of protein and fats. Save the grease from bacon for cooking. Canadian bacon is canned, but it is such a dense and concentrated source of nutriment that you may be justified in carrying it despite the can. It depends on the length of the trip.

Fresh eggs can be carried for several days even in hot summer weather; if you hardboil them, they last even longer. I carry fresh eggs in the original carton, liberally padded inside with shredded and crumpled newspaper, and with the carton tightly closed with cellophane tape and enclosed in a plastic bag. However, some people remove the shell and carry the eggs in liquid form in a plastic bag or bottle. Others use the special aluminum or plastic egg carriers that are sold in outdoor stores. I've never lost an egg my way, but take your pick.

Durkee makes a unit pouch of scrambled eggs with bacon bits and a western omelet mix, both of which are quite good if they are prepared properly. As with all true dehydrates, you must follow the directions for mixing and cooking very closely.

That's about it, if you accept the standard American approach to breakfast. I have a little broader view. In fact, I'll eat anything for breakfast that I would eat at any other meal, only less of it. In Japan, for example, I had a delicious meal of cold rice mixed with soy sauce, a raw egg, and seaweed, pickled sour cherries, cheese, canned fish, and a soybean curd soup. It was a surprisingly light meal that sat well while hiking.

If you can't quite make that scene, then let me advocate the last bit of beef stew or whatever that was left over from dinner the night before. It is invariably more delicious after sitting overnight and being reheated. In fact, one of my friends insists that I increase my stew recipe by at least two quarts just so he can gorge himself on my special hunter's recipe in the morning. Oh, all right! Stay with your old bacon and eggs. Let's get on to lunch.

*Lunch Is Trail Food*

In Chapter 8, we discussed the two approaches to eating on the trail. For myself, snacking on a high-energy food whenever I feel like it makes more sense than a large, formal lunch.

Therefore, I like a preparation variously called "gorp" or "birdseed" that provides the kind of quick energy and protein that can keep you going over a lot of tough miles. There are many mixtures—in fact, part of the fun is making up your own concoction. My own basic mix is peanuts, M&M candies, and raisins. To this I also add on occasion sunflower, sesame, or pumpkin seeds or soybeans. If you don't like peanuts, try cashews, walnuts, almonds, or a mixture of nuts. Dates may be included. Bacon Bits add an unusual flavor. Corn Flakes, Rice Krispies, or Grape Nuts provide some bulk. I mix the stuff up and put it in a twist-tied plastic bag. Carried in my pocket, it is ready at all times without my even breaking stride.

I also carry a small bag of lemon drops or sour balls. These not only quench thirst, they are also a powerful and instant source of sugar energy that will really pick you up when you start to flag. These concentrates should be accompanied by occasional sips of water at springs that you pass and should be supplemented with a good deal of liquid in the middle of the day and at the nighttime camp.

At the midday stop, brew up a cup of tea or bouillon, either chicken or beef. Bouillon is available in cubes or as a powder in a foil pouch. The powder dissolves better, I find. A packaged dehydrated soup is also good. Lipton makes Cup-A-Soup in one-cup units and in many flavors (see the master list) that require only the addition of hot water. However, watch it. This soup is measured for a standard 6-ounce household teacup. The first time I mixed it up in my 10-ounce camping cup, I thought the stuff was terrible.

Soups that require 10 minutes or so of cooking are also made in many flavors by Lipton, Goodman's, and Knorr. These unit pouches generally make up into a quart of hot soup. My favorites for lunch are pea, vegetable, tomato, and onion soups and chicken and beef bouillon.

You may also want a cooling drink of lemonade or oranageade or one of the other fruit or punch mixes. They come with sugar already added and are fortified with vitamin C; they also provide an important source of water.

If you believe in regular lunches at midday, a broad variety of goodies are available from which to choose. For the first day out, you may elect bread and cheese and fruit and a bota of wine—a tradition with many hikers.

A big loaf of French or Italian bread, sliced thin, and a cheese such as Gouda, Edam, Cheddar, Swiss, Brie, Tilsit, or Port Salut—generally selected in contrasting pairs—go fabulously well with fresh pears or apples. A good French, American, or Chianti wine turns such a meal into a banquet.

After the first day, you will be a little more restricted. Breadstuffs can be supplied by rusk, melba toast, graham crackers, matzos, or Ry-Krisp. Only the last two, though, are really easy to keep whole when toted on the trail. The first four hard cheeses mentioned above keep well for a long time, too, particularly if they are coated with wax or are tightly wrapped in Saran Wrap or in a cloth that is then dipped in melted wax. Butter or margarine will keep quite a while in cool weather. Canned butter keeps just about forever and is worth the weight of the can on a long trip since it is an important source of fats and fat-soluble vitamins. Vegetable shortening, lard, and cooking oils are also useful and a good source of fats.

Peanut butter can be carried in a plastic jar, or you can re-package it in clip-closed tubes, which are available at outdoor stores. The tubes can also be used to re-package butter, jams, and jellies. Jams and jellies and honey can also be bought in unit portions.

Nuts, dried fruit, chocolate, and fruit bars are also natural luncheon choices. Dry Italian sausage, jerked beef, and hot sausage sticks keep for a long time and are concentrated protein. But every now and then it is nice to add a canned meat or fish dish, despite the slight additional weight of the can. There are many possibilities on our master list. But since they do add weight, I would plan on this change of pace only every third day. Don't forget to crush your cans and tote them along!

### *Dinner Is a Special Occasion*

When you finally make camp, you have the time to relax and spread yourself a bit in the way of eating. This may not be a great luxury, especially in the case of high-mountain expeditions, or it may be a gourmet meal if you have the time and talent on a shorter trip. But it is the end of the day and your system has the time to concentrate on digestion to the exclusion of most other physical activity.

For this reason, dinner is the time for packing in the harder-to-digest foods with bulk that are necessary in the diet. Since you will usually be eating rather early, don't worry about going to bed with a full stomach. Civilized eating habits must give way to practicality in the woods or mountains.

As you can see on the master list, a wide variety of dehydrated foods are available in supermarkets for dinners. They are, perhaps, a little shy of meat proteins, but since everything else is reasonably priced, we can afford to include meat from the special camping foods to compensate.

One of the first things you should do while waiting for the main course to cook is to have a hearty cup of soup or bouillon. It is relaxing and provides a much-needed shot of water, salt, and nutriments. You can prepare soup minutes after camp is set up and the stove or fire is ablaze. My favorites for this time of day are onion, leek, mushroom, or tomato soup and either of the bouillons.

You may also want to have a little shot of schnapps or whatever with the pre-dinner conversation. It is also a time for snacking on whatever goodies are left over from lunch. Watch the booze, though, at high altitudes. Over 10,000 feet a little goes a long way, and it's easy to get so bombed that you burn the dinner.

One-pot dinners are the goal for backpackers, because they are complete and save time and utensils. There are a number of complete meals—or nearly complete—already prepackaged in supermarkets.

Among the best are Lipton's beef and chicken stroganoffs and the Kraft macaroni-and-cheese and spaghetti-and-tomato-sauce dinners (even if you do have to haul along a can of tomato paste for the latter). In fact, I rate these as all excellent. Another good line is by Pennsylvania Dutch: egg noodles with butter, chicken, cheese, or beef sauce—one-pouch meals that take only seven minutes to cook.

For the first night out you may carry some fresh meat, frozen or chilled and thoroughly wrapped in a plastic bag so it won't juice up your pack. Traditionally, this is a steak, grilled over hardwood coals and accompanied by baked potatoes in foil and a fresh vegetable (my favorites are green beans or summer or zucchini squashes, or the two squashes mixed and delicately sautéed in butter with mushrooms).

After the first day you'll have to be a little more ingenious. Basic meat proteins can be supplied by dried beef or jerky, hard salami, dried salt fish, or small cans of meat, chicken, clams, tuna, or other fishes.

These meats or fishes are used by some hikers instead of fresh hamburger, with one of the new Hamburger Helpers, completely flavored dinners in several flavors (see the list). You can also try them with Hunt's Skillet dinners. McCormick has a Taco Casserole and Chun King can give you several oriental dishes. Some very unusual taste sensations can be achieved by experimenting with these products, which normally require the addition of ground meat.

Many of these dishes should be baked for best results. The easiest way to do it is in your frying pan, as described in the preceding chapter.

Another source of meat is dehydrated vegetable-beef or chicken soups, which can serve as the basis for a wide variety of stews and other one-pot meals. Vegetable foods high in protein are beans and lentils. There is even a precooked baked bean by Hallmark that just needs the addition of bacon or salt pork and boiling water, and a short bake.

These vegetable dishes can be served as a change of pace from meat dishes and can be mixed with dried soups or vegetable flakes to create a number of tasty and hearty meals. In fact, I rate a dish of lentils, cooked with salt pork or bacon and, perhaps, a carefully treasured tomato, as a great delicacy. I seem to stand alone in this, alas. Several years ago, I strong-armed a bunch of boys into agreeing to this dish for one meal and they have never let me forget it.

Rice, of course, has always been regarded as a backpacking staple. Almost anything you add to it goes well with this grain. If you don't think so, look at all of the pilafs listed in cookbooks; rice has been used as the basis of meals all over the world for many centuries. Many of the dehydrated soups go well with rice and you can add any dried meat, fish, or vegetable. Also, try rice cooked with one of the prepackaged gravies or with bouillon. And don't forget to try barley as a substitute. It is good for a change.

Goodman's has a variety of soups—vegetable and mushroom, split pea, minestrone, and mushroom and barley—that are really complete meals, particularly if you whip up a batch of cornbread, regular bread, or biscuits to go with them.

Naturally, no one is going to waste space in the pack after the first day on store bread, unless it might be the black pumpernickel that lasts forever and is as dense as plutonium. But when you have a little time, you can bake some bread or biscuits of one kind or another. Any of the pre-mixes, such as Bisquick, are fine for bread or biscuits. Repackage the mix in a plastic bag and include the recipe panel from the box. Bread and biscuits are easy to make in camp. Just add water to the mix and form the stiff dough into a cake about ½ to ¾ inch thick, lightly dust both sides with dry mix, and flop it into a hot, greased pan over coals.

Arrange the heat so the bottom browns in about ten minutes. Then prop up the pan at about a 45-degree angle in front of a brisk fire at the back of the fireplace, with the top of the bread facing the fire so it will brown; turn the pan every few minutes to insure even cooking.

Biscuits or higher-rising bread or cornbread can be baked in a covered frying pan over and under coals or in the Dutch oven arrangement, both of which were detailed in Chapter 9. Various fruits and meats can also be added to breads and biscuits for variety. When baking, prepare enough for several meals and carry it along with you wrapped in foil.

You can also make dumplings from biscuit pre-mix. Make a soft dough very quickly and drop globs of it into a briskly boiling stew or soup. The pot must be covered because dumplings are cooked by a combination of boiling and steaming.

Since potatoes are an important staple in this country, packaged spuds crowd the market shelves: mashed, hashed brown, and scalloped. They can be prepared and then mixed with other foods in a frying pan or pot to make a complete meal. Or you can top a stew with mashed-potato crust and bake it to form a sort of shepherd's pie. The same crust can be made with a pre-mix dough. There are also flavored croutons that can be used in soups as a potato substitute. Several mixes for potato pancakes and potato dumplings are also good.

I require one more essential food that will leave many people cold. I am a salad nut. I would just as soon leave my pants at home as go on a backpacking trip without at least one head of lettuce. On short trips, I have even carried mushrooms, a green pepper, a head of cauliflower, radishes, and carrots with which to create a big vegetable-salad orgy at night. Naturally, I also carry a small plastic bottle of dressing (my favorite is Italian) with a piece of foil under the cap and over the threads to prevent leakage. It doesn't make weight sense, maybe, but it is my one luxury. And as far as I'm concerned, I'm only going this way once, so it might as well be first class.

Desserts are not my thing. I never eat them. But they are a good source of food value and most people like some sweet after dinner. The supermarket is a rich source.

There are cookies beyond description (and I do like Fig Newtons). Many people love milk puddings, which are nutritious and easy to make. Flavored gelatins make a light dessert. A favorite with many young people are s'mores. They are created from a marshmallow and a square of sweet chocolate sandwiched between graham crackers. This is toasted and melted into a gooey mess over coals on the grill or a forked stick, and you can't carry enough makings.

My six-year-old Chris just brought home a dandy from first grade. You melt up a bunch of chocolate drops and mix in Rice Krispies, then dig out globs of the stuff and let the clusters chill. It makes a crazy, light confection.

Today a whole range of cake, fudge, and brownie mixes glut the shelves. To be perfect, most require an egg. But we have cooked them without and they aren't bad, just a little flat. But there is a new line of Snackin' Cakes by Betty Crocker in four flavors that merely require the addition of water and a little vinegar.

### *What About Camping Dehydrates?*

Advanced methods of drying foods, particularly freeze dehydration, have opened up a whole new world of eating and weight reduction for backpackers. And although we have already seen that a hiker can get along in the supermarket, that's no reason to reject the newer products.

They are rather expensive. So most people will probably choose to use them as supplements and a change of pace rather than as a sole diet, except on extra-long or very difficult trips where every ounce is critical. In such circumstances, only the special dehydrates make sense because they provide a balanced diet with the absolute minimum of bulk and weight.

There are a growing number of suppliers, as shown in Appendix B, and while not all of the items they purvey are exactly great eating, the quality does appear to be steadily increasing. Some of the foods, of course, are the same as those that can be purchased in supermarkets—soups, pre-mixes for bread, cereals, powdered milk, and puddings, to name a few. Most suppliers stress their complete prepackaged meals in two- and four-man sizes and some even offer twenty-man bulk meals. But most also sell individual items. And for my money, that is the way to buy, getting only those foods that can't be acquired at less cost in the supermarket.

An example of value is dehydrated meats. You can really extend the versatility of your meals with such dehydrates as beef and pork patties, hamburgers, meatballs, ham cubes, pork chops, beef steaks, and meat and bacon bars—all by Wilson's. Others also supply freeze-dried chicken and shrimp.

The individual vegetables—peas, green beans, carrots, and corn—are valuable additions to stews and other dinner dishes. And it is also hard to beat the freeze-dried fruits shown in the special master list. I also have a weakness for the pure fruit crystals of orange, grapefruit, lime, and pineapple juices that I feel are infinitely tastier than store-bought synthetics.

For fancy lunches, Kellogg is now marketing a line of dehydrated salads through the outdoor stores—egg, tuna, crabmeat, and chicken, all with integral dressings that are just mixed with water. And there are quick-mix ice creams in pouches, too. Canned fruit pemmicans and special fortified bars and cookies also pack more nutrition in small bulk. One new line of foods by Mountain House is actually precooked as well as dehydrated. All you have to do is add hot water, according to this company.

Although most of the dehydrated dishes are at least fairly good in texture, to my way of thinking, they lack flavor. They are probably formulated for bland palates. That's one of the reasons why I carry the spice bag noted in Chapter 7. The trick is to prepare the food as directed, taste it, and adjust it by the addition of a complementary

A spice bag is useful for pepping up dishes, particularly dehydrates. Mine contains (left to right), in addition to six containers of spices, various dehydrated gravies; flour, salt, sugar, and pepper in plastic bottles; bouillon and tea bags, and powdered milk. In the foreground are some extra dehydrated soups in cup and quart portions.

spice or two. Perhaps even an added sauce or gravy is indicated.

For example, the Mountain House beef stew is of good quality but blah in flavor when merely heated. However, a pinch of thyme, marjoram, savory, and garlic plus a pouch of mushroom gravy turns this dish into a real winner. A soupçon of wine creates a memorable meal.

It's not fair to single this supplier out, though, because all foods—dehydrated or fresh—can stand help. Applesauce and stewed fruit come alive with a zip of cinnamon and lemon juice or crystals. A chicken dish blossoms with a pinch of sage or poultry seasoning. A squirt of soy sauce transforms vegetables—and so on. Just remember that the love of good food and the ability to prepare it are cultivated. You can learn them, if you wish, by studying basic cooking theory and then practicing and experimenting constantly.

*Food from the Wild*

Our pioneering heritage encourages all of us to believe that we should be able to shoulder a pack and stride forth to live off the land. But for most urban creatures, at the time that they go into the woods and in the locations to which they travel, this is a futile dream.

During the summer backpacking "season" when most hikers are out, most game is out of season. That leaves the backpacker only fish, frogs, and certain varmints. Furthermore, neither animals nor much edible vegetable matter inhabits the heavy forests and high-mountain areas that many backpackers consider their goals. Both types of edibles prefer low meadows with open sunshine where both the prey and the predator can thrive.

That doesn't mean you should give up on wilderness food. A knowledge of wild edibles and the preparation of game can be obtained from the many excellent books on these subjects. Firsthand knowledge can be gained in the field on special foraging trips that concentrate in low-lying meadows and spring holes and swamps and ponds where such provender abounds.

Then when you are on a serious backpacking trip, you can keep your eyes open and collect whatever comes your way. The rule is never pass up likely food when you see it. This may mean a pause to pick berries or greens at the edge of a glade or an hour spent with a fly rod beside a pond or stream.

If that's your bag—as it is mine at times—have fun. But make sure your companions feel the same way about it. If your partners want to climb six mountains, or even just one, they will feel that anyone who dawdles to pick "weeds" when he has a pack full of perfectly good civilized food ought to be locked up or, preferably, pushed off a cliff.

There are volumes more to be said about eating—in fact many volumes have already been said on the subject because everyone has a different idea of what constitutes good food. There are campers who use only basic ingredients, grinding grains and making up all of their own mixes. Others experiment with drying or smoking in homemade rigs. Some extremists eat only natural vegetable foods.

Camp cooks vary from "chemists" who simply follow instructions to the letter to creative cooks like Napoleon's chef, Dunan, who rose to the occasion after the Battle of Marengo when the army had outrun its baggage train. For the celebration ordained by his boss, M. Dunan liberated a chicken and some fresh tomatoes and garlic from a farmyard and, with the flasks of olive oil and cognac he always carried on his belt, turned out a dish so memorable that it lives today (no, I don't believe he also found any eggs or crawfish, as some recipes specify).

My point is that if you eat to live, it's all there in packages for you with the directions in black-and-white. If you live to eat, you will somehow turn every trip into a gourmet experience whenever the opportunity presents itself on the basis of an experience that is far too broad to compress into this or any other single book.

## MASTER LIST OF SUPERMARKET FOODS

BEVERAGES
- Cherryade
- Cocoa
- Coffee
- Instant breakfast protein supplement
- Lemonade
- Orangeade
- Orange drink
- Punch
- Tea

BREADS AND MIXES
- Bread crumbs
- Biscuit and bread pre-mix
- Corn-bread mix
- Flavored croutons
- Graham crackers
- Matzos
- Melba toast
- Pancake mix
- Pumpernickel (black)
- Rusk

Ry-Krisp
Soda crackers
Zwieback

CEREALS

Bircher müsli
Chex; Wheat, Rice, and Corn
Corn Flakes
Cornmeal for mush
Cream of Rice
Cream of Wheat
Farina
Grape Nuts and Flakes
Grits
Oatmeal, instant
 Apples and cinnamon
 Dates
 Maple and brown sugar
 Natural flavor
 Raisins
Oatmeal, regular
Raisin Bran
Rice Krispies
Wheatena

EGGS

Fresh
Omelet, western
Powdered with bacon bits
Scrambled

FRUITS, DRIED

Apricots
Cranberries
Currants
Dates
Figs
Mixed fruits
Peaches
Pears
Prunes
Raisins

COMPLETE DINNERS

Beef stroganoff
Chicken stroganoff
Egg noodles with:
 Beef sauce
 Butter
 Cheese sauce
 Chicken sauce
Macaroni and cheese
Spaghetti and tomato sauce

DINNERS REQUIRING ADDED MEAT

Hamburger Helpers
Oriental dishes (Chun King)
Hunt's Skillet dinners
Taco Casserole

MEATS AND FISH, DRIED

Bacon
Beef
Chicken
Fish—cod and herring
Salt pork
Sausage and salami, hard

MEATS AND FISH, CANNED

Anchovies
Canadian bacon
Caviar
Clams
Kippers (herring)
Liver pate
Liverwurst
Lobster
Oysters
Salmon
Sardines
Shrimp
Spreads
 Chicken
 Corned beef
 Ham
Tuna
Vienna sausages

GRAINS, SEEDS, AND VEGETABLES

Barley

- Beans, dried
  - Black-eyed peas
  - Great Northern
  - Lentils
  - Lima
  - Navy
  - Pinto
  - Split peas
- Millet
- Nuts
  - Almonds
  - Cashews
  - Mixed nuts
  - Peanut butter
  - Peanuts
  - Pecans
- Potatoes, dried
  - Dumplings
  - Hash brown
  - Mashed (flakes)
  - Pancakes
  - Scalloped
- Rice
- Seeds
  - Pumpkin
  - Sesame
  - Sunflower
- Soybeans
- Vegetable flakes, dehydrated

PASTA

- Macaroni
- Noodles
- Spaghetti

SOUPS

- Beef bouillon
- Beef and noodle or vegetable
- Chicken bouillon
- Chicken noodle
- Chicken rice
- Cream of chicken
- Cream of mushroom
- Green pea
- Leek
- Minestrone
- Mushroom and barley
- Onion
- Potato
- Tomato
- Vegetable

GRAVIES AND SAUCES, DEHYDRATED

- Brown
- Chicken
- Chili
- Ground beef, with and without onions
- Hollandaise
- Mushroom
- Onion
- Pork
- Spaghetti
- Turkey

DESSERTS

- Cookies
- Gelatin, flavored
- Pre-mixes
  - Brownies
  - Fudge
  - Gingerbread
  - Snackin' Cakes
    - Banana walnut
    - Chocolate almond
    - Chocolate chip
    - Coconut pecan
- Puddings
  - Butterscotch
  - Chocolate
  - Tapioca
  - Vanilla

SWEETENINGS

- Chocolate bars
- Hard candies

Honey
Jams
Jellies
Maple syrup
Molasses
Sugar
  Brown
  Rock
  White

DAIRY FOODS AND FATS
Butter, fresh and canned
Cheeses
  Edam
  Cheddar
  Goat's milk
  Gouda
  Parmesan
  Romano
  Swiss
Lard
Margarine
Olive oil
Vegetable oil
Vegetable shortening

## MASTER LIST OF SPECIAL CAMPING FOODS

BREAKFAST FOODS
Juice crystals
  Grapefruit
  Orange
  Pineapple
  Tomato
Mixes
  Biscuit
  Blueberry syrup
  Coffee cake
  Corn bread
  French toast
  Maple syrup
  Pancake
Oatmeal with cinnamon, sugar, and fruit
Oatmeal with sugar and milk
Scrambled eggs
Scrambled eggs with ham or bacon bits

LUNCHEON FOODS
Bolton biscuits
Chocolate bars, tropical
Fruit, dried
Fruit chips
  Pineapple chunks
Fruit pemmican, canned
Gorp (nuts, chocolate, raisins)
Jams and jellies
Nuts
Peanut butter
Salads
  Chicken
  Egg
  Ham
  Potato
Trail cookies

DINNER DISHES
Bean pot
Beef almondine
Beef and noodles
Beef and potatoes
Beef chop suey
Beef hash
Beef, rice, and peas
Beefsteak dinner
Beef stew
Beef stroganoff
Beef tacos
Chicken a la king
Chicken and dumplings
Chicken and noodles

- Chicken and rice
- Chicken chop suey
- Chicken pilaf
- Chicken romanoff
- Chicken stew
- Chili con carne
- Corn chowder
- Corned beef dinner
- Goulash
- Ham a la king
- Ham and beans
- Ham and cheese
- Ham and potatoes
- Macaroni and cheese with ham
- Meatball dinner
- Pork and potatoes
- Pork chop dinner
- Shrimp creole
- Spaghetti dinner
- Spanish rice
- Tuna a la neptune
- Tuna casserole
- Turkey supreme
- Turkey tetrazzini

MEATS

- Bacon bar
- Beef, diced
- Beef patties
- Beefsteak
- Chicken, diced
- Ham
- Hamburgers
- Meatballs
- Meat bar
- Pork chops
- Pork patties
- Sausage patties
- Shrimp

VEGETABLES

- Carrot slices
- Corn
- Green beans
- Green cabbage
- Mushrooms
- Onions, chopped, sliced, and toasted
- Peas
- Peas and carrots
- Peppers, red and green
- Potatoes
  - Diced
  - Flaked
  - Hash brown
  - Sliced
- Rice a l'orientale
- Spinach flakes
- Sweet potatoes

FRUITS

- Apple/blueberry
- Apple/cherry
- Apple/raspberry
- Applesauce with cinnamon
- Apple slices
- Apricot slices
- Banana chips
- Date nuggets
- Fig slices with sugar
- Fruit cocktail with sugar
- Grapes
- Peach slices
- Pears
- Prunes with sugar

DAIRY FOODS

- Cottage cheese
- Ice cream
  - Chocolate
  - Strawberry
  - Vanilla

DRINKS

- Chocolate malt
- Cocoa

- Fruit-flavored with vitamin C
  - Boysenberry
  - Cherry
  - Grape
  - Lemon
  - Lemonade, pink
  - Orange
  - Pineapple/orange
  - Punch
  - Raspberry
  - Tangerine
- Meal beverages
  - Cherry
  - Chocolate
  - Coconut
- Milk
  - Nonfat
  - Whole
- Milk shake
  - Chocolate
  - Strawberry
  - Vanilla
- Ovaltine, chocolate
- Vanilla eggnog

DESSERTS

- Gelatins, flavored
  - Apple Splendor
  - Cherry/apple
  - Lemon/lime
  - Orange
  - Raspberry
  - Raspberry/apple
  - Strawberry
- Pies
  - Apple delight
  - Blueberry cobbler
  - Chocolate creme
  - Lemon
  - Pineapple cheesecake
  - Raspberry cobbler
- Puddings
  - Banana creme
  - Butterscotch
  - Chocolate
  - Lemon
  - Vanilla
- Smashes
  - Blueberry
  - Cherry
  - Raspberry

## SAMPLE ONE-WEEK MENU

MONDAY

- Lunch
  - French bread
  - Salami
  - Swiss cheese
  - Edam cheese
  - Mustard, pouched
  - Red wine
  - Sourballs
- Dinner
  - Chicken bouillon
  - Steak
  - Baked potato
  - Green beans
  - Butter
  - Coffee
  - Cognac
  - Cookies

TUESDAY

- Breakfast
  - Grapefruit crystals

Oatmeal with maple and brown sugar and milk
Tea with sugar
Lunch
Tea
Lemonade
Gorp
Sourballs
Dinner
Leek soup
Beef stroganoff
Cookies
Coffee
Cognac

WEDNESDAY
Breakfast
Stewed apricots
Oatmeal, natural, with milk
Tea with sugar
Lunch
Onion soup
Orangeade
Rusk
Chocolate bars
Raisins
Sourballs
Dinner
Tomato soup
Chicken a la king with peas
Biscuits with butter
Strawberry pudding
Coffee
Cognac

THURSDAY (layover day)
Breakfast
Orange crystals
Biscuits with pork gravy
Tea with sugar
Lunch
Pea soup
Ham spread, canned
Rusk
Punch
Dinner
Beef bouillon
Spaghetti and tomato sauce
Brownies and butter
Coffee
Cognac

FRIDAY
Breakfast
Pineapple crystals
Scrambled eggs with bacon bits
Tea with sugar
Lunch
Onion soup
Pink lemonade
Gorp
Sourballs
Dinner
Rice and cream of chicken and mushroom soups
Corn bread and butter
Coffee
Cognac

Saturday
Breakfast
Stewed mixed fruit
Bircher müsli and milk
Tea with sugar
Lunch
Chicken bouillon
Ry-Krisp
Peanut butter
Jelly
Sourballs
Dinner
Cream of mushroom soup
Beef-soup stew with vegetable flakes and diced potatoes

Corn bread
Gingerbread and butter
Coffee
Cognac

SUNDAY

Breakfast
Orange crystals
Pancakes
Maple syrup or brown sugar syrup
Tea with sugar

Lunch
Beef bouillon
Punch
Gorp

# 11

# DO-IT-YOURSELF GEAR

Despite the wealth of new gear available today to backpackers, the time always comes when a person thinks he can do it better. Or sometimes, a hiker wants a piece of equipment that runs to $150 and, short of money, he has to make do with what's at hand.

For whatever reason, the personal construction of camping gear—either at home or at the campsite—is an ancient and honorable practice. And all through this book I've been promising to describe how to make this or that piece of equipment. So, this is it. We'll start with sleeping gear, then tents and packs, mention some of the kits available for making gear, and finally describe a few of the things that can be made in the woods to make camp life more comfortable.

*Sleeping Blankets and Bags*

As I mentioned before, when I was young and when my kids started backpacking, we didn't rush right out and buy sleeping bags. We made do with pairs of old blankets that were already on hand. For summer camping, I still think they may be as practical as some of the low-cost sleeping bags that are being peddled today.

There are three ways to use them. First, you can just roll up in a blanket or two, tucking the loose end under you to keep it snug, and raising and lowering your feet briskly to flip the loose bottom under your feet. But, it won't stay that way all night, unless you sleep like the dead.

The next approach is to interfold the two blankets, as shown, putting the folds on opposite sides and tucking the

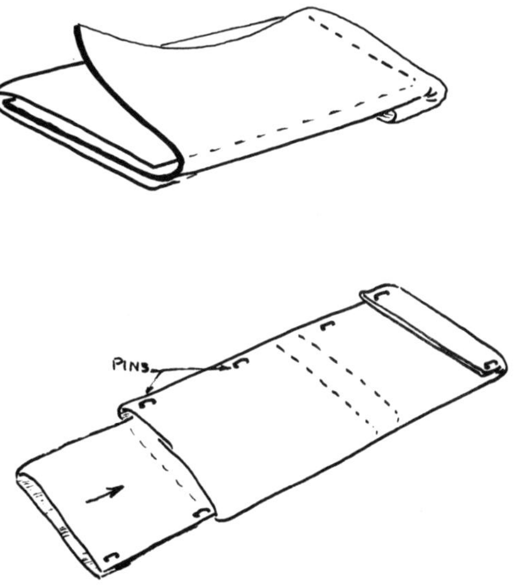


Low-cost blanket rolls can be folded in two ways: a simple interlocking fold (above) and two nested bags secured by large safety pins (below).

bottom under. An advantage of these two methods is that they require no pins.

But with some big blanket pins, you can construct an even better bag like the ones we used for our children. As in the second diagram shown here, you make an interfolded bag, then pin through both layers to secure the arrangement. A few more pins in the bottom fold keeps your feet warm.

With a blanket roll, if you want to live like a mountain man, you will get along without an air mattress or a sleeping pad. Just dig two shallow pits in the ground, one at the hip and the other at the shoulder. Cover this with a ground cloth, of course, to prevent ground moisture from soaking your blankets.

There are limitations to this rig, though. On a wooden floor in a hut or lean-to it leaves much to be desired. I spent a night rolled up in a blanket on the tatami-mat floor of a Japanese mountain hut that was anything but comfortable, even lying flat on my back. And, of course, for modern people, blanket rolls would be acutely uncomfortable in winter weather.

But there are limitations in conventional sleeping bags, too. A bag that's good for below-zero sleeping is uncomfortable at summer temperatures for most people. That's how I got interested some years ago in sleeping-bag design. I was looking for something that would be more flexible, suitable for all times of the year, and low in cost.

Talking over the problem with a friend who is a chemist, we decided that modern technology must have something to offer that could solve this problem. After listing and rejecting several possibilities, we settled on urethane foam in sheet form as a likely solution. It is flexible and resilient, has great insulating value in relatively thin layers, and is permeable to water vapor—a necessity if one is not to drown in his own exhalation.

From there, it was a simple step to visualize a bag made from several envelopes; the foam in the middle, sandwiched between materials that would protect it on the outside and would be comfortable to sleep on inside. The foam envelope would be interchangeable to provide different levels of insulation.

After some further experimenting, we came up with the final solution. It requires only low-cost materials available locally. The outer envelope is made from waterproof nylon on the bottom to help keep out ground moisture. The top of the outer pocket is permeable nylon to let out body moisture during sleep. The middle envelope is, of course, a folded and cemented length of urethane foam in any desired thickness. The inner sleeping surface is a bag created from either a common sheet blanket or, for extreme cold, a nylon-pile material. A few snaps and two luggage straps complete the list of materials.

The waterproof nylon, gray in color, was obtained from Morsan; the blue dress-weight nylon was bought at a fabric discount center. The white foam and the special adhesive were also obtained at a discount house, but they can also be obtained from one of the catalog stores. For my first test, the sheet blanket came from a department store. Later, the nylon pile, intended for coat linings, was found in the fabric outlet. I started with ½-inch-thick foam and later tried several other thicknesses.

Since I am large enough to want plenty of room, we decided to make the bag 36 inches wide by 96 inches long. Folded in half and rolled tightly, we later found, it makes a bundle only 18 inches long and 6 inches in diameter with a weight of 2 pounds—no bigger than commercial bags and half as heavy.

Construction starts by folding the 16-foot length of foam in half, trimming the two corners at the fold into curves that look better and help protect the easily frangible foam. The adhesive is painted on the four side edges of the foam in 1-inch stripes with an old paint brush (see drawing). As per instructions on the can, this adhesive sets up in a few minutes and the foam is then carefully folded into a long envelope. The edges are pressed firmly together to adhere them, and the envelope is left overnight for the adhesive to cure fully.

The second step is to create the outer cover. A 10-foot length of waterproof nylon is pinned to a length of regular

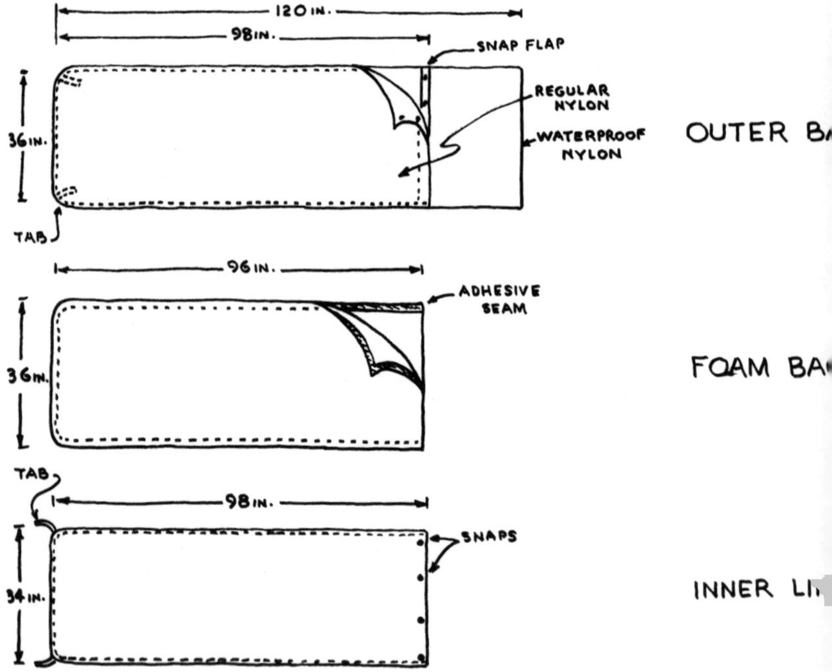


A versatile sleeping bag that can be made at home has three components: an outer shell of regular and waterproof nylon (top), an insulating section of urethane foam sheet that can be purchased in different thicknesses for different seasons of the year (center), and an inner liner made from nylon fleece or a cotton sheet blanket (bottom).

nylon measuring 8 feet 3 inches long; both webs are 3 feet 1 inch wide. The two are folded together along the bottom and sides in conventional felled seams. The top edge of the regular nylon and the extension flap of waterproof nylon are also hemmed to prevent fraying. This extension flap serves as a wrapper for the rolled bag and as a head rest in use.

A flap of regular nylon 2 inches long and the width of the bag is also seamed and sewn by its top edge to the waterproof sheet at the level of the upper nylon cover, as per the drawing. This is later used to secure the inner liner.

The double sheet blanket is then folded, trimmed to size, and hemmed to form an envelope 2 feet 10 inches wide and 8 feet 2 inches long. Then, the three envelopes are put together.

I found that static electricity in the foam makes it almost impossible to insert the sheet blanket or to keep it in place during use without some assists. So we sewed cotton tapes to the bottom outer corners of the sheet-blanket liner and to the inner corners of the outer nylon shell.

Two coat hangers were cut and straightened out and pushed through the seams in the bottom corners of the foam envelope. With the liner tapes tied to the hooks in these wires, two people can easily draw the sheet-blanket liner into place. The tapes are then tied to their opposite numbers on the outer shell, which is turned inside out for the operation and is then skinned back over the foam.

The final step is to install four snaps in each of the top two edges of the sheet-blanket liner, which should protrude about 2 inches above the foam and match a similar extension in the top of the outer liner. The matching halves of the snaps are inserted in the top nylon cover and in the flap of nylon on the bottom layer. These enable the inner shell to be fastened to the outer one, protecting the upper edges of the foam from wear and also securing the liners in place. Two luggage straps secure the tightly rolled bundle for carrying. Since the foam resists compression by any other means than an orderly rolling action, it seems to me that this is a more practical way to decrease bulk with this material than is the stuff-bag approach used for the new foam sleeping bag mentioned in Chapter 4.

Results with my bag have exceeded expectations. I have experimented with several foam thicknesses, always with success.

For me, the ½-inch foam is comfortable on chilly nights. I have been satisfied with a ¼-inch foam envelope on warm summer nights. I have used a 1-inch foam and have kept warm at temperatures below 20 degrees Fahrenheit. The supreme test was a winter mountaineering expedition, for which I created an envelope with 1-inch foam on top and 2 inches of foam underneath. With a nylon-pile liner—and no pad or air mattress below me—I was warm at sub-zero temperatures.

However, I wouldn't really advise this latter rig for backpacking. While warm, it is very bulky since it can't be folded in half and then rolled. As a result, you end up with a sausage 3 feet long and a foot in diameter. It catches on every tree you pass, dislodging a shower of snow from the branches that winds up down the back of your neck.

However, I have used all of the other combinations for more than seven years now, and the bag is still going strong, although much patched and battered. Originally, it cost exactly $14.53 to build, and each additional foam envelope costs less than $5.

### *Special Tents You Can Make*

Having solved the sleeping-bag business, I next turned my attention to tents. I really don't like to sleep under canvas or nylon. I'd much rather be under the stars. But weather and insect conditions in the East—in fact, in most backpacking areas—make it difficult. Often it's nice and clear when you hit the sack, but, about three in the morning, you awake to a driving rain or a thunderstorm. The only time I tried it in the High Sierra, I was almost eaten alive by snow mosquitoes.

So I started to ponder about a way to live in a tent and still be outside. It didn't take long to work it out. Teddy and I decided (long before the commercial tent described in Chapter 6 was on the market) that we would build a tent with a waterproof bottom and a mosquito-netting top. Over this we would pitch a clear-plastic sheet tarp that would normally be secured only at the foot of the tent; the upper edge would be folded back so I could have a clear view of the stars. If a rainstorm came up, it would be a simple matter to lean out and pull the tarp up into place, securing it with two more tent pins. And that's just what we did for a cost of less than $20. This is a one-man unit for a lone backpacker and the whole tent with tarp and

This open-air tent is nylon netting at the top. The base can be made from waterproofed nylon and extends up the sides to protect the sleeping bag inside. Three zippers give access. The tent is supported by jointed aluminum poles.

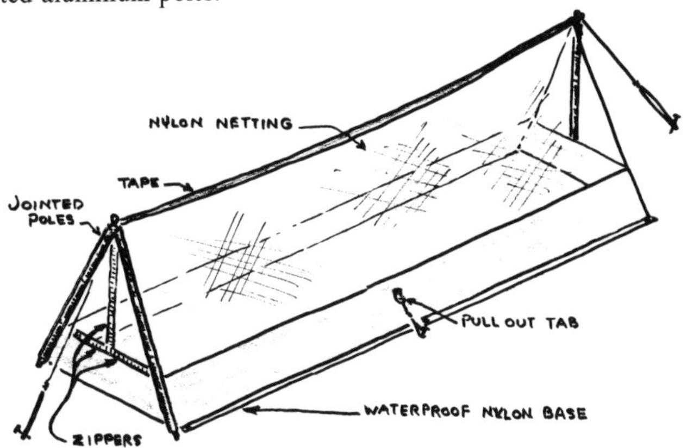

jointed aluminum poles weighs just about exactly a pound and rolls into a bundle 12 inches long and 6 inches in diameter.

The tent is 8 feet long and is an isosceles triangle, measuring 2 feet on the base and on each slanting side. There are three zippers in the front for a full opening. The plastic tarp measures 12 feet long and 8 feet wide, thus extending beyond each end of the tent for full protection even during the most driving storm. It is wider than the tent to avoid condensation problems. The tarp is reinforced at the grommet points with "air conditioning" tape. Obviously, all of these dimensions could be increased to form a two- or three-man shelter.

The waterproof base is made from Coverall, the polyethylene-extrusion-coated nylon scrim mentioned in Chapter 6 as the material in my tarp tent. It extends 6 inches up the sides and ends of this tent to prevent water from getting at my sleeping bag or gear. There are two pull-outs, one on each side, to keep the tent taut and fully roomy. The diagram shows construction.

There are several tricks to making any tent. For one thing, the ridge cannot be a straight line if the tent is to pitch smooth and free from wrinkles. Fabric will sag under its own weight unless a rigid ridge pole is employed. My tent, like most, pitches via cords tied at either end to a tape that is sewn into the ridge. Therefore, the side panels at the ridge seam must be cut in a curve.

This curve is best described by Gerry Cunningham and Margaret Hansson in their book *Lightweight Camping Equipment and How to Make It*, which is a must for any backpacker who seriously wants to construct his own camping gear (see the book list). Anyway, this curve amounts to ¼ inch for every foot of ridge.

I plotted it out on newspapers taped together on the

floor. The squared outline of the side panels was drawn with a Magic Marker pen, using a big T-square and a long board as straight edges. (Check the measurements of the two diagonals to make sure they are the same and, therefore, that your plan is truly squared up.) Then I marked out the successive ¼-inch deviations every foot and was able to draw a very satisfactory free-hand curve between them that was right on the marks. The mosquito netting was pinned to this plan and the lines were re-drawn on the material with the felt pen.

The second trick involves the sewing of synthetic materials. It's not the easiest thing in the world. But I'll let Teddy tell you about it. She's the expert.

"When I made this tent, I used nylon thread because it was the only kind then available with the necessary strength. Today I would probably use cotton-covered polyester, which is even stronger and sews easier. The problem with synthetics is that they tend to overheat the needle. So you have to use a slower sewing speed and less tension on the thread. I use a medium-length stitch that will stretch a bit when the material is put under tension in use.

"If your machine has it, use a zigzag stitch with nylon thread. A straight stitch is probably okay with the polyester thread. All seams should be felled for strength and to make the tent bottom waterproof."

Okay, now you know how to sew synthetics. You can put that knowledge to work in two other tents that must be homemade, too, since I don't know any outfitter that offers them: the forester and the Whelen tents.

These two tarp tents have one great common advantage. They can be heated efficiently with a campfire. They are also simple and light. In buggy conditions, a mosquito bar can be hung in the Whelen tent to improve the situation.

Mosquito netting can be sewn in the back of the forester, and with sod cloths and mosquito doors in front, it would be quite satisfactory, if a little bulkier.

The diagrams are just about self-explanatory for these tents. The forester is really a tapering and angularly cut tarpaulin and could be fashioned from a reinforced plastic sheet as well as not. I would recommend making it from the lightest available urethane-coated nylon, 1.9 ounces per square yard. The complete ventilation from front to back should minimize condensation, particularly if you sleep with your head to the front, as you should. The dimensions given will make an adequate two-man shelter. Obviously, these measurements can be scaled either up or down, but I think it would be unwieldy if made for any more than four people.

The Whelen lean-to, a bit more complicated, is still essentially an oddly cut tarp. It is not completely necessary to have the attached awning front, but this device does give a great deal of added protection in a driving rain.

Some additional explanation is needed about the various tapes and ties on the Whelen, though. The ridge is a rugged cloth tape that has five pairs of ties outside two pairs inside. The outside ties enable the tarp to be supported from the ridge pole lashed between two trees. The inside loops hold gear or a pole from which clothes can be hung.

There are four pairs of ties on the underside of the tarp that can be used to hang the mosquito netting bar. Even if you don't plan to use a mosquito bar, sew the tapes in anyway. In a high wind they allow the tarp to be lashed to two long poles that, in turn, are lashed at an angle to the ridge pole. This creates a very stable and windproof structure. The tapes in the middle of the outside roof are

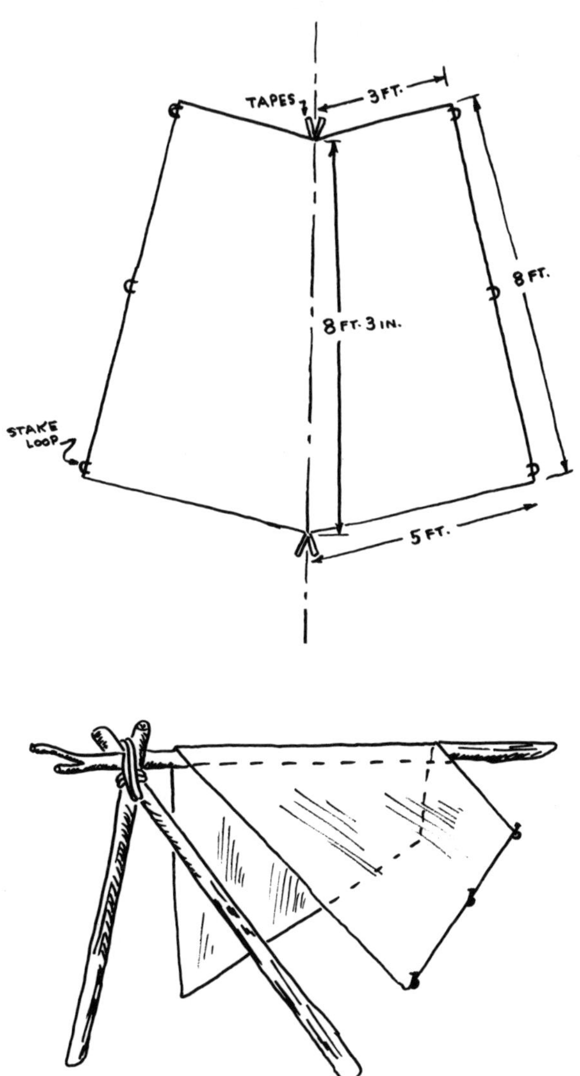


The forester tent, actually a form of tarp, is easy to heat. This size will hold two comfortably.

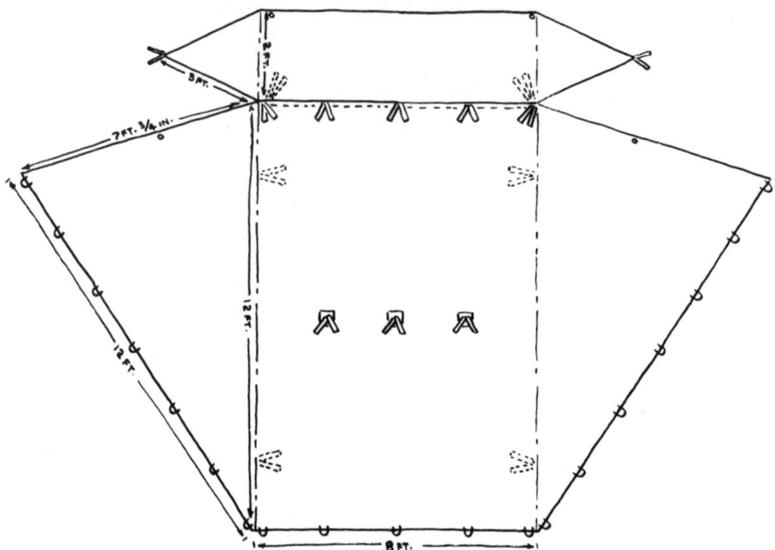


The Whelen tent gives more protection than a simple tarp. It has an awning in front and side panels to ward off rain and wind. This size will hold four people comfortably.

for attaching ropes to take the belly out of the tarp, particularly in heavy snowstorms.

I would also make this tent out of 1.9-ounce urethane-coated nylon. All tapes should be reinforced with patches and the seams must be waterproofed with nylon tent compound. The dimensions given are for a two-man unit. They can, of course, be scaled up or down, but I would think that a four-man unit would be the practical maximum.

One more tent has been promised—a polyethylene tube tent that is a little more practical than the commercial models. This tent was invented, I believe, by Scouts going to Philmont, the great Scout camp in New Mexico. They needed low-cost one-man structures that would last through two weeks of rugged backpacking in the high country of this beautiful mountain area. This tent just about fills the bill.

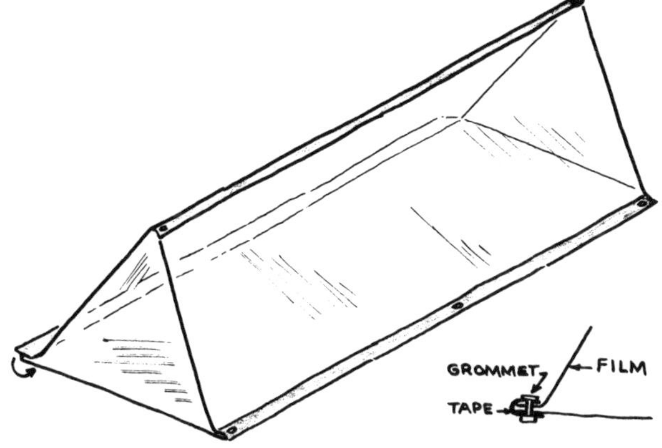


A plastic tube tent can be constructed in almost any size, but generally is a one-man shelter measuring 8 feet long and 3 feet on a side of the prism. The tape, 2-inch gray air-conditioning tape, is used to secure both sides of the base. A strip is run through the inside of the top ridge to support the rope that holds the tent up. Grommets are put in each side of the base and in each end of the top.

We used them, at first, for a group of boys that I lead on an annual week-long backpacking trip in eastern mountains (now all of these boys have two-man mountain tents). But when we were building them, we developed a few improvements that we thought were useful.

This tent is made from a sheet of 5-mil polyethylene film 8 feet long and 9 feet wide. As shown in the diagram, the two sides are folded over and taped together with a strip of 2-inch air-conditioning tape, 1 inch of tape on each side. Then, at 3-foot intervals, the film is folded again and another strip of tape is applied with 1 inch of the tape on either side of the fold.

Three grommets are applied in each tape, passing through both layers of film and tape to hold them together, to form the base of the tent and to form points for securing the tent with stakes. At a spot equidistant from the two base tapes (a little less than 3 feet), a tape is run through the inside of the film tube and adhered to form a ridge line. It helps if it is longer than the film tube and is folded up and over the top of the film at either end. A grommet is placed in the film at either end through these reinforced sections.

Parachute cord is used to pitch the tent and is run through the entire length of the tent as well as through the two grommets in the ridge. Aluminum gutter nails are used to stake down the tent and also to support the ends over poles cut in the woods if trees are not available to tie to. Despite the impervious film, this tent is not too bad for condensation, at least in high and dry climates. In bug country, some ingenious boys cut a full panel of netting and taped it into the foot of the tent with the air-conditioning tape. A split panel of netting was then taped into the head of the tent and tied together in the center with lengths of string after the tent was entered.

The cost of such a tent is a little over $3, and while it

isn't the greatest in the world, it serves a purpose on a one-shot trip. It will last even longer with care.

### *How to Make Frames and Packs*

With the advances in pack frame construction that have taken place during the last few years, there is little technical reason to build your own. But prices being what they are, you may not be able to afford the latest gear. Or you may need an extra frame for such heavy work as toting a chain saw to use in clearing trails or building a cabin. So it's a good idea to know how to go about it.

The classic is the Trapper Nelson or Alaskan Sourdough packboard. Everyone has his own idea on exactly how this should be built. The accompanying diagram shows my concept, with an added shelf, which Nelson (whoever he was) never thought of, for helping to tote a chain saw and a can of gas.

The top and bottom frame extensions and the center bar extension are rounded for securing a tarpaulin-wrapped load quickly with a standard diamond hitch, which can be looped on these extensions without having to thread the rope through eyelets. Screwed-in hooks on the sides of the frame can be used, too.

The webbing straps shown here are the lowest-cost approach to carrying the frame. But I think I'd pop a few dollars more and buy the standard padded replacement straps sold in outdoor stores for regular frames. You will probably be using this frame for heavy loads.

Any tough hardwood—such as spruce, oak, or maple—can be used for the construction. The shelf is ¾-inch outdoor plywood with ¼-inch side panels and is sized to take both my saw and a standard 2-gallon gasoline can (I pile a musette bag containing my oil bottle and tools on top). Heavy nylon webbing or canvas can be used for the

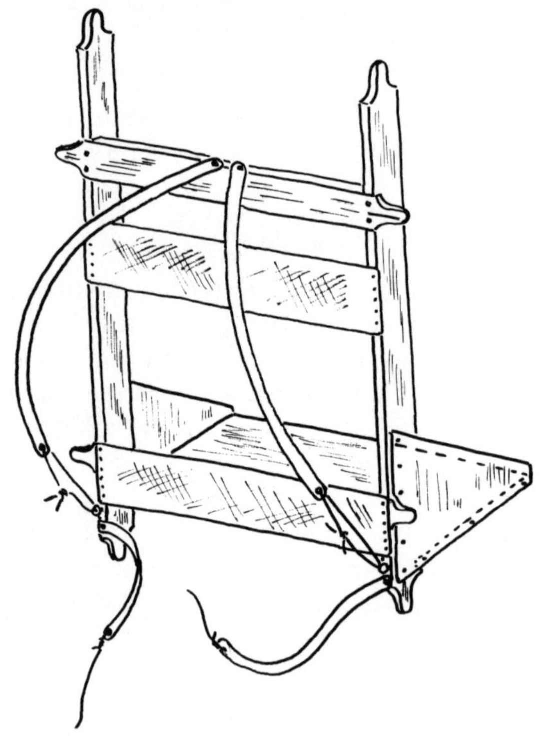

The Trapper Nelson pack frame can be made in many configurations, but should be about 14½ to 15½ inches wide and from 20 to 30 inches long. This one has an added shelf to carry a chain saw and accessories. The back support bands can be either canvas or nylon and are either nailed on or laced around the frame with cord. The rounded posts allow a load to be lashed on quickly with a diamond hitch, but hooks can also be screwed into the frame for this purpose. The simple tied shoulder straps could be improved with regulation pack straps.

supporting bands, which are seamed, grommeted, and either screwed or nailed in place. Round the edges of the frame to prevent the splintering and abrasion of the cloth bands.

The straps are grommeted and screwed in place on the top frame brace and are laced through eyelets at the bottom, which allows them to be adjusted to the proper length. While the diagram shows a tied webbing waist belt, a standard buckled belt would be more comfortable.

There are variations on this theme. One of the oldest is to use cord—today, preferably nylon parachute cord—for the supporting webbing that rests against your back. It's threaded back and forth through holes drilled in the frame. It is light and airy, but can only support a light load. Another approach is to lash a full-length strip of canvas or nylon across the frame on the back-support side, with the lashings going completely around the frame and supporting the load on the other side. This is a very strong rig but rather hot on the back.

The frame need not be rectangular, either. It can be tapered from a wider bottom to a narrower top, or vice versa if you want to put more of the load at the top over the shoulders. A tumpline can be attached for help in supporting the load on portages. But get your neck muscles in shape before you try this for a very heavy load or a long carry.

Either eyes or hooks can be screwed down each side of the frame for securing the load with a simple back-and-forth lashing instead of a diamond hitch. All in all, it is a very simple and easy-to-make frame that can be put together for a very few dollars.

Some people are not satisfied to work in wood, though, and have experimented with frames made from aluminum, magnesium, and molded glass fiber. Magnesium is not easy to find, but do-it-yourself aluminum is available in many hardware stores in rods, angles, and tubing. It is a soft material that can be formed easily.

To bend aluminum tubing, fill it with wet sand to prevent it from collapsing while it is being worked. The problem with this stuff is the welding, which you will probably not be able to do yourself. So after you have cut and shaped your pieces, take them to a shop that specializes in heli-arc welding (welding conducted in an inert-gas atmosphere). It might be a good idea to take some scrap pieces with you and let the welder practice a little at first. Every aluminum alloy has its own characteristics, and he may not be familiar with the stuff you are using.

If you want to work with fiber-filled epoxy, you can get kits from any major catalog store. Frames can be made from light wood, composition board, or even paperboard. The glass fiber is soaked with the resin and is stretched into place, with successive coatings added to build up the structure. A lot of interesting shapes and constructions can be devised with this modern stuff.

Obviously, you can also design and make your own packs. I used to draw up a new concept about once a week. But the modern packs have satisfied me enough so that I have given up trying to figure out new ones. Tomorrow, of course, I may be dissatisfied again and start all over. If you want to try, it is a good idea to cut templates from stiff brown wrapping paper, which can be pinned together or glued in place to see how the final pack will look and perform. These templates can then be used to cut the fabric, allowing some extra for felled seams.

### *Equipment from Kits*

A number of years ago outfitters carried materials and quilted down that could be bought by the yard, but that seems to have gone out of fashion, judging by the latest catalogs. However, as the cost of equipment has gone up—particularly down garments, sleeping bags, and tents—a few specialty companies that sell only do-it-yourself kits for fabricating such equipment (see Appendix A) have entered the field.

I have never bought any, but judging by the catalog illustrations, the prices, and the description of the instructions that are sent with the cut-out pieces, most of this gear looks like a good buy.

The closest I have come to a finished product was at the Avalanche Pass lean-tos in the Adirondacks one bright winter day when I met a fella who was sporting a down parka made from a kit by his wife. It looked just about as good as my Eddie Bauer down jacket, and he wasn't bashful about telling me that his cost about a third of what mine did. If this is any indication of the quality and value to be found in such outlets, I wouldn't hesitate to buy.

One company, Carikit, sells the down compressed in plastic tubes for both its garments and sleeping bags. The tube is inserted in the channels in the fabric and then broken open in place. The plastic, apparently, is a polyvinyl alcohol film, because the pitch is that it dissolves on washing or dry cleaning, leaving the down fluffed into place and secured by the channel construction. Very neat.

## *Campsite Do-It-Yourself*

Whittling is an art that is definitely on the decline in today's hurry-hurry society. But I have noticed in camp that when you put a man with some time on his hands together with a knife, he inevitably starts shaving sticks. It seems to come naturally.

Since this is so, a person might as well be doing something useful at the same time. That's what whittling used to be all about. There are many simple little things that can be created from sticks with either a knife, a saw, or an axe that make life easier around camp—particularly a long-term base camp. Since most of these items are made from wood, they can be discarded when you leave and will return to the soil. The following suggestions are just that. Any imaginative person will think of many more on his own.

For example, a handy table for meal preparation and eating can be constructed beside the fireplace in front of your log seat by driving four forked sticks into the ground the desired length and width apart. Lash two straight poles between each pair of forks in the long direction. Then cut a series of shorter sticks for crosspieces that are slightly longer than the distance between the long stringers. These short sticks are lashed onto the long poles by first knotting a cord around each stringer with a clove hitch placed close to the fork. Now wind this string over each stick as it is put in place close to the preceding one, continuing until the

Woods table created by lashing sticks to long braces.

entire tabletop is in place and finish off with a final clove hitch.

The smaller the diameter of the crosspieces, consistent with the load they will have to carry, the smoother the top of the table. If you want to get really fancy, you can plane off the top of each stick with your knife and notch the undersides to fit the long stringers.

For that log seat in front of the fire, you can make a backrest. Take two heavy poles and sharpen one end of each; drive the pointed ends into the ground in front of the log seat at a 45-degree angle so that the stakes lean against the log. One or two poles are then lashed between these two uprights near their upper ends and behind the log seat to create the backrest.

Backrest for log seat in front of campfire.

A very neat rack for packs, food bags, and towels can also be created by lashing two poles one above the other about 2 feet apart between two trees. The top pole should be about 4 feet from the ground. The packs are lashed to both the top and bottom poles. Food bags are suspended from the upper pole and towels are hung over the lower one. Everything is neat and in one place. And the rig can be covered with a poncho or ground cloth, tied in place, in the event of a storm.

A substitute for the dingle stick, a fire crane, was apparently created by the Scouts. It is a neat piece of mortise-and-tenon work created with only a saw and knife. A heavy pole about 3 inches in diameter and 3 feet or more long is first sharpened at one end. A mortise is cut near the other end with three cuts of the saw, one straight in and two at a diagonal on either side. The wood is pried out of the mortise with a knife.

A tapering tenon is cut in the end of a 2-foot pole of slightly less diameter than the first pole. It is made with

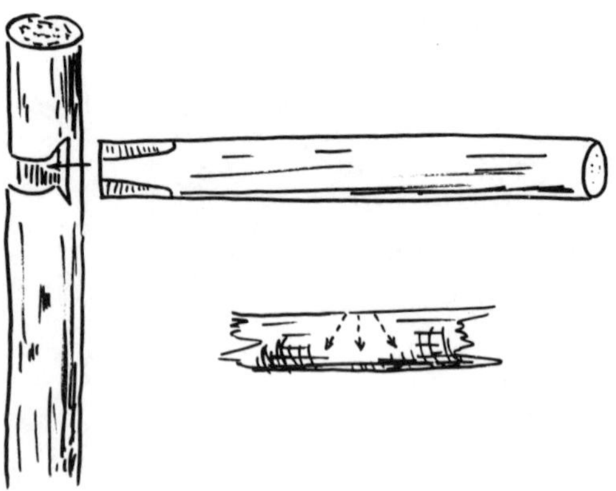

Fire crane from two logs has mortise cut with three saw kerfs (inset). The tenon is shaved with an axe or knife.

two diagonal saw cuts and some knife whittling. It is adjusted with the knife until it can be forced firmly into the mortise.

The sharpened end of the pole is driven into the ground beside the fireplace with the smaller pole extending horizontally over the fire. Pots can be slid directly on the pole or hung from this strong support by hangers.

A pair of tongs will help move burning wood or pick up hot objects. To make them, take a green stick from a windfall of some tough wood, such as maple, that is twice as long as the desired tongs. Shave it down in the center on one side until less than half the diameter is left. Flatten both ends or cut saw teeth in them with your knife to serve as grippers, then bend the two ends of the stick slowly until they touch. A loop of string part way down the handles will prevent the tongs from springing back open.

Makeshift grills for toasting bread or marshmallows or grilling a steak can also be made from green windfall sticks. A small one is made from a forked stick, the end of which has been laced back and forth with wire. A larger grill can be made for meats from a larger fork and more wire. Or a long and limber branch can be bent into a loop and fastened to itself with wire. Next weave green twigs in cross directions to form a lattice. A very green and poor-burning wood is best for this device, and it must be kept a sensible distance above the coals and watched closely for burning.

However, we once made such a grill from aspen, which burns very well, when we were encamped at Long Lake in the Colorado Rockies on a fishing trip. We had a couple of steaks we wanted to grill—and we managed to do them to perfection before the grill caught fire. Since there were no stones on this little spruce hummock, we used a hunter's fire and made a tiny bed of coals between the two logs with spruce wood so old and weathered it had no pitch left in it, an exception to the rule that softwood makes a poor cooking fire.

One tool that Teddy always has me make as soon as we get to a lean-to is a broom so that she can clean up the area. This is created quickly from a straight pole about 5 feet long, to which is bound a large handful of limber twigs, or better, a handful of evergreen boughs secured from a windfall. A rake can be made by using slightly larger twigs, spreading them apart, and lashing each one to a crosspiece.

Woodland toothbrushes, which are made from soft twigs of birch, were a favorite with our kids when they were little. The end of a 3-inch twig is barked and many longitudinal slices are made with a knife in the end until the wood is reduced over a length of about a ½ inch to a mass of soft bristles. We always used salt for brushing instead of toothpaste, and the kids got a big kick out of the departure from the usual.

Hangers for clothes can be made from a stick that is bowed and held in place with a lashed cross stick. It is hung up with either a piece of string or is hooked into the fork of a branch. Pot hangers or clothes hooks can also be made from old wire coat hangers at home or from the

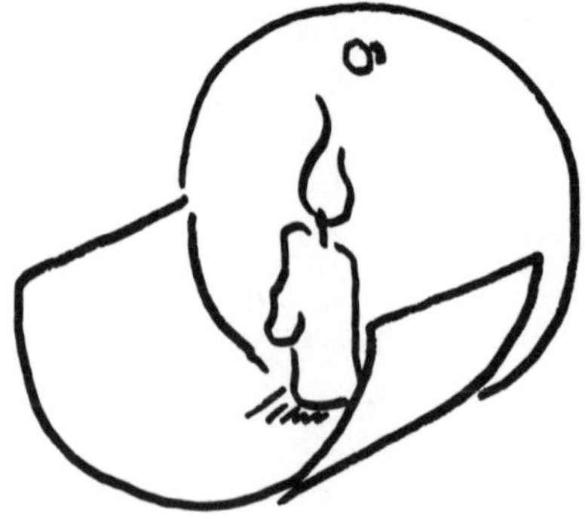

Candle holder cut from can prevents drips, and reflects light.

inevitable length of heavy wire that you always seem to find on the trail. These are handy tools that I don't mind leaving behind at a lean-to.

If you propose to burn a candle in a hut or a lean-to for light, then you might make a candle holder to prevent the charring of the logs or the wax from spilling. It's easily done by cutting down a small tin or aluminum can. First make a straight cut from top to bottom with a swift blow from your axe, leaving the bottom intact; then use your can opener to cut the can into a scoop shape.

The can is nailed in place or fastened by a hardwood splinter, which is pushed through a hole in the base of the can and tapped firmly into a slit made in a back log with your knife. The metal interior of the can reflects more light and shields the flame from drafts, and the bottom catches the dripping wax.

Advanced whittlers can also make forks and spoons from such softwoods as birch. Or you can turn out chopsticks from hardwood, if you like to eat oriental style.

On days when you may be pinned down with the kids in a tent, lean-to, or hut by a major storm, it is amazing what a quickly whittled toy will do to keep the tads entertained. One such time in the Smokies, I made Pat a little doll; a small canoe with seats and a paddle was turned out for Chuck, and Rob had a small mechanized army of cannon and tanks—all whittled from handy softwood kindling. I don't remember that it took me more than an hour, and the kids were happy all day while Teddy and I read paperbacks that we always bring along for such contingencies.

These few projects suggest many more. But since backpacking is primarily a game of movement, time for such diversions is somewhat limited and their usefulness is restricted unless you practice the base-camp day-trip strategy.

# 12

# WHAT TO DO IN AN EMERGENCY

Civilized people tend to get a little careless at home because they know that the police, the family doctor, and the emergency room at the local hospital are always within quick call. This type of thinking—or lack of it—just has to change when you get into the woods. Even a few miles from the road, you are your own rescue party.

For this reason, considerations of safety should not only always be uppermost in the mind of the leader, but also with every member of the party. This cannot be stressed too strongly. Because I love the wilderness, I hate to tell horror stories to scare people into acting sensibly. But I have seen too many foolish accidents not to realize that people must be made to respect natural forces.

Dire injury is not the only hazard on a backpacking trip. A severe sunburn, a twisted ankle, or a badly blistered foot may not endanger the life of the hiker under normal circumstances, but any of these "accidents" may so incapacitate him that continuing the trip becomes impossible. Then at least one other person must abort his trip, too, to accompany the injured party back to civilization. These injuries are, in fact, far more common than major disasters and are to a great extent preventable.

It is not the intention of this chapter to deal exhaustively with the subject of first aid. There are several top-notch books on the subject that are listed in the book list. I urge you to get an appropriate text and study it. Then, restudy it every year or so. A major problem in the woods is that too few people learn the basic elements of first aid for either major or minor injuries and, therefore, are unprepared to do the right thing when an emergency arises.

A basic definition of an accident is that it happens when it is not expected, perhaps on a sunny afternoon stroll in a nearby woodland. You are not keyed up there, as you might be on a major expedition in remote and possibly dangerous territory.

What I want to do is describe the most common accidents that happen on camping trips and how they can be avoided or dealt with. I hope this will impress you with the need for deeper knowledge. We will first describe the basic first-aid kits that should be carried by backpackers. Then, the most common hazards, in my experience, are an upset stomach, blisters, sprains, broken bones, burns, cuts, splinters, a foreign object in the eye, insect bites, and frostbite or "exposure."

### *The Basic First-Aid Kits*

I believe that every hiking party should carry two fundamental sources of first-aid supplies. Each hiker ought to have his own little kit to take care of minor injuries and to hold his personal supply of special medicines or favorite patent remedies. This takes the pressure off the main first-aid kit, which is carried by the leader.

The personal kit should have a few adhesive bandages, a couple of sterile gauze pads, some antiseptic such as first-aid cream or Merthiolate, a few aspirin, and, of course, any special medication, such as allergy pills, that the bearer has to take. It can also contain a small vial of Alka-Seltzer, Kaopectate, or Milk of Magnesia, whatever your preference is for settling an upset stomach. In snake country, a compact snake-bite kit, such as the Cutter unit, which all packs inside a small rubber suction cup, can be tucked in, too. The whole bit can be packed into a Band-Aid can. There are also first-aid kits on the market that are this size.

For the group kit, more equipment is needed. I will use mine as an example, because I think it is a good one. I carry a Sportsman first-aid kit by Johnson & Johnson that comes in a plastic box, to which I have made a few additions. The J&J kit, as bought, has Band-Aids, gauze pads in two sizes, a roll of gauze bandage, a triangular bandage, a snake-bite kit, ammonia ampules, first-aid cream, bottles of salt, dextrose, and halazone tablets, tweezers, and scissors. It also has a preposterous little information card on survival and a very good little booklet on first aid.

To this, for the ordinary trip, I have added a tin of aspirin, a needle, some adhesive tape wound on a toothpick to take up less space, some moleskin, a long elastic bandage, and a small bottle of Kaopectate. The last two are not in the plastic first-aid kit, but are in the upper right-hand pocket of my pack.

I have been able to get by with this collection very well in several hairy situations. Of course, if you are going on a

My first-aid kit for the trail is a standard model with a few additions. On the rock at the left is moleskin; in front of it is a roll of elastic bandage and a small bottle of Kaopectate. Behind it is a tube of first-aid cream and to the right are ammonia ampules, adhesive tape on toothpicks, salt and dextrose tablets, and a bottle of halazone. In the kit lid are dressings, tweezers, and scissors, and a needle is taped to the lid. Also available are a triangular bandage, Band-Aids, aspirin, rolled bandage, and a snake-bite kit.

long expedition in remote country, you will have to carry a much bigger medical kit that will include sutures and antibiotics. But this is beyond the scope of first aid.

The first requirement in being prepared for any eventuality is to check out your first-aid kit every time you prepare for an outing. It won't do you any good if you haven't replenished supplies—or if it got dropped into a pool of water which soaked and ruined everything in the kit, as happened to a friend of mine—or if someone in the house just happened to need some bandages and took them out of the camping kit because there weren't any in the home medicine chest. So check out your kit to make sure you have everything you need.

In good shape? Okay, on to actual cases.

*My Stomach Hurts!*

No matter how you boil your water and dishes, no matter that you serve food so light and easily digestible that it all but floats off the plate, some fink will eventually come down with a stomachache. It results, in almost every case, from bowels that are too loose or not loose enough. How's that for a diagnosis!

If too loose, trot out your little bottle of Kaopectate. Dosage: two big tablespoons, with the sufferer's spoon. Perhaps another dosage will be necessary in a few hours. That should take care of his trots.

If nausea accompanies a stomach upset, I have found that thinning out Kaopectate with water has a very settling effect. Feed it to the patient a spoonful at a time. He may toss up the first couple, given an hour or so apart, but usually the third will stay down. Keep the patient in bed until you are sure it is just a "little bug" and nothing more serious.

If one person comes down with such a bug, keep his utensils separate from everyone else's. If two people have the same symptoms, gather up all the utensils and pots and pans and boil them thoroughly for ten minutes. It could be sloppy dishwashing practices that have come home to roost, or it may be a contagion that can be transmitted from person to person through the cookware.

If you follow the rules of feeding that we discussed in Chapters 9 and 10, constipation should not be a problem. But humans are ornery critters, so you may have one who turns cranky. Here's where you trot out a bottle of Milk of Magnesia, if you have it. Personally, I believe in a strong infusion of stewed prunes. Mash them up as they simmer and give him a big glass of the dark brown liquid from the pot. I've never seen any constipation that this won't handle.

Just make sure that the stomach pains stem from either of the two causes mentioned above. If the pain occurs with normal bowels and is localized in an area that is sore to the touch, then you had better get the victim to a doctor, because it could be appendicitis.

### *My Feet Are Killing Me!*

We have already described in Chapter 2 how to avoid blisters on the feet. There is no improvement on well-fitting stockings and boots. But even so, a blister will occasionally develop because of the severity or length of the trip or because the feet were too tender at the start.

If an irritation develops, try to catch it before it becomes a blister. Stop immediately and remove both boots and stockings. Wash the feet and dry them completely. Cover the irritated area with a piece of moleskin, which is self-adhesive and is obtainable at any drugstore. A sizable piece should always be in the first-aid kit. Then put on a pair of fresh, dry stockings and try again.

If in spite of all precautions a small blister develops, try to catch it before it bursts. The area can be padded with a piece of moleskin in which a hole has been cut that is slightly larger than the blister. This is then covered with another solid piece of moleskin. Hopefully, this will carry you until you get home or to camp.

If a large blister develops or a small one must be taken care of, relieve the blister by carefully draining it. This is accomplished by sterilizing a needle in a match flame, holding the needle high in the hottest part of the flame so that it doesn't get coated with carbon. Pierce the blister carefully near the base after sterilizing the skin in the immediate area with whatever antiseptic you have with you, or with a good soap-and-hot-water washing if you are in camp. Drain the blister carefully by pressing it with a sterile gauze pad. Then cover the area with a piece of moleskin.

Blisters can also occur on hands, particularly if you live a normally sedentary city life and are suddenly called upon to use an axe or saw to any great extent. The best protection is a good pair of deerskin or horsehide gloves worn at all times when you are working. Get a pair that are smooth on the inside, without rough seams. Naturally, such gloves are a bit more expensive, but gloves with rough interiors are worse than no gloves at all. If you should start to get an irritation, stop before it becomes a blister and pad the area with a gauze pad covered with several smoothly applied strips of adhesive tape. A conventional Band-Aid is almost useless in this area because it tends to roll up. However, some of the new plastic-strip bandages hang on a lot tighter and are fine.

If you develop and break a blister on your hands—usually between the thumb and forefinger or on the palm—it is very prone to infection because of the grime to which hands are constantly exposed. Therefore, it is particularly important to clean the area thoroughly with soap and water and an antiseptic. Cover the wound with a clean bandage and replace it as often as necessary.

Broken nails and hangnails are very common on feet as well as hands. A close trimming of the nails both at home and on the trail will help. Toenails should be cut squarely, fingernails rounded. Fingernails, in particular, tend to get dry and brittle with exposure and break readily, generally down into the quick.

If this should happen, don't just tear or bite off the loose nail. This will almost surely tear it deeper, and wounds in this area are very susceptible to infection. Trim the nail as carefully and as closely as possible. Treat the area with an antiseptic, then cover it with an adhesive bandage or a strip of adhesive that will protect the loose edges from tearing any more.

### *I Think I Sprained It!*

Far too common are sprained ankles, and they can be as disastrous to a backpacking trip as a broken bone. In fact, such an injury usually takes longer to heal. To avoid sprains, constantly watch where you are walking. You are carrying a heavy load on your back, so never allow yourself to be caught off-balance. Don't jump over an obstacle or from rock to rock. Step over or around them. Watch the trail sharply for loose rocks, and redouble your attention on talus or scree slopes. If you want to look around at the view or at wildlife, stop while you do it.

If in spite of this care you stumble, let's hope you only suffer a minor sprain. The most modern treatment is not heat, but an icy bath for several days. Try to get your ankle into a cold stream or spring or a snowbank as soon as possible and soak it for an hour or so. Repeat this treatment several times a day as the opportunity arises. If snow is available, make a cold compress with it in a triangular bandage. Between times, support the injured ankle with an elastic bandage.

You can also use your triangular bandage for support. Fold it into a narrow band and pass it under the instep and up around the heel, crossing the ends over and bringing them around to the front of the ankle. Then cross the ends again and loop them through that portion of the bandage that extends up from instep to heel. Pull the ends back up to the front of the ankle and pull them snug enough to support the ankle but not so tight as to cut off circulation. Finish off with a square knot.

An ankle bandage is made by folding a triangular bandage into a narrow band. It is passed under the instep and around the heel (1). Then the ends are crossed over the front of the ankle and looped through the instep portion (2). The ends are then brought back up to the front where they are pulled tight and tied off (3).

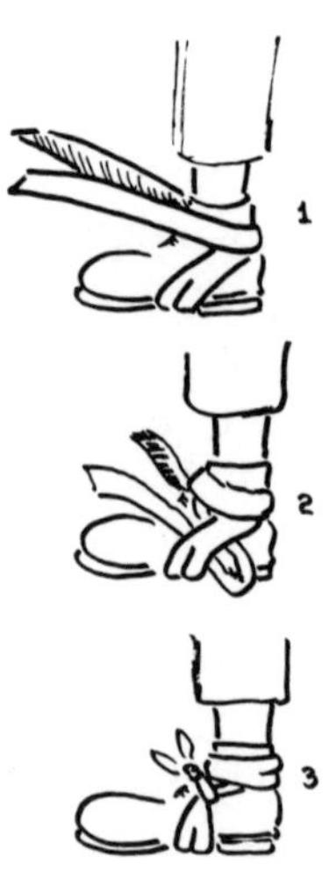


These measures are useful, though, only in the case of a minor sprain, and continued walking on such an injury should be done with great caution to avoid a second wrench that can totally incapacitate a hiker.

A severe sprain should be treated as a serious injury. In such an unfortunate circumstance, cold compresses are of course immediately applied, the joint is immobilized, and the hiker will have to be evacuated by some means.

*Evacuation Techniques*

The best answer is a stretcher, and one can be built in the woods from available materials. It isn't as hard as it sounds. First cut two sturdy, *green* saplings (I'll forgive you just this once!) about 14 feet long with a minimum diameter of 1½ to 2 inches. Then saw off about 3 feet from each pole for cross braces; lash the cross braces between the poles about 7 feet apart, leaving 2-foot handles at either end. Wind the body of the stretcher with a long rope or several short ones, zigzagging close together from pole to pole.

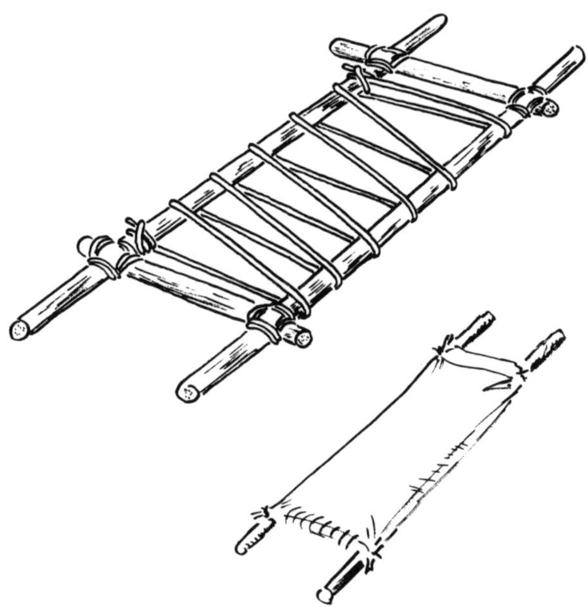

A trail stretcher is created by lashing four branches together, as shown, and then winding a rope around them to create a base. Finally, a sleeping bag is lashed over the framework.

If you don't have enough rope, use what you have and also lash a double-folded ground cloth over the frame. Or remove the bottom corner seams from a sleeping bag (the cheapest bag) and slide the frame through the inside of the bag, lashing it at the four corners. For a long trail evacuation, I prefer these stronger rigs to the folded-blanket routine (folded over the poles in thirds and held in place by the patient's weight). But test any stretcher with the full weight of a well person before putting the victim to the test.

Next put the injured party's sleeping bag on the stretcher and bunch the corners to tie them to the handles with short cords. The victim should be put in the bag and gently but firmly tied to the stretcher with soft ropes or spare clothing. If you accidentally roll him off the stretcher while handling him on rough trails you may cause a worse injury.

The whole thing can be accomplished in no more than fifteen minutes by an experienced team. I know, because three years ago I had to lead the evacuation of a boy in shock from a badly broken arm on such a rig for eight miles from behind Mount Marcy in the Adirondacks.

The evacuation is not fast, though. Carrying a dead weight over rough trails and trying to do it with both speed and gentleness is extremely exhausting. If there are only two stretcher-bearers, it may be very slow. Four are better, one for each handle. Hell, a dozen are not too many! Then you can take turns. But whatever, hang in there.

If there are only two of you to begin with, you've got trouble. You may be able to cut a pair of crutches on which your partner can hobble, but this isn't very satisfactory. The crotch must be just the right height and must be padded with some clothing. The limb stub for the handgrip must also be just the right distance from the crotch. If not, the user may suffer pinched nerves in the armpit, a "crutch palsy" that can be as damaging as anything else that's wrong with him.

An alternative is to drag the victim out on a travois, a triangular Indian device that is made from two long poles lashed together at one end and held apart halfway down by a lashed crosspiece. The victim can sit on the crosspiece or can recline in a sling made with a ground cloth or sleeping bag lashed above and below the crosspiece. The lashed end of the poles is supported on the shoulders of the "horse" who pulls it. This device will work only on broad trails, though, and is a rough ride that may be too much for the victim.

During our first winter camping expedition, Chuck and I used to theorize about what we would do if I were injured. We decided we could load me in a sleeping bag and put it on top of the other one for insulation, then put everything in a plastic ground cloth, tied at both ends to form a sort of boat. Plastic slides very well over snow. It works, but the ride is too rough for a person suffering from either broken bones or a head injury.

Another alternative is to cache the packs and support or carry the injured hiker out on your back. Lacking every other possibility, you will have to leave the injured person at an emergency camp with everything needed for life support within reach and go for help. But these are all desperate measures that underscore the necessity for avoiding injuries, as well as the advisability of hiking in groups of three or more people.

### *Other Twists and Strains*

An equally bad accident on the trail is a twisted knee. As the possessor of two bad knees suffered in ancient skiing accidents, I am particularly conscious of this

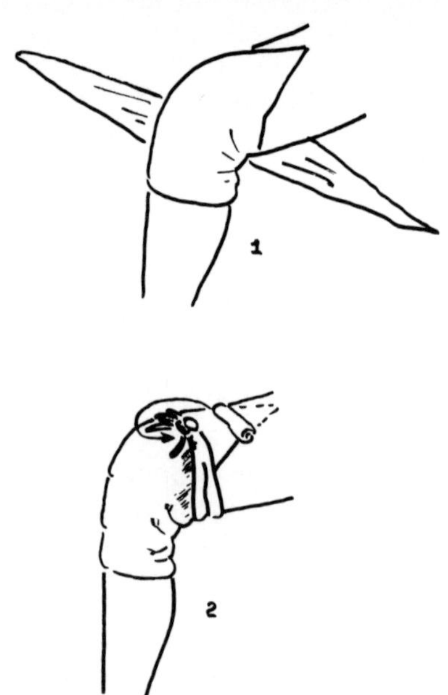


A knee bandage starts with triangular bandage laid on top of leg, with the point on the thigh. The ends are wrapped around behind the knee (1) and then are tied above knee. Finally, the point is rolled down and tucked in under the tied ends (2).

possibility. Avoid twisting turns with the feet while carrying a heavy load that put undue strain on the knees. Be particularly careful at muddy or icy spots, where a slip can cause such a rotation—or can spread the legs suddenly and drastically to throw a strain on groin muscles and tendons.

Little can be done on the trail to relieve the latter. Only rest will work. A twisted knee needs the same care, but you can pack it in cold compresses and support it. The elastic bandage is the best. But if you are already using that for another disaster, try the triangular bandage. The broad, folded edge is placed around the leg below the knee with the pointed end above the knee on the thigh. Bring the loose ends around the leg behind the knee, cross them, and bring them around again above the knee, tying them off with a square knot. Then roll the pointed end down and tuck it under the knotted portion. Don't make this bandage so tight it cuts off circulation.

Other strains and sprains can be acquired in arms and shoulders by unaccustomed exercise, such as sawing and chopping, if you are not in shape for it. Take it easy when you first start to work, particularly if it is cold. Take easy strokes and don't bear down with all your strength when it isn't necessary. If a strain occurs despite these precautions, immobilize the arm or shoulder with a sling, perhaps even binding the arm to the body with a strip bandage across the chest and back. In severe cases, the victim will not be able to carry a pack or, at the most, will only be able to tote a minimum weight. So everyone else has to shoulder the extra load.

### *I Think It's Broken!*

Which brings us to the ugly subject of broken bones. When a person falls, you may not always know whether anything is broken or not. Not every break is a compound fracture with a piece of splintered white bone sticking up through the wound to telegraph itself. And if only one bone is broken in an arm or leg, the limb may not be displaced.

For these reasons, keep the victim lying down while you examine things methodically. The pause also gives him time to recover his senses and get over the shock and impact of the fall. Gradually, feel over the various limbs, neck, and head. Ask for pain and try to localize areas that hurt very badly. Ask him to wiggle this and that. Even then, you may not be sure. Bones can crack but not separate until a further stress is put on them. A broken

Severe injuries, such as a suspected broken back or multiple fractures, must be immobilized completely before evacuation. Create a solid stretcher with cross branches and then bind the patient to the stretcher to prevent any movement. At least three people should lift the patient onto this stretcher without allowing his body to twist or flex.

back is not always signaled by paralysis in the extremities. Internal injuries may have no external symptoms.

The first judgment is the severity of the fall. How far was it and how did the victim land, and on what? Then, if he is in deep shock with no visible wound, or is unconscious, or has an obvious head wound and is scatterbrained, or has paralysis of the fingers or toes—treat for a possible internal injury, fractured skull, or broken back.

This means trying to get professional help before you move him or you may make matters worse. If this is clearly impossible, evacuate the victim on a stretcher with the maximum of care. Lift the body with a minimum of three people supporting the head and shoulders, the torso and buttocks, and the legs—and lift only high enough to slide a ground cloth or sleeping bag underneath. Then everyone grasps this "stretcher" and carries the patient the shortest distance to an evacuation point. Treat the victim for shock and attend to any bleeding wounds, of course, as will be described later. If you must evacuate by stretcher, it should be done with the greatest of gentleness.

Suspected broken back victims should be carefully placed on a solid surface such as smooth poles lashed rigidly to the stretcher. The victim must be tied carefully and gently to this immovable platform at two points on the legs and two on the torso; the shoulders and the head should also be immobilized with padding and supports. But let me reemphasize that these measures should be taken only if there is no other possible alternative for evacuation, which we will discuss presently.

More common are simple fractures of arms or legs, although no break is really simple. If you can't fully determine whether an injury is a break or a severe sprain, then treat it as a break.

The limb must be immobilized with splints. These are easily cut from straight-grained hardwood with an axe. Split off as thin a slab as possible from a billet that is long enough to extend well beyond both sides of the suspected

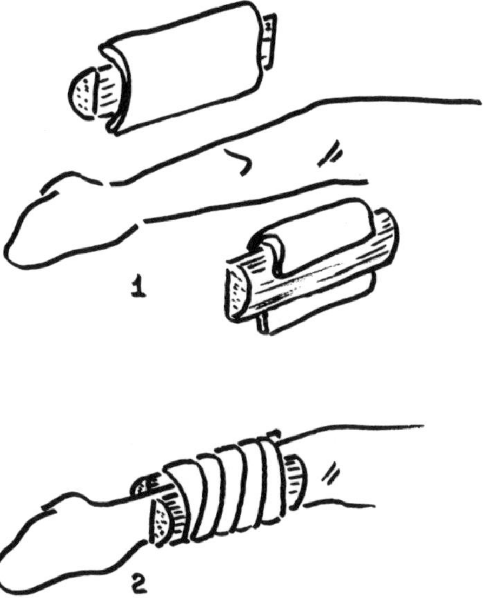


A broken limb must be immobilized with splints, which can be split with an axe from straight-grained hardwood. The splints are padded with whatever soft material is handy (1) and then are bound gently but firmly on either side of the break with an elastic bandage (2) or lengths of cloth or handkerchiefs.

break. Smooth the splints off and pad them with clothing. Gently bind two splints to the limb, one on each side. I like to wind them on with an elastic bandage, but a gauze bandage, handkerchiefs, or strips of cloth can also be used. If the latter, make at least two ties above and below the break. Do not try to set the bone if you can get the victim to a doctor within a week! You'll just mess things up.

If the injury is to an arm, use the triangular bandage to form a sling, then bind the whole thing gently to the body. The patient can probably walk out slowly. But have someone beside him to help keep him in balance and look for signs of shock. If a leg or ankle is broken, you'll have to make a stretcher and carry him out.

But before charging down the mountain with a stretcher in tow, first consider the various other means of evacuation that are available today. In many areas, civilian or military helicopters are on hand (and expensive) for aid in serious accidents. Is the injury serious enough to consider such an effort? How long will it take for a member of the party to summon such aid? Can you get the patient out as fast and as safely yourself? Is there landing room in the woods or on the mountain for a helicopter? Or is there a nearby lake that can handle a float plane? Or can you use both techniques, evacuating the patient part way to a better pick-up point by plane?

The hike leader has to make these determinations. Don't rush it. The life of your friend may rest on your picking the right answers.

### *Boy, Is That Hot!*

For some reason, fooling around campfires sooner or later leads to a burn. The use of a hot mitt or a well-padded pair of gloves or even a doubled-up handkerchief minimizes the possibility. But sooner or later you will grab a hot pot bail or bobble a boiling kettle of water. Burns are bad news and should not be treated lightly. They are also very likely with children, small ones in particular. A campfire is a magnet for kids, so be careful how you let them play with burning sticks or around boiling pots of water or food.

If a burn happens, assess its nature. A first-degree burn is characterized by a reddening of the skin. It can be treated with first-aid ointment to exclude air and soothe the irritation. Petroleum jelly, lotion, or sweet butter or lard are also okay, if nothing else is available. Cover the area loosely with a gauze bandage to keep it clean.

A second-degree burn develops blisters and is more alarming because the area is particularly prone to infection if the blisters break. Many first-aid books advise covering blisters with a dry gauze bandage. I disagree. First of all, the first-aid cream soothes the great pain; second, it lubricates the skin and prevents it from drying out and causing the blisters to break; and, third, it provides an antiseptic area if the blister should break. But spread the ointment on very carefully and cover the area carefully with a large, loose bandage held in place by tape.

Third-degree burns, which are very serious, may show as burned skin or as dead white or charred flesh. The patient should always be treated for shock, which will be described shortly. Do not try to remove any clothing that may be stuck to the burn. Do not put any ointments on the wound; they would just make the doctor's job more difficult. Cover the burned area loosely with a cloth or bandage. Give the victim fluids, preferably those containing salt and sugar, and rush him to a hospital.

Sunburn is not a different kind of burn; it is just a first- or second-degree burn from a different source. It is hard to convince sun worshippers of the dangers of sunburn, but let me tell you a little story.

I was making a whitewater trip for the first time with Rob, when he was twelve. We were going down the upper Delaware River in early spring with a bunch of young fellows, one of whom insisted on wearing shorts and no shirt despite all advice. He had a tan too. By four o'clock in the afternoon and twenty miles downriver, he was virtually in shock with an acute burn, low pulse, and nausea. We had to evacuate him for medical attention and his trip was finished.

Sunburn or heat prostration or "stroke" are real hazards, particularly where the rays of the sun are intensified by water, snow, white sand, or high altitude—or to a person who simply is unaccustomed to long outdoor exposure. The preventive is to cover up; this includes the head and eyes. If you insist on getting a tan, sun yourself for short periods only and copiously apply one of the lotions that block ultraviolet light. Don't worry, more than enough tanning rays will get through.

If you notice a companion staggering and feeling faint from heat exhaustion, get him into the shade and lying down. Symptoms are a pale face, clammy skin, the shivers and, possibly, nausea. Bathe the entire head and neck and wrists with cold water. If the victim is conscious, give him salted water. Look out for those salt tablets. I can't take them at any time; they make me sick. Simple salted water is safer.

Since the victim is suffering from a form of shock, treat him for it. We might as well discuss the procedure right now. Keep the victim flat with his feet and legs elevated on a pack or padded rock. Cover him with a light blanket or sleeping bag to ward off the chills, unless the temperature of the air is so high that he would be uncomfortable.

Shock can accompany any injury or severe emotional

stress. It's the body's way of copping out for a while. It can occur immediately after the incident or hours afterward. The victim may appear dazed, seeming to have only a hazy idea of what is going on. In extreme cases, the victim may be unconscious. In any event, he does not respond intelligently, and it is the height of stupidity to question him sharply or to try to bring him around by slapping his face, as I once saw a woman try to do with an accident victim. If he doesn't come around in a reasonable time, evacuate him to a doctor.

Another form of sun damage is sunstroke, suffered by prolonged exposure to powerful and direct radiation. It is usually accompanied by a dry, flushed face and raspy, shallow breathing. Get the victim into the shade and treat as for heat exhaustion.

### *Hey, Look, I'm Bleeding!*

The best way to avoid getting cut is to keep all edged tools—your knife and axe and saw—very sharp. Also, keep your hands covered with gloves, keep your arms and legs out of the way, and learn how to use the tools properly. Ironically, while this will prevent accidents, if an accident does happen it is likely to be severe because of the sharpness of the blades.

Small cuts are very simply treated by washing the area thoroughly, applying an antiseptic cream, and bandaging with either an adhesive bandage or a gauze pad and tape. Big cuts usually occur on the hands, arms, or, less likely, the legs, and are often accompanied by severe bleeding from severed veins. This blood is a dark red in color. Your first job is to stop the bleeding fast.

Grab the wound with a hand immediately, preferably a hand holding a clean handkerchief, but with the hand alone if getting a handkerchief means fumbling around. Apply a firm pressure directly to the wound, squeezing the torn flesh back together gently.

Then get someone to fetch the first-aid kit or have the victim apply pressure himself if there are only two of you. Release pressure only long enough to slip a large sterile pad over the wound. Reapply pressure at once, adding other pads, handkerchiefs, or even clothing as the blood soaks through. Keep up the pressure until the bleeding ceases. Bind the pads to the wound with whatever is handy—adhesive tape, gauze bandage, handkerchiefs, or strips of cloth—which will keep pressure on the wound. You can also learn the key pressure points of the body, which restrict blood flow in the major arteries to the extremities, and use this technique to supplement—but not replace—direct pressure.

A victim with bleeding of this intensity will probably suffer shock, which should be treated as described earlier. Then he should be evacuated to a doctor by the fastest means. If you are alone with him, and he can't walk, you may just have to tough it out until he can. But don't leave him alone under any circumstances. He may not be able to help himself if the bleeding begins again.

People who have lost a lot of blood are thirsty and should be given fluids in small and continuous amounts. Soups and broth are particularly good because they contain both salt and nourishment. But only give them if the patient is conscious and not sick to his stomach.

Tourniquets should be avoided except in the most extreme cases of life and death. About the only thing that qualifies is when a major artery is severed. Since these are protected deep within the body, only a severe accident to the extremities will expose this bright red blood flow. Since you can't put a successful tourniquet on the neck, the legs and arms are the only areas that qualify. That's how rare the accident will be.

If it should occur, grab a handkerchief or the triangular bandage and fold it into a band, which is wrapped twice around the limb just above the injury and is fastened with an overhand knot. Place a sturdy stick across this knot and tie a square knot on top. Twist the stick and bandage until the bleeding stops. Then tie the stick in place on the limb to keep it from unwinding and rush the victim to a doctor or, preferably, directly to a hospital.

You must be able to tell the doctor how long the tourniquet has been in place so he can take appropriate remedies, but don't try to take the tourniquet off yourself. You won't be able to stop the bleeding and a victim with an injury this severe will bleed to death in a few minutes.

Most doctors advise wilderness wanderers to keep up to date on their antitetanus shots, which is a good idea, since you will then only have to have a booster in the event of an injury. This is particularly recommended for fishermen, who are prone to suffer from another kind of cut—a puncture wound from a fishhook.

Favorite spots for the accidental repose of flies or small lures seem to be the back of the neck, ear, cheek, arm, or hand. I found a new one last summer on a canoe trip when a companion plunged his hand into a pack pocket and came up with a hook imbedded in the back of his finger. Naturally, the barb was out of sight in the meat. What to do?

A relatively new technique for removing fishhooks that has aroused some controversy aims at avoiding further puncture by withdrawing the hook by the path in which it entered. To perform this feat, you grasp the meat in the direction of the fishhook and pinch it. Grasping the hook firmly with the other hand, you deftly and swiftly press forward on the hook and rotate it outward. The theory is that squeezing the flesh causes the hole to elongate, and outward pressure away from the barb gives it more space to slip out without tearing. It's an interesting concept and I have wanted to try it—on someone else first.

Unfortunately, this was not the time. I found after gentle examination that the hook was firmly imbedded in the tendons in the back of my friend's finger. Any experimentation might permanently damage them. So I went back to old-fashioned ground.

In this approach, you manipulate the flesh around the hook until you get a minimum in front of where the barb is imbedded. Then the hook is grasped firmly with the other hand and deliberately pushed through the flesh until the barb is well out into the open. This is no time for squeamishness if you value your buddy's comfort. It is also a time when everyone around hopes he is a good fisherman who keeps his points sharp.

Take your needle-nosed pliers (now you know why I always carry them) and snip off the barb with the wire-cutter portion. Retract the now barbless hook through the wound. At this point, a tube of first-aid cream comes in handy. By applying the spout to one side of the puncture, it is often possible with a little massaging to force antiseptic ointment completely through the wound, which helps prevent infection. Naturally, the victim should see a doctor for a tetanus booster as soon as possible. In my friend's case, the operation was so successful that the wound was practically healed when he got to the doctor.

A similar accident is the ubiquitous splinter. And here I will probably outrage half the medical profession, but I believe in leaving reasonably small splinters alone for about a day rather than digging them out at once. In about twenty-four hours, a splinter will fester and can usually be popped from the puncture by gently squeezing around it.

Then treat the wound with antiseptic before releasing the pressure and the ointment will be sucked into the puncture, which can be virtually forgotten.

Immediate digging with a sterilized needle, in my experience, not only causes a great deal of pain and irritation, but enlarges the wound and seems to encourage infection or at least inflammation. Naturally, if the splinter is very large or in an awkward place, you will have to remove it. The tools are the needle and a pair of fine tweezers, both of which are standard in your first-aid kit.

### *Something's in My Eye!*

Only once in my life did I ever get something serious into my eye—a simple little fleck of sawdust. But I wasn't able to get it out and I spent several miserable days until I could get to a doctor. By that time I had a good old infection in the underside of the lid and a scratched eyeball. This is an accident well worth preventing, believe me. As an old parental admonition goes, you have only one pair of eyes (which always seemed rather silly to me as a kid, because there were many other things that I also had only one pair of to which I was equally attached).

In any event, a good way to avoid eye damage is to wear a pair of safety sunglasses whenever you are sawing wood or doing any other activity that produces flying debris. Since my eyes are rather sensitive to strong sunlight, I wear sunglasses most of the time outdoors anyway.

If you should get something in your eye, resist the impulse to rub it, which can damage the delicate membrane covering the eyeball or imbed the particle in it. Instead, close the eye gently and encourage the tears to wash it out. Vigorously blowing the nose will clear the duct in the inner corner of the eye that leads to the nose and will encourage a speedy flow of tears.

If this doesn't work and you can feel the object at the top of the eyeball, try holding the upper lid out and down while the tears flow. If it is behind the lower lid, pull down on the flesh under the eye, causing the lower lid to spring out, and repeat the gentle blinking. Perhaps a buddy can spot the particle as he holds your eye open by pressure above and below the eye and remove the offending body with the corner of a clean handkerchief.

Still got it? Then, there is one more safe trick before heading for the doctor. Form an eyecup from your versatile pack of foil with a smooth folded-over rim and flush the eye with clean spring water. Hold the full cup up to the eye with your head bent over, then rotate the head up with the cup in place to spill the water into the eye while blinking. If that doesn't work after a try or two, put a clean pad over the eye, held in place with tape above and below, and head for that poor overworked doctor. Generally, though, foreign objects can be removed with no more than temporary annoyance.

### *Something Just Bit Me!*

Equally annoying are insect bites or stings, particularly if you are one of those poor unfortunates, like Chuck, who are allergic to foreign proteins. And if you don't think you are because your experience has been solely with those effete little suburban bugs, wait until you get bitten by a hairy-chested black or deer fly, which literally removes a chunk from you. A wasp, hornet, or bee sting can also sometimes be a source of continued swelling and pain. For some people, these stings can be fatal without immediate antidote. If you are one of these unfortunates, don't forget to take along your pills in the first-aid kit.

If the pain gets unbearable, try a paste of common baking soda, smearing it liberally over the bite and letting it dry in place. Several applications will usually reduce the swelling and the itching or sting. I have been told that a weak solution of common household ammonia is just as good, but you probably won't have it along on a backpacking trip. An old-fashioned remedy that I can vouch for is the use of a poultice made up of mud or the partially decomposed vegetable matter from a swamp.

In most cases, insect bites are simply annoying. But there are a few creatures that are actively poisonous or, at least, hostile. One of the worst you can run into, in my opinion, is a scorpion, either the desert or subtropical variety. Inhabitants of both areas proudly claim their scorpion is the worst, but having been stung once by each, I think I can dispassionately proclaim that both are equally bad.

When I was a boy, I was stung on the arm by the desert variety while tussling on the ground with a buddy at a campsite in the Mohave. I rolled on the little arachnid while he was minding his own business. Fortunately, it was a little one; even so, I couldn't use my arm for three days. While living in Florida, later, I jumped into my boots one morning at a fishing camp and slid a foot right into the southern variety, which had picked my boot as a warm place to snooze. I couldn't get my shoe on for three days.

You will have to watch out for these creatures because they are so confident of the prowess in their stinging tail that they won't retreat if they feel threatened. Fortunately, they aren't so abundant that you will meet them every day. If you should be stung, don't panic—you probably won't die, even though the sting of a large scorpion can make you feel like it. Try compresses of soda paste or weak ammonia to draw the pain. Oh, yes, as a preventive, shake out your boots in the morning before you put them on. I still do even when there isn't a scorpion within a thousand miles of me.

In the same class are tarantulas, ticks, chiggers, and sand fleas that also bite, itch, and generally drive you mad. Contrary to popular opinion, the tarantula is not poisonous, but it can deliver a painful bite if you ram your finger into its jaws. So much for him. I will have more to say about the others in a minute.

In the truly dangerous class in the United States are black widow spiders, the brown recluse spider, and, while we're at it, Gila monsters (a lizard), rattlers, moccasins, copperheads, and coral snakes. Each of these critters has a harmless cousin that looks almost like it, so don't flip the minute you see something that looks like the "sudden death" pictured in your insect or reptile books. But do study the poisonous ones and the nonpoisonous "imposters" so that you can recognize them. Then file the descriptions away for future recall. Chances are you will never have to.

I don't want to pooh-pooh dangerous wildlife, but black widows, brown recluses, Gila monsters, and coral snakes occur only in rare pockets. And the other snakes tend to occur in significant numbers only in limited areas. And as we said in other chapters, these creatures are not out to get you, with the possible exception of the water moccasin, which can be rather belligerent at times, standing its ground instead of retreating. To repeat previous advice, keep your bare paws out of holes and from under ledges and stones in country where there are poisonous varieties. Watch out in old abandoned buildings out West for concentrations of the "bad" spiders. And in the South, watch how you thrash around in swamp country.

In such places, have your snake-bite kit handy and read the instructions beforehand so you know how to use it. Basically, the procedure is to put a snug band around the limb above the bite to restrict circulation, cut open the punctures with a small blade in the kit, then suck out the blood and poison with an aspirator, either a rubber suction cup or a small plastic pump device. Naturally, you want to get medical attention as soon as possible.

But the main thing is to keep calm. Few people die of snakebite in this country, particularly when they follow established procedures and don't run around in a panic pumping the venom throughout their systems. The two spiders are more dangerous, I believe, but even here it is my understanding that a bite is not necessarily fatal. Victims of such bites should lie down and keep calm and must be evacuated by stretcher. Don't give them liquor. It is not true that it offsets the poison, and some reports claim it is actually a detriment.

Much more common—and occasionally even dangerous—are the tinier Arachnida and Siphonaptera. Some areas of the country, particularly in wet seasons, are loaded with ticks. These obnoxious creatures are also the bearers of several diseases, among them Rocky Mountain spotted fever.

Therefore, in tick country, examine your body every night. The same for your dog, if you take him backpacking in such areas. Pups can actually become debilitated simply by being drained by a host of ticks. If you find one running around loose on your body, just pluck it off. If it is already attached, don't yank it off or you will undoubtedly leave the head in your skin to fester and infect. Instead, hold a lighted cigarette *near* its body or put a drop of oil, gasoline, or alcohol on it. Discomfort in the one case and the closing of its breathing pores in the other will cause the tick to withdraw. The same procedure is used for your dog.

With chiggers, the best advice is don't! Don't get anywhere near them. But since some parts of the South are virtually alive with these minute "red bugs," this isn't really practical advice. They inhabit heavy brush, Spanish moss, and so on. Before going into this kind of country, liberally spread insect repellent, powdered sulfur, or kerosene around every entrance port to your clothing—neck, waistband, and ankles. Then try to avoid pushing through heavy undergrowth. Don't picnic or stop to rest under heavy clumps of Spanish moss. Chiggers are constantly dropping out of these havens.

If you gather up a collection, they will burrow into your skin to lay their eggs and you are in for one of life's more exquisite torments. They itch and burn like the very devil. However, the agony can be minimized and shortened by covering the area with an impervious layer that shuts off their air supply. Grease or oil will help; a paste of strong soap, too. But I have found the best bet to be colorless nail polish, dabbed over each little red-flecked burrow. Then, try to keep from clawing yourself to death until they have died in two or three days.

Biting fleas are a specialty of some beach areas and some tall-grass pampas. They can be discouraged from attack by liberal applications of an insect repellent, as for chiggers.

These precautions and remedies are adequate for the United States. But if you are going into foreign areas—such as Central and South America, Africa, and southern Asia—there are much more dangerous insects and snakes that require special precautions, even specific antidotes. Be sure to read up on such areas before you take off.

*I Have a Strange Itch!*

Another hazard that you are likely to encounter is one of the topically poisonous plants. These are generally summed up as poison ivy (or poison oak in the South and West) and poison sumac; but nettles, thistles, and other thorny growth can also be irritating.

Two stories will sum up the poison-plant situation. A Scout troop I once knew made two memorable trips in a single year. One was a canoe trip that took them across a large lake. Reaching an island after dark and in a rainstorm that they thought was their camping objective, they piled out and into their bags on the soft and resilient undergrowth. In the morning they saw to their horror that they were not on the right island and, furthermore, that their campsite was a solid carpet of poison ivy. All contracted a good itch and about half of the troop needed medical attention.

On the next occasion, this ill-starred bunch made a fall camp and considered themselves fortunate to find an abundance of dried bushes for kindling right next to the camp. The next day almost the entire troop was very sick and a few required emergency attention at a hospital. Their kindling was dried stalks of poison sumac and they had all inhaled quantities of the poison in the smoke (equally dangerous with poison ivy and oak, incidentally).

There is little reason ever to make these mistakes. Poison ivy is a low-growing plant or shrub or high-climbing vine that is very easy to distinguish. In summer, it bears glossy leaves in threes that are sometimes coarsely toothed. Poison oak, which is closely related, often grows as a shrub and has from three to seven leaflets that are hairy underneath. In the fall in frosty climates the leaves of these two turn bright red, then brown, but are still recognizable by shape.

Unlike harmless red sumac—which has slender, flat compound leaves and is generally covered with erect clusters of red berries—the poison sumac has smooth compound leaves that grow in a V from the stem. And this shrub or small tree has clusters of waxy white berries that droop on the stem.

If you should handle either of these poisonous varieties or push through them in the undergrowth, wash the affected parts with strong soap. A prompt wash with alcohol will also wash away the poisonous sap.

All parts of these plants are equally poisonous, too. Now I also know that some people are less susceptible than others to these poisons. They are usually the ones that are never bitten by insects either. But I would like to caution you that resistances seem to change for inexplicable reasons and these plants also seem to be more toxic at some seasons of the year than at others. So take care.

If you should get a mild case of poisoning from any of these plants, try covering it with a drying compound such as zinc ointment or calamine lotion. Severe cases should be treated by a doctor. Never scratch this rash, which can be spread by the fingernails. For the milder irritations of nettles, thistles, and briars, wash the skin with a good strong soap solution and put on a soothing lotion as soon as you get to camp.

### *Wow, I'm Cold!*

A special form of accident is called freezing to death. It is characterized by frostbite. And there is plenty of misinformation floating around about this winter malady.

While it is true that the lower the temperature, the more danger there is of frostbite, it does not follow that frostbite can only occur at very low temperatures. It is a function of temperature, wind, and humidity, but there is always a possibility of frostbite at temperatures of 20 degrees Fahrenheit or lower. Children, with their tender skins, are even more prone to frostbite than adults.

The prevention is to keep covered up and warm and to keep a sharp eye on exposed parts of the body for numbness or the telltale patches of white skin that signify freezing flesh. Frostbite can also occur by restricting circulation and is most common in feet that are bound too tightly by boots or by snowshoe or crampon harnesses.

Starting the morning out by putting on frozen boots at low temperatures is an invitation to frostbitten toes. When I first went winter mountaineering, I left my boots out one night (only once!). It was 30 below when I bailed out in the morning, and within minutes of hitting the trail with an overly tight left snowshoe harness, I could feel my toes going on that side. By loosening the harness and vigorously wiggling my toes at every step, I restored feeling. But I still frosted my little toe enough so that the skin died and peeled and that toe was sensitive to cold for several years. It was a near miss that taught me a lesson.

That's why I sleep with my boots (in a plastic bag) and such vital clothing as mittens and socks arranged around me to dry out. It is the only guarantee of dry gear, even if it does cost you a truly comfortable night's sleep.

If you discover a numb spot, take immediate measures to ward off freezing. *Do not* rub the spot and do not apply snow. Where these insane notions came from, I don't know, but they are as widespread as they are idiotic. Rubbing will simply abrade sensitive flesh. Snow will insure freezing. The best thing is to warm the area with hands or arms. In the case of freezing feet, they can also be tucked into the groin or inside the shirt against the stomach or under the armpits of a helpful companion.

Under these circumstances, it is advisable to stop immediately and make camp. Build a fire and cautiously warm the affected members near the blaze. Be sure you also keep an unaffected member at the same distance from the fire to judge the heat or you may burn yourself without immediately knowing it.

If you get caught out in a storm without adequate gear, shift your mind and efforts immediately from your hiking goals to survival. Many people have died on Mount Washington in the White Mountains of New Hampshire, for example, despite the warning signs on all trail approaches, because they started up the mountain on a hot summer day wearing only a T-shirt and shorts.

But this massif, only 6,288 feet high, is noted for the most treacherous weather anywhere in the world, except for a few mountains in Antarctica. At a temperature of 80 degrees Fahrenheit in the valley, the normal summit temperature is in the low 60s. But a storm can blow up at this end of a long mountain funnel in about thirty minutes, and when it does, the temperature can drop 20 or 30 degrees with a very high wind. The resultant wind-chill factor on the summit can be below zero—in mid-August!

Several people have died of hypothermia—a net loss of body heat—within normal shouting distance of the summit house under these extreme conditions. The obvious answer is to be prepared for such an event. But if not, then at least hikers should be prepared to abandon an unprofitable course of action and promptly retreat to the lee side of the mountain below timberline, where a bivouac can be established with a snug fire.

I guess that is the final message. A backpacker should never be afraid to bow before superior force. It is not a sign of either intelligence or maturity to suffer injury or death from a sense of false pride that demands going on when all signs point to a retreat.

Writers have said that nature is "harsh" and "unforgiving" and "cruel." This is giving nature human characteristics and is untrue. Nature is none of these things. Nature is indifferent to puny little man. It just flows along following its own basic laws of physics and chemistry.

Men who have lived with nature a long time understand this and don't try to overpower giant natural forces. But civilization has caused many of us to withdraw more and more from the reality of nature. This is at the same time the challenge and the excitement of returning along backpacking trails. We can rediscover the thrill, not of mastering nature, but of flowing with it as the surf rider lives for an instant on the power of a huge comber or a skier swoops at the edge of inexorable gravity.

Life on the trail is not one of brute force, but of a delicate attuning to the rhythm and surges of natural forces. It is a never-ending process of learning, of advancing farther, and of retreating less. Its reward is the feel of a rock under the hands that transmits the magnetism of a whole mountain, of a wilderness stillness so profound that it creates a faint melody in the mind's ear. These experiences restore both the soul and the body. Who could ask for a greater reward?

# APPENDIX A
## *Equipment Suppliers*

Note: Many of the companies listed here also supply dehydrated camping foods by the manufacturers listed in Appendix B, and most have mail-order departments.

Alpine Designs
6185 E. Arapahoe
P.O. Box 3561
Boulder, Colo. 80303

Alpine Recreation
455 Central Park Ave.
Scarsdale, N.Y. 10583

3214 Erie Blvd. East
Syracuse, N.Y. 13214

Eddie Bauer
1737 Airport Way South
P.O. Box 3700
Seattle, Wash. 98124

L. L. Bean, Inc.
Freeport, Me. 04032

Bishop's Ultimate Outdoor Equipment
6804 Wedgewood Rd.
Bethesda, Md. 20034

Thomas Black & Sons, Inc.
930 Ford St.
Ogdensburg, N.Y. 13669

Camp 7, Inc.
3235 Prairie Ave.
Boulder, Colo. 80301

Camp Supply Co.
1151 S. Seventh St.
St. Louis, Mo. 63104

Camp Trails
4111 W. Clarendon Ave.
P.O. Box 14500
Phoenix, Ariz. 85019

Carikit Outdoor Equipment
P.O. Box 1153
Boulder, Colo. 80302

Class 5
2010 Seventh Ave.
Berkeley, Calif. 94710

Climbers and Campers
510 Main St.
Springfield, Mass. 01105

Climbers' Corner
55 River St.
Cambridge, Mass. 02139

4B Henshaw St.
Woburn, Mass. 01801

Cloud Cap Chalet
625 S.W. 12th Ave.
Portland, Ore. 97205

Comfy-Seattle Quilt Div.
Olin, Inc.
310 First Ave. South
Seattle, Wash. 98104

Dave Cook Sporting Goods Co.
16th and Market
Denver, Colo. 80202

Dunham's Shoes
Brattleboro, Vt. 05301

Eastern Mountain Sports, Inc.
1041 Commonwealth Ave.
Boston, Mass. 02215

Eureka Tent Co.
Box 986
Binghamton, N.Y. 13902

Fabiano Shoe Co., Inc.
South Station
Boston, Mass. 02210

Frostline
Box 2190
Boulder, Colo. 80302

Gabriel's
1436 Easton Ave.
Madison, Ohio 44057

Gander Mountain, Inc.
Box 248
Wilmot, Wisc. 53192

The Garcia Corp.
329 Alfred Ave.
Teaneck, N.J. 07666

Gerry Div. of Outdoor Sports Industries, Inc.
5450 North Valley Highway
Denver, Colo. 80216

Gokey Co.
21 W. Fifth St.
St. Paul, Minn. 55102

Leon R. Greenman, Inc.
132 Spring St.
New York, N.Y. 10012

Herters, Inc.
Waseca, Minn. 56093

Himalayan Back Packs
P.O. Box 5668
Pine Bluff, Ark. 71601

Hirsch-Weis Div. White Stag
5203 S.E. Johnson Creek Blvd.
Portland, Ore. 97206

Holubar
1975 30th St.
Box 7
Boulder, Colo. 80302

Hudson's
105 Third Ave.
New York, N.Y. 10003

Jonas Bros. of Seattle
1507 12th Ave.
Seattle, Wash. 98122

Kelty
1801 Victory Blvd.
Glendale, Calif. 91201

Kreeger & Son, Ltd.
30 W. 46th St.
New York, N.Y. 10036

K2 Jan Sport
Vashon Island, Wash. 98070

Moor and Mountain
67 Main st.
Concord, Mass. 01742

Morsan
810 Rt. 17
Paramus, N.J. 07652

2485 Rt. 22
Union, N.J. 07083

269 Rt. 18
East Brunswick, N.J. 08816

1999 Rt. 110
Farmingdale, N.Y. 11735

2257 Rt. 112
Coram, N.Y. 11727

3560 Long Beach Rd.
Oceanside, N.Y. 11572

515 Boston Post Rd.
Orange, Conn. 06477

Mountain Sports
821 Pearl St.
Boulder, Colo. 80302

Mountaineering Recreation
960-A Troy Schenectady Rd.
Latham, N.Y. 12110

268 Central Ave.
Albany, N.Y. 12206

The North Face
P.O. Box 2399
Station A
Berkeley, Calif. 94702

The Orvis Co., Inc.
Manchester, Vt. 05254

P&S Sales
P.O. Box 45095
Tulsa, Okla. 74145

H. H. Petrie Sporting Goods, Inc.
702 N. Midvale Blvd.
P.O. Box 5427
Madison, Wisc. 53705

Ptarmigan, Inc.
821 17th St.
Denver, Colo. 80202

Recreation Unlimited
926 Rt. 17
Ramsey, N.J. 07446

Recreational Equipment, Inc.
1525 11th Ave.
Seattle, Wash. 98122

Sierra Designs
Fourth & Addison Sts.
Berkeley, Calif. 94710

Sport Chalet
951 Foothill Blvd.
La Canada, Calif. 91011

Stow-A-Way Sports Industries
166 Cushing Highway
Cohasset, Mass. 02025

Sunbird Industries, Inc.
5368 N. Sterling Center Dr.
Westlake Village, Calif. 91301

Swiss Ski Sports
559 Clay St.
San Francisco, Calif. 94111

Tight Lines, Inc.
220 S. Main St.
West Bridgewater, Mass. 02379

Trailblazer by Winchester
Taylorville Rd.
Statesville, N.C. 28677

Vasque Div. Red Wing Shoe Co.
Red Wing, Minn. 55066

West Ridge Mountaineering
13808 Casimir Ave.
Gardena, Calif. 90249

# APPENDIX B
## *Camping Food Producers*

Chuck Wagon Foods
Micro Drive
Woburn, Mass. 01801

Dri-Lite Foods
11333 Atlantic
Lynwood, Calif. 90262

F.S.P. Foods
Trail Chef and Mountain House
P.O. Box 6128
Albany, Calif. 94706

National Packaged Trail Foods
632 E. 185th St.
Cleveland, Ohio 44119

Perma-Pak Camping Foods
40 E. 2430 South
Salt Lake City, Utah 84115

Rich-Moor Corp.
P.O. Box 2728
Van Nuys, Calif. 91404

Stow-A-Way Sports Industries
166 Cushing Highway
Cohasset, Mass. 02025

Trail Chef
1109 S. Wall St.
Los Angeles, Calif. 90015

Wilson Certified Foods, Inc.
Freeze-Dried Div.
4545 Lincoln Blvd.
Oklahoma City, Okla. 73105

# SELECTED OUTDOOR READING

*Adirondack Winter Mountaineering Manual* (paperback). Adirondack Mountain Club, Inc., Gabriels, N.Y., 1972.

*America's Camping Book*, Paul Cardwell, Jr., Scribner's, New York, 1969.

*The Art and Science of Taking to the Woods*, C. B. Colby and Bradford Angier. Stackpole, Harrisburg, 1970.

*At Home in the Wilderness*, Sun Bear (paperback). Naturegraph, Healdsburg, Calif., 1970.

*Backpack Cookery*, Ruth D. Mendenhall (paperback). La Siesta, Glendale, Calif., 1966.

*Backpack Techniques*, Ruth D. Mendenhall (paperback). La Siesta, Glendale, Calif., 1968.

*The Backpacker's Handbook*, George Sullivan. Grosset & Dunlap, New York, 1972.

*Backpacking*, R. C. Rethmel (paperback). Alamogordo Printing, Alamogordo, N.M., 1968.

*Backpacking: One Step at a Time*, Harvey Manning. Random House, New York, 1973.

*Beachcomber's Handbook*, Euell Gibbons. McKay, Inc., New York, 1967.

*Be Expert With Map and Compass*, Bjorn Kjellstrom, (paperback). American Orienteering Service, La Porte, Inc., 1955.

*Campcraft*, Catherine T. Hammett (paperback). Pocket Books, New York, 1961.

*The Camper's Bible*, Bill Riviere (paperback). Doubleday, Garden City, N.Y., 1970.

*Camping and Camp Cookery*, staff of *Hunter's Encyclopedia* (paperback). Collier, New York, 1962.

*Camping and Woodcraft*, Horace Kephart. Macmillan, New York, 1965.

*Camping by Backpack and Canoe*, Theodore A. Cheney. Funk & Wagnalls, New York, 1970.

*Camping Equipment*, C. B. Colby. Coward-McCann, 1972.

*Camping for Boys and Girls*, Tom McNally (paperback). Follett, Chicago, 1966.

*Complete Book of Camping*, Leonard Miracle with Maurice Decker. Outdoor Life and Harper, New York, 1961.

*Complete Book of Nature Photography*, Russ Kinne. Chilton, Philadelphia, 1971.

*Complete Book of Outdoor Lore*, Clyde Ormond. Outdoor Life and Harper & Row, New York, 1964.

*Complete Cross Country Skiing and Ski Touring*, William J. Lederer and Joe P. Wilson. Norton, New York, 1972.

*The Complete Guide to Family Camping*, Bill Riviere. Doubleday, Garden City, N.Y., 1966.

*The Complete Snow Camper's Guide*, Raymond Bridge. Scribner's, New York, 1972.

*The Complete Walker*, Colin Fletcher. Knopf, New York, 1972.

*Cooking for Camp and Trail*, Hasse Bunnelle with Shirley Sarvis (paperback). Sierra Club, San Francisco, 1972.

*The Cross-Country Ski Book*, John Caldwell (paperback). Greene, Brattleboro, Vt., 1968.

*The Edible Wild*, Berndt Berglund and Clare E. Bolsby. Scribner's, New York, 1971.

*Field Guide to Animal Tracks*, Olaus Murie and Roger T. Peterson. Houghton Mifflin, Boston, 1954.

*Field Guide to the Mammals*, William H. Burt and R. P. Grossenheider. Houghton Mifflin, Boston, 1964.

*Field Guide to Rocks and Minerals*, Frederick H. Pough and Roger T. Peterson. Houghton Mifflin, Boston, 1953.

*Field Guide to Trees and Shrubs*, George A. Petrides. Houghton Mifflin, Boston, 1972.

*Field Guide to Wildflowers*, Roger T. Peterson and Margaret McKenny. Houghton Mifflin, Boston, 1968.

*First Aid Textbook*, American Red Cross (paperback). Doubleday, Garden City, N.Y., 1957.

*Food for Knapsackers*, Hasse Bunnelle with Winnie Thomas (paperback). Sierra Club, San Francisco, 1971.

*Free for the Eating*, Bradford Angier. Stackpole, Harrisburg.

*Fundamentals of Rock Climbing*, (paperback). MIT Outing Club, Cambridge, Mass., 1966.

*Going Light With Backpack or Burro*, David R. Brower (paperback). Sierra Club, San Francisco, 1956.

*Guide to Adirondack Trails.* Adirondack Mountain Club, Inc., Gabriels, N.Y., 1972.

*Guide to the Appalachian Trail.* Appalachian Trail Conference, Inc., Washington, D.C.

*The Hiker's and Backpacker's Handbook*, Bill Merrill. Winchester, New York, 1971.

*Hiking-Climbing Handbook*, Curtis Casewit. Hawthorn, New York, 1969.

*Horses, Hitches and Rocky Trails*, Joe Back. Swallow, Chicago, 1959.

*Introduction to Foot Trails in America*, Robert Colwell. Stackpole, Harrisburg, 1972.

*Knots and How to Tie Them* (paperback). Boy Scouts of America, New Brunswick, N.J., 1969.

*Knots and Splices*, Percy W. Blandford. Bell, New York, 1965.

*Light Weight Camping Equipment*, Gerry Cunningham and Margaret Hansson (paperback). Colorado Outdoor Sports Corp., Denver, 1968.

*Living off the Country*, Bradford Angier. Stackpole, Harrisburg, 1968.

*The Long Trail.* Green Mountain Club, Rutland, Vt.

*Maine Mountain Guide.* Appalachian Mountain Club, Boston.

*The Man Who Walked Through Time*, Colin Fletcher. Knopf, New York, 1968.

*Manual of Ski Mountaineering*, David R. Brower (paperback). Sierra Club, San Francisco, 1962.

*Medicine for Mountaineering* (paperback). Sierra Club, San Francisco.

*More Free-for-the-Eating Wild Foods*, Bradford Angier. Stackpole, Harrisburg, 1969.

*Mountaineering—Freedom of the Hills*, Harvey Manning. Mountaineers of Washington State, Seattle.

*Mountaineering: From Hill Walking to Alpine Climbing*, Alan Blackshaw (paperback). Penguin, Baltimore, 1968.

*The Mountaineering Handbook*, Curtis W. Casewit and Dick Pownall. Lippincott, Philadelphia, 1968.

*On Snow and Rock*, Gaston Rebuffat. Kaye, London, 1967.

*On Your Own in the Wilderness*, Townsend Whelen and Bradford Angier. Stackpole, Harrisburg, 1964.

*The Outdoor Cook's Bible*, Joseph D. Bates, Jr. Doubleday, Garden City, N.Y., 1963.

*Outdoor Survival Skills*, Larry D. Olsen. Brigham Young University Press, Provo, Utah, 1967.

*Outdoorsman's Cookbook*, Arthur H. Carhart (paperback). Collier, New York, 1962.

*Outdoorsman's Handbook*, Clyde Ormond. Outdoor Life and Dutton, New York, 1970.

*Reading the Woods*, Vinson Brown. Stackpole, Harrisburg, 1969.

*Snow Camping and Mountaineering*, Edward A. Rossit. Funk & Wagnalls, New York, 1970.

*Sportsman's Camping Guide*, Leonard Miracle (paperback). Outdoor Life and Dutton, New York, 1969.

*Stalking the Blue-Eyed Scallop*, Euell Gibbons. McKay, New York, 1964.

*Stalking the Good Life*, Euell Gibbons. McKay, New York, 1971.

*Stalking Healthful Herbs*, Euell Gibbons. McKay, New York, 1966.

*Stalking the Wild Asparagus*, Euell Gibbons. McKay, New York, 1962.

*Suggestions for Appalachian Trail Users* (publication 15). Appalachian Trail Conference, Washington, D.C.

*Survival*, (manual no. AFM 64-5). Dept. of the Air Force, Washington, D.C., 1969.

*Survival and Escape*, (field manual no. FM 21-76) Dept. of the Army, Washington, D.C., 1969.

*White Mountain Guide*. Appalachian Mountain Club, Boston.

*Wilderness Cookery*, Bradford Angier. Stackpole, Harrisburg.

*Wilderness Handbook* (paperback). Sierra Club, San Francisco, 1967.

*Wood Craft*, "Nessmuk" (paperback). Dover, New York, 1963.

# INDEX